Crimes and Punishment

THIS PAGE (TOP TO BOTTOM): Family Feud/Maurizio Gucci; Heaven's Gate Suicides/Marshall Applewhite; Peruvian Hostage Crisis/Tupac Amaru; Death of a Princess/JonBenet Ramsey. FACING PAGE (LEFT TO RIGHT): Oklahoma Verdict/Timothy McVeigh; Flight to Oblivion/TWA Flight 800.

Crimes and Punishment

BLITZ EDITIONS

CI
4-2·00
24.95

Published by Blitz Editions
an imprint of Bookmart Ltd
Registered Number 2372865
Trading as Bookmart Ltd
Desford Road
Enderby
Leicester LE9 5AD

ISBN 1-85605-415-2

Editorial and design by Brown Packaging Books Ltd
Bradley's Close
74–77 White Lion Street
London N1 9PF

Editor: Nina Hathaway
Design: wda
Picture Research: Adrian Bentley
Authors: J. Anderson Black
    Owen Booth
    Holly North

Printed in Singapore

CONTENTS

Wiping Out Crime

The year 1996-97 saw a significant drop in crime rates throughout the United States. While this is obviously welcome news, the question is why? Is it just a glitch in the statistics or are the new approaches to policing and sentencing really having an effect? Even more important, is the fall going to be sustainable?

An FBI survey showed that in 1996 there was a 7 percent drop in the number of murders nationwide, continuing a three-year downward trend. This was one element of an overall fall of 3 percent in serious crime across the board: aggravated assault, down 5 percent; vehicle theft, down 3 percent. In the nine major cities of the Unites States—those with a population of a million or more—violent crime was down by an average of 8 percent. Violent crimes in the suburbs also showed a significant fall. There were black-spots, nevertheless; police in Minneapolis were bewildered and dismayed as their city bucked the national trend with a 56 percent rise in murders. Overall, however, the picture is encouraging.

President Bill Clinton, who had made being "tough on crime," a central plank of his reelection campaign, crowed at the figures. "We are making a difference," he said. "Today our neighborhoods are safer, and we are restoring people's confidence that crime can be reduced." Janet Reno, the Attorney General, attributed the fall to: "More police on the streets, fewer guns in the wrong hands, more prosecutors and more jail cells to keep criminals behind bars."

A CHANGING SOCIETY

While there is undoubtedly some truth in Ms. Reno's claims—the country's prison population has more than doubled since the mid-1960s to over one million criminals—other factors are also involved. Criminologists attribute the fall in the crime rate, in part at least, to the changing demographics of American society. Percentage-wise, there are simply fewer people in the most crime-prone category—males between the age of 15 and 29.

The trade in "crack" cocaine has also changed. It became so common in the late 1980s that it lost its fashion status.

FEWER CRIMINALS: The crime rate among the youth of America continues to fall.

This is significant because much of the violent crime in the United States is drug-based. Crack is particularly addictive and in itself induces psychotic behavior, a deadly combination which spawned its own crime wave.

As for the increase in the prison population, most criminologists agree that a relatively small number of people are responsible for the vast majority of serious crimes. It makes sense, therefore, that if more than a million hardened criminals are kept out of circulation at any one time, crime as a whole will fall. Former Secretary for Education, William Bennett, is a strong advocate of incarceration. "Most prisoners are violent or repeat offenders," he says. "Prisons do cut crime."

BACK TO THE BEAT

Much credit must also be given to radical changes in policing methods, particularly in the big cities. There has been a move away from car-bound cops back toward traditional foot patrols, and a more proactive approach to policing generally. The emphasis now is to attempt to tackle the problem before it happens, rather than just racking up impressive arrest rates.

The "Zero Tolerance" policy, pioneered in New York City by the then police chief, William Bratton, has been widely copied. Bratton's theory was that if he got tough on petty crime—graffiti and littering—the serious crime would take care of itself. It was a controversial approach but it had dramatic results. In 1995, New York City saw an unprecedented fall in serious crime of 17.5 percent, with murders dropping below the thousand mark for the first time since 1968.

The endless debate on gun control and how it affects crime statistics is as yet unresolved. There are those states that favor the outright banning of handguns, a measure which is generally agreed to be unenforceable. Yet there are others that favor a measure of deregulation. In 1987, Florida passed a law that allowed private citizens to apply for licenses to carry concealed weapons. The theory was that potential street criminals would be discouraged if they thought they had a fair chance of being shot for their day's work. Lobbyists for gun control were outraged at the move,

PRESIDENTIAL INITIATIVE: Attorney General Janet Reno talks to Indianapolis residents about community policing, a strategy embraced by the Clinton administration.

MAKING CONTACT: A police officer talks to a young girl living in a housing project in Bensalem, Pennsylvania.

but the fact remains that, since the law was passed, 150,000 citizens of Florida have applied for concealed weapons licenses, and the homicide rate has fallen by 29 percent. Impressed by this statistic, 27 other states have introduced similar legislation.

The paradox is that cities where stricter gun control has been introduced have also seen dramatic falls in homicides. In Chicago, for instance, where moves were made to stem the flow of cheap, illegal firearms, and penalties for carrying firearms were stiffened, the number of murders dropped from 930 in 1994 to 823 in 1995. Paul Jenkins of the Chicago Police Department is in no doubt that his force's approach to the gun problem has had results. Gang members and drug dealers are simply leaving their guns at home, rather than risking long prison sentences for carrying firearms during a felony. "We'll arrest a whole crew," explained Jenkins, "and find no guns."

BATTLE FOR NEW ORLEANS

Perhaps one of the most impressive success stories can be found in New Orleans, a city with an appalling crime record. Here a "good cop—bad cop" approach was adopted. Lieutenant Edwin Compass explained his force's Community Oriented Policing Squads (COPS) initiative. The basic idea is to get tough and proactive. "If we see someone we don't know," said Compass, "we ask them what they're doing there. If the story doesn't check out, we arrest them for trespassing. Now we don't see as many drug dealers around here."

This aggressive tactic is balanced by a gentler hands-on approach to the wider populace. Squad cars have been largely replaced by foot patrols. "We do neighborhood clean ups, counseling on child abuse, you name it," said New Orleans police officer Djuana Adams.

To highlight the success of COPS, Compass cited a housing project at the junction of Congress and Law Streets, just outside the city's French Quarter. "A few years ago, it was a war zone," he explained. In the late 1980s, drug dealers had claimed the place as their own and the various gangs fought over the territory with regular shoot-outs and drive-bys. At a nearby kindergarten, preschool children had regular "shooting drills." An alarm would be sounded and they would dive under their desks until they were given the all clear. By 1994, there were at least three shootings a month in that single city block. "I'd bet it was the most dangerous block in the United States," Compass commented.

COPS was established in 1995 with federal backing. Police set up round-the-clock substations in vacant apartments on Congress and Law, and some of the city's other crime-ridden housing projects. The 50 officers who man these substations, patrol the projects on foot and get to know the residents on a one-to-one basis; they clear out the drug dealers, organize squads to remove graffiti and pick up trash, and send truants back to school. The results have been nothing short of miraculous. By the end of 1995, the murder rate had dropped by 75 percent. "The rate is still unacceptable." said Lieutenant Compass, "but we're getting there."

The law-abiding residents of the housing projects, once afraid to leave their homes, feel a measure of security again. "I felt better almost as soon as the police moved in," said Brenda Holmes, a resident of the Desire housing project. "They've given us our lives back."

COMMUNITY POWER

While the move back to community policing was pioneered in the big cities, it is by no means restricted to them. In 1993, the small cotton town of Taylor, Texas, was invaded by crack dealers, and with them came an epidemic of murder, rape, and burglary. Crime got so bad 79-year-old Mae Willie Turner was afraid to sit out on her porch at night. "The place was infested," she said.

Then came Turn Around Taylor, a community action group aimed at helping the good citizens of Taylor to regain control of their town. In 1993, after a teenager was murdered in a gang fight, police chief Fred Stansbury called in Herman Wrice, a Philadelphia management consultant who helps organize anti-crime groups as part of a federal program. "We wanted a program where the community felt it had a proprietary interest," said Stansbury.

The citizens of Taylor, including Mae Willie Turner, took to the streets, decked out in jackets emblazoned with the slogan "Up With Hope—Down With Dope." They demonstrated in the areas worst affected by the drug epidemic. Chief Stansbury had the downtown district of the town declared a historic area, which meant a ban on the public consumption of alcohol.

The citizens' group even managed to persuade the National Guard to level 50 derelict buildings which had become a haven for drug dealers and their customers. The campaign was an unqualified success and the dealers left town. "I can sit on my porch anytime now," said Mae Willie Turner.

In a world where politicians like to take the credit for everything good that happens, it is only fair to give some credit to President Clinton for his police initiatives. When elected to the White House for the first time in 1992, Clinton vowed to put 100,000 new police on the

MAN OF VISION: New York Police Commissioner William Bratton is credited with pioneering the zero tolerance policy.

SUCCESS STORY: Lieutenant Edwin Compass at a Community Oriented Policing Squads' substation in New Orleans. The crime rate here has been greatly reduced.

beat in the United States. He applauded the numerous subsequent community policing initiatives, along with the fall in crime generally. "What's happening across America," he said, "essentially closes the door on what began with the Kitty Genovese case 30 years ago."

He was referring to an appalling example of public indifference to the plight of others, when Kitty, a young woman from New York City, was murdered while dozens of people ignored her cries for help. "I know now that we have ended both the isolation of the police from the community and the idea that the community doesn't have a responsibility to work with the police or with its neighbors . . . I don't tell these folks how to deploy the police or what they should do all day. All I say is that there has to be a community policing strategy because that's by definition a grass-roots reform, and we know that it works."

There is no doubt that the new policing approach is one of many factors which has helped reduce the nation's appalling crime rate. Whether it can be sustained remains a matter for conjecture.

PEACEFUL LIVING: The residents of many New Orleans' housing projects now feel more confident about the security of their possessions.

Fall of an Icon

Bill Cosby is the most successful black actor ever. More than that, he became a role model who transcended the racial divide, representing to many the perfect family man. Then, in the space of a few days, his life was shattered: his son was murdered, and his good reputation was destroyed when he admitted infidelity to his wife of 35 years.

On January 1, 1996, Bill Cosby had everything—success, fortune, and the unbridled love of the American public. Two weeks later, the 59-year-old entertainer's life was dragged through hell.

The saga started on January 14, when 22-year-old Autumn Jackson faxed Cosby's lawyer claiming to be his illegitimate daughter, demanding $40 million for her silence, and threatening to sell her story to the *Globe*, a supermarket tabloid, if her terms were not met. Cosby contacted the FBI and Jackson was arrested, along with her accomplice, 51-year-old Jose Medina. They were charged with conspiracy and extortion.

CRIME SCENE: Police officers search for clues beside Ennis Cosby's convertible. Cosby was shot to death in Los Angeles on January 16, 1996.

FATHER AND SON: Bill Cosby and his only son Ennis sit courtside at a New York Knicks basketball game in Madison Square Garden.

said, "and I'm very sorry." The terrrible news was that Bill Cosby's only son, 27-year-old Ennis, had been gunned down in Los Angeles. His body had been found at 1:45 a.m. lying in a pool of blood outside the driver's door of his Mercedes-Benz sports car. The car's hazard lights were flashing and the trunk of the car was open. Ennis Cosby had apparently been changing a flat tire when he was killed by a single shot to the head. L.A. police chief Willie Williams said he believed that the motive for the killing was robbery, adding that "the perpetrator was only there for a few moments or even seconds."

On hearing the news of his son's death, Cosby climbed into his Range Rover and headed back to his Manhattan brownstone. Scores of reporters were waiting on his doorstep when he got home and the actor told them: "He was my hero. This is a life experience too difficult to share."

RANDOM ATTACK?

The police believed that the murder had been random and opportunistic, always the most difficult type of crime to solve, but at least they had one witness, 47-year-old screenwriter Stephanie Crane. Ennis Cosby had been driving to see Ms. Crane when he had a blowout on the Mullholland Drive slip road of the I 405 freeway. He called her on his mobile phone and asked her to drive over from her home to where he was stranded. He

Cosby flatly denied that Autumn Jackson was his daughter, but freely admitted that he had paid for her college tuition. He pointed out that he had helped pay for the education of dozens of impoverished black youth through a trust he had set up in the late 1970s. The press and the public, who identified him so closely with Dr. Heathcliffe Huxtable, the lovable family man he portrays in The Bill Cosby Show, seemed inclined to take him at his word. Only Cosby himself knew that it was only a question of time before the truth came out and his squeaky-clean image would be damaged beyond repair.

GUNNED DOWN

There was much, much worse in store for Bill Cosby. Two days after the extortion attempt, Cosby was called out of rehearsals in a television studio in Queens, New York, to take a phone call from his publicist, David Brokaw. "I've got the worst news to tell you," Brokaw

ALLEGED DAUGHTER: Autumn Jackson leaves federal custody on the arm of her attorney, Robert Baum, after posting $250,000 bail.

said he needed her to shine her headlights onto his car so that he could see what he was doing while he changed the tire. Ms. Crane claimed that she reached Ennis at about 1:40 a.m., 15 minutes after receiving his call, and focused her headlights on the Mercedes while Ennis replaced the lug nuts.

Moments later, she said, she became very frightened when she saw a "suspicious-looking" man walking toward Cosby. She panicked and drove off. A few minutes later she returned to the scene to find Ennis lying beside his car in a pool of blood.

Crane called the police immediately. A police officer was on the scene just minutes later and found Crane standing over Ennis's body. "She was freaking out," reported the officer, "sobbing and saying: 'Why, why, why?'"

Crane told police that she had only met Ennis the previous week at a party given by a mutual friend. She described the man she had seen approaching Ennis's car as white, about 5ft 7in (1.75m) tall, in his early twenties, and wearing a woollen cap. She was taken to police headquarters to help a sketch artist to construct a composite of the suspect.

PUZZLES

There were several things about the murder that puzzled the police. The killing had happened in one of the city's safest neighborhoods where there is very little crime. Nothing had been taken from the car, and Ennis's wallet was still in his pocket containing what police described as "a decent amount of cash." Officers also described the flat tire on the car as being "unusual," and said that they were investigating the possibility that it had been deliberately slashed after the murder.

Investigators were anxious to trace Ennis Cosby's movements earlier on the night of the murder. He had worked out at Los Angeles' exclusive Sports Center, between 6:30 and 10:30 p.m., but the staff knew nothing of his whereabouts between the time he left the club and calling Stephanie Crane.

Police made a statement saying that they considered it unlikely that Ennis was killed by anyone he knew. He had only recently arrived in Los Angeles from New York to embark on a postgraduate degree course and, apart from colleagues of his father, knew virtually nobody in the city.

PUBLIC GRIEF

The Cosby family were not alone in mourning the death of Ennis Cosby, who was not just Bill's son, but was an outstanding role model for young black Americans in his own right. Having struggled to overcome dyslexia, he had gone on to excel as a student, graduated from Morehouse College in Atlanta, taught special needs students in New York City, and was about to embark on a doctorate in education.

When one of Ennis's special needs students, Walter Stephen Douglas, heard of his murder, he was devastated. "I cried all day," he said, "I put a picture of Ennis on the bed and cried myself to sleep. He just went away and part of me went with him. I understand why his dad said he was his hero. He was a hero to me too. I wanted to be like him. The way he got over his problem. I thought I could do the same thing. I wanted to do what he wanted to do—open a school for kids like me. I figure if I put myself to it, I could be a teacher and make it fun . . . just like Ennis."

Few of the countless people who mourned Ennis Cosby had actually met him, but they seemed to feel connected through his screen alter ego, Theo Huxtable, Bill Cosby's son on *The Bill Cosby Show*. "It feels like losing a relative," said Kai Brooks, a student at Howard University. "I mean, my God, we grew up with Bill Cosby."

It was a shared intimate grief with the

BRIGHT FUTURE: A smiling Ennis Cosby poses for his high school yearbook. Cosby overcame his dyslexia to become a brilliant academic.

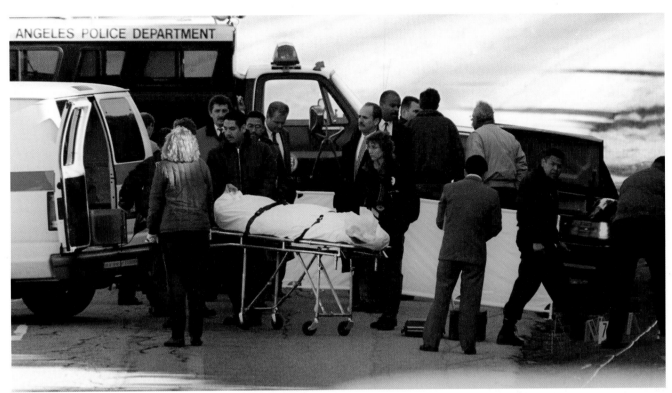

SAD DEMISE: Officers from the Los Angeles Police Department remove Ennis Cosby's body from the scene of the crime.

treasured entertainer and philanthropist, like some universal family agonizing for a kindly uncle who was struggling to handle the worst personal tragedy a father could imagine.

Ennis's murder prompted eulogies about Bill Cosby himself. David Marc, a lecturer at UCLA film school, spoke for countless millions when he said: "He's a black man that white America dreams of, anti-O.J., anti-Farrakhan." Charles B. Rangel, a Democratic Congressman from New York and a friend of Cosby, said: "Bill Cosby epitomizes how we want America to be. When he talked about his make-believe family, he was talking about his own family, about our own families, our own lives. Now Bill has lost a son and the country has lost a family member."

Within days of this outpouring of goodwill, however, Bill Cosby would not only have lost his son, but also his precious reputation.

CONFESSION

As police continued their investigation into the murder of Ennis Cosby, the Autumn Jackson affair refused to go away. In an attempt to quell rumors that he was indeed the girl's father, Bill

SHATTERED: Bill Cosby leaves his home with his wife Camille, just hours after receiving the news of their son's death.

ARTIST'S IMPRESSION: A composite drawing of the suspect in the Ennis Cosby murder case. The likeness was created with the help of key witness Stephanie Crane.

A caller to a New York radio show spoke for an untold number of black Americans: "I really looked up to him. He made me feel good about being black. Now I feel ashamed for him and I feel foolish that I gave him my trust."

Bill Cosby's wife, Camille, however, found it in her heart to be more forgiving. "We are a united couple," she told the press with great dignity. "What occured 23 years ago is not important to me except for the current issue of extortion. What is very important to me is the apprehension of the person or persons who killed our son."

Attorneys for Autumn Jackson, who was on remand in New York, were quick to grasp the opportunity Cosby's confession offered. "If she's his daughter," said a spokesman, "she's committed no crime. She has a perfect right to tell the world." It is highly unlikely that the courts will view the extortion attempt in such a benevolent light.

TABLOIDS TO THE RESCUE

Within days of Ennis Cosby's murder, *The National Enquirer* posted a $100,000 reward for information leading to the arrest and conviction of his killer. In the following issue, however, they published the Autumn Jackson story.

Cosby agreed to do an in-depth interview with CBS news anchorman, Dan Rather. The program, which was aired on Monday, January 27, 1997, was a bombshell. The interview initially concentrated on the murder but then moved on to the attempted extortion. Asked by Rather if he knew Autumn Jackson's mother, Shawn Thompson, Cosby admitted that he did and then went on to say: "If you are asking, 'Did you make love to this woman?' the answer is yes." Asked if he was the father of Autumn Jackson, Cosby said: "There is that possibility."

America was shocked, and the press, which had spent the past week eulogizing Cosby, turned on him. The headlines screamed "I've Strayed" and "Cosby's Cheated Wife!" The family's recent tragedy was forgotten as the press pilloried Cosby as a hypocrite.

"The Cosby-Jackson affair has set back the black community," said Professor James Barnett, a New York political scientist. "Many whites suspected that Cosby was too good to be true. They resented his power and money. Now they have found that his house is also made of glass. It will reinforce all the negative stereotypes of black males."

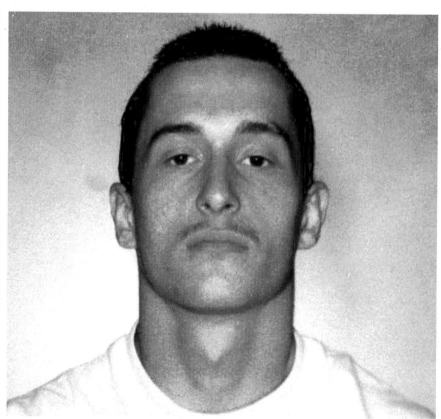

PRIME SUSPECT: Eighteen-year-old Ukranian immigrant Mikhail Markhasev was arrested for the murder of Ennis Cosby after a tip off to a leading tabloid.

PRESS CONFERENCE: Defence attorney Charles Lindner (left) entered a plea of innocent to murder on behalf of his client Mikail Markhasev.

The Cosby family reacted with rage and indignation. Camille Cosby called the editor of the *Enquirer*, Steve Coz, personally, requesting that he withdrew the reward. "I do not want their money to be associated with our son," she said.

Unbeknown to her, however, the tabloid had already received a tip-off which they had handed on to the police and which would eventually lead to an arrest in the Ennis Cosby case. Showing uncharacteristic restraint, Coz had agreed to delay publishing the story lest it jeopardized the police's attempt to build up a case against the suspect. "We were sitting there with a dynamite story that we could have splashed," said Coz.

On Wednesday, March 12, Los Angeles Police Chief Willie Williams announced that an 18-year-old Ukranian immigrant, Mikail Markhasev, had been arrested and charged with the murder of Ennis Cosby. They made no mention of the *Enquirer*, which had given them his name more than six weeks earlier.

Steve Coz later said that, after offering the reward, the magazine had received hundreds of calls, most of which were obviously bogus. One, however, sounded hopeful. On January 26, ten days after the murder, a man who wished to remain anonymous, called the *Enquirer*, and spoke to reporter John South. He claimed to know the identity of Cosby's killer. South had heard it all before, but this tipster seemed to know details about the case which had been deliberately suppressed by the police.

MYSTERY TIP OFF

A meeting was arranged between the "tipster" and reporters from the *Enquirer*. Explaining how he had first met Mikail Markhasev, the tipster said, "Mike [Mikail] was going to give my friend [also anonymous] a gun. It was about a week after the shooting. My friend knew Mike from the Youth Authority juvenile work camp. My friend and I drove up to see Mike in the North

Hollywood area. We stopped at a phone booth at the corner of Laurel Canyon and Magnolia and my friend called Mike.

"Ten minutes later, the guy showed up. He was about 6ft (1.82m) tall, wearing a dark blue coat with a hood. The first thing I noticed about Mike was how jumpy he was. He was nervous, seemed to be on speed, and talked non-stop.

"As he got into the car, he asked us to drive some place quick. We went down a street near the Los Angeles River and I parked near some residential buildings. While I waited in the car, my friend and Mike started going through the bushes, looking for what I later found out was a gun. Within a few minutes they came out of the bushes. As I sat in the front seat, Mike and my friend stopped about 10ft (3.04m) from the car and started talking. That's when I overheard Mike say, 'I just shot a nigger and it's all over the news.'

"When he got back into the car, Mike said, 'I've got to get home. I've got to lay low for a very long time.'

PUBLIC GRIEF: A young girl takes flowers to the gate of Bill Cosby's country home in Shelburne, Mass. All America shared Cosby's sense of loss.

"I didn't believe him at first. I thought he was just a young kid on drugs talking out of his hat. He said, 'Well, we didn't find the gun. I'm worried it might have been washed away. I hid it in the bushes in a knit cap.'

"By this time I was getting pretty nervous because Mike was so jumpy. My only thought was: 'I want this guy out of my car.' We drove back to Mike's home, a big apartment complex on the corner of Whitsett and Magnolia. He invited us in for a Russian beer, but I said: 'No, we've got things to do.' As we drove off, I told my friend: 'That guy isn't all there. I'm glad we had no part of that gun. He's crazy even to talk like that.'

"Then my friend said: 'Man, he's the guy who killed Bill Cosby's son. He told me he's the one. Mike was on crack. He walked up to Ennis and put the gun in his face. Ennis told him: 'Take it easy, man. Calm down. I've never had a gun flashed in my face before.' Ennis was really nervous and that made Mike nervous. Ennis probably took too long to give Mike what he wanted, which was money. He was just out to mug the guy."

The tipster went on to say that he still didn't really believe that Mikail was the killer until he saw the police sketch of the suspect, and noticed the likeness. He and his friend had then discussed what they should do about the situation.

PUBLIC CONFESSION: Bill Cosby during his revealing interview with Dan Rather when he shocked the American public by admitting to his infidelity.

TRIBUTE: The scoreboard for a basketball game in the CoreStates Center calls for a moment of silence in respect for Ennis Cosby's murder.

His friend had not wanted to get involved. The tipster, who had read about the reward, contacted *The National Enquirer*, and they had handed over the information to the LAPD, giving the tipster's name and beeper number.

On March 7, more than a month after they had been contacted by the *Enquirer*, the LAPD finally got round to approaching the tipster. He repeated his story, and then accompanied police officers along the route he had taken with Mikail and his friend some weeks earlier, showing them the phone booth where they had met and the bushes where the two men had looked for the gun.

A police search of the area eventually turned up a .38 caliber handgun, tightly wrapped up in a woollen hat. Subsequent ballistic reports confirmed that it was the weapon used to murder Ennis Cosby.

Police kept Mikail Markhasev under surveillance for five days before finally arresting him and then charging him with the killing.

David Brokaw, Cosby's publicist, said Bill Cosby and his wife were greatly relieved by the arrest. "I sense a real sense of triumph, exuberance, and something along the lines of closure," Brokaw said. "Everybody recognizes that these processes don't come and go in a week or two. But at least now there's great hope that the police can jump on what looks like a promising lead and pursue the case to its conclusion. Mrs. Cosby wants this man and she wants him now and wants him appropriately prosecuted and convicted."

On March 15, Mikail Markhasev made a brief appearance in Los Angeles County Court and was charged with murder "with special circumstances," a charge which allows the prosecutors to seek the death penalty.

THE SUSPECT AND THE VICTIM

The murder of Ennis Cosby is doubly tragic because of its random and futile nature. A young man is mending a flat tire in the early hours of the morning and another young man, whom he has never set eyes on, walks up and shoots him dead. For what? A few dollars which he didn't even take.

The background of the two men could not have been more different.

Ennis Cosby was well educated, privileged, and born into a celebrity family. Markhasev came to the United States with his mother in 1989, aged 10, an impoverished immigrant from the crumbling Soviet Union.

Like Ennis, he was a potentially bright youth and was initially enrolled in a gifted student's program, but it was not long before he fell into bad company and he spent the next few years drifting in and out of schools in Los Angeles, West Hollywood, and Orange County. During this time he picked up the nickname "Pee-wee," because of his supposed resemblance to the comic actor Pee-wee Herman.

By the time he was in his mid-teens, Markhasev was on the streets of Los Angeles, running with the Mexican gangs and involved with the petty street crime they espouse.

In 1995, Markhasev, still only 16 years old, was found guilty of possession of marijuana and assault with a deadly weapon. He was sentenced to six months in an Orange County juvenile probation camp. There was only one direction for him after that—down.

Flight to Oblivion

When TWA Flight 800 exploded and crashed into the sea south of Long Island on the evening of July 17, 1996, killing all 228 people onboard, the immediate assumption was that the aircraft had been the victim of a terrorist bomb. After more than a year of investigation, the FBI and the National Transportation Safety Board still cannot answer the question, did the plane fall or was it pushed?

There was nothing extraordinary about the scene outside Gate 27 of JFK International Airport, New York, on the evening of Wednesday, July 17, 1996. A couple of hundred passengers were milling around, clutching their boarding passes and waiting to be ushered aboard TWA Flight 800, bound for Paris, France. There was the usual gamut of emotions: anticipation, excitement, apprehension, and downright boredom at the prospect of the 7¼-hour flight.

There was nothing unusual about the waiting passengers either. Three school teachers from Montoursville High School were trying to keep track of the 16 students in their charge. Ruth and Edwin Brooks, an octogenarian couple from Edgartown, Massachusetts, seasoned travelers who had visited every continent in the world save Antarctica, were relishing the prospect of what might be their last trip overseas. Jack O'Hara, a producer for ABC Television who was on his way to cover the Tour de France cycle race, was far from relishing the trip, however. He hated flying and, to ease his anxiety, the network had agreed to throw in tickets for his wife and 13-year-old daughter. Little Larkyn Dwyer from New River, Arizona, was excited about the prospect of celebrating her twelfth birthday under the Eiffel Tower. Michel Breistroff, a 29-year-old star ice hockey player, was looking forward to rejoining his team after a vacation in New England where he had been a student. It was the usual eclectic mixture of men, women, and children who made up a scene that is repeated in departure lounges around the world every day of the year.

LONG SEARCH: Divers unload equipment from a rubber raft after finishing their day's search for the wreckage of TWA Flight 800.

RELIABLE CRAFT: A TWA 747 touches down at the airline's St. Louis headquarters. It was an aircraft of this type that carried the passengers of Flight 800 to their deaths.

The boarding call came shortly after 7:30 p.m. and the passengers started to file onto the aircraft, little realizing what fate had in store for them that night.

The plane allocated to Flight 800 was one of the oldest Boeing 747s still in service. Built in 1971, Boeing 747 #N93119 had flown to every corner of the world during its quarter-century of service, but more recently had been restricted to the transatlantic routes, flying out of Washington DC and New York to Paris and various destinations on the Mediterranean, including Athens and Tel Aviv. Not that its age was any reflection on the aircraft itself. Officers who had flown her spoke highly of #N93119, an opinion which is backed up by its Federal Aviation Record. In 25 years of service, only two minor mishaps were recorded: a blown tire on take-off in 1987, and a faulty oil line, which caused an engine to shut down in 1988. Overall, it was an enviable record.

And so, at 8:02 p.m., with all the final flight checks completed, the passengers and crew safely strapped in their seats, Flight 800 trundled down the runway and took off. It flew south briefly and then headed east along the southern coast of Long Island.

FIREBALL
It was a warm evening and at 8:48 p.m. many of the residents of East Moriches were still enjoying barbecues in their yards. Randy and Cecelia Penney were among the many who saw the explosion, a fireball in the sky to the south. Cecelia said later, "I thought, is this nuclear war? It was like I was watching it on TV." Randy, however, was in absolutely no

doubt about the source of the fireball. He rushed down to the dock to join a rescue party which was already assembling. They all piled aboard the six small boats at their disposal and headed for the crash site. They had no trouble locating it. "The water was on fire with fuel," Randy said later. "We pulled three bodies out of the water; two of them were still strapped into their seats. We had to get them out of there quick because we didn't want them to sink." Of the 18 people Randy saw pulled out of the water, most had their clothes blown off. "I tried not to look at them, at their faces. I didn't have time to think about what I was seeing. We were out there looking for survivors. At about 3:00 a.m., it became apparent there were none."

Long before Randy Penney and the little armada from East Moriches had

abandoned hope, a massive rescue operation had been mounted. The crew of a National Guard C-130 had been on an air-sea rescue training exercise not far from the crash site. They radioed in a mayday signal and then headed for the wreckage. Within minutes of the alert, an official rescue operation was under way, with craft heading to the site from as far away as New York City and Cape Cod, Massachusetts.

The rescuers spent all night hauling lifeless bodies out of the sea, most of which had all their limbs broken. By dawn the rescuers were forced to accept that their task was hopeless. There was no chance of anyone having survived the crash. The 210 passengers and 18 crew of TWA Flight 800 were officially pronounced dead.

NO WARNING
Flight 800 had taken off without incident and then, 45 minutes later, it had simply disappeared off the radar screen. There had been no message from the pilot to indicate that the aircraft was in any sort of trouble. There was no question of a mid-air collision, so it appeared that Flight 800 had simply, but catastrophically, disintegrated in mid-air. A veteran TWA pilot spoke volumes when he said: "747s don't just fall out of the sky. There is nothing a crew member can do to make a plane blow up like that."

Speculation that Flight 800 might have been the target of a terrorist bomb was immediate. The authorities added considerable weight to that theory by assigning more than a hundred FBI agents to the crash investigation. Within hours of the disaster, the agents were

SPELLED OUT: The information board at Charles de Gaulle Airport in Paris announced euphemistically that TWA Flight 800 had been "cancelled."

studying the passenger manifest in search of possible leads.

The National Transportation Safety Board was more circumspect about the possible cause of the demise of Flight 800. Its decisions are based on painstaking research and reconstruction, rather than gut instinct. The first, and most vital task was to recover the so-called "black boxes," two heavily armored electronic devices, one of which records the communications between the cockpit and ground control, the other which monitors the aircraft's vital signs. Both boxes, along with the shattered carcass of Flight 800, were currently resting on the ocean bed at a depth of about 140 feet (43m). Other wreckage was scattered over a vast area, and the hunt for debris promised to be long, hazardous, and far from pleasant. And so it proved.

The job fell to the US Coast Guard to search an area of seabed that covered more than 232 sq miles (600sq km). At least 400 personnel were seconded to the search, along with four helicopters, nine Coast Guard cutters, and a C-130 plane. The crash site was split into grids, and each subsection was systematically combed, inch by inch. Every fragment of the Boeing 747, every human body part, and every item of personal effects was

SHATTERED REMAINS: A piece of debris from TWA Flight 800 floats in the waters off Long Island. It took weeks of searching before the bulk of the wreckage was discovered.

YOUNG VICTIM: Larkyn Dwyer (left) and her friend Charlotte Cain in a photograph signed by President Bill Clinton. Larkyn was on her way to see Charlotte in Paris aboard Flight 800.

picked up and shipped immediately to the FBI forensic laboratory.

The working conditions for the hundred or so divers were appalling. At a depth of 120 feet (36.5m), the water temperature was less than 50°F (10°C); the water pressure was horrendous and visibility virtually nonexistent. "It was a scene from hell," said one of the divers, "decapitated corpses, severed limbs, chunks of aircraft, a kid's teddy bear. You couldn't stay down there for long."

THEORIES

While the debris was being retrieved, and the search for the black boxes continued, innumerable theories were put forward as to what had caused the explosion of Flight 800. They varied from the probable, that a bomb had somehow been smuggled aboard the airliner, to the implausible, that it had been shot down by a surface-to-air missile.

The FBI were anxious to reconstruct an exact history of the plane in the 24 hours before the crash. Boeing 747 #N93119 had left Athens at 1:25 p.m. (local time) on the morning of July 17, and landed at JFK at 4:38 p.m. (local time) on the same day. The immediate

THE JIGSAW: Bit by bit, the wreck was pieced together in Calverton, New York. This section comprises more than 700 individual fragments.

suspicion was that a bomb had been smuggled aboard in Athens, then hidden aboard the plane, and timed to detonate shortly after it took off again from New York for Paris.

DENIALS
The Greek authorities were less than impressed by this. Dionyssios Kalofonos, Director of the Greek Civil Aviation Authority, did not conceal his anger when he said: "Before the TWA Boeing aircraft left for Kennedy airport, it was parked in Pit #22, where some 15 maintenance experts inspected it. The plane was not left unattended for a minute."

Evangelos Markoulis, spokesman for the Greek Public Order Ministry, was equally adamant that the favored theory was impossible. "To be precise, a time-bomb has 12 hours less one minute to blow up. The flight to Kennedy is 10 hours. Therefore, if such a device had been planted on board the aircraft, it would have gone off after it landed at Kennedy and before it departed for Paris." He added that there had been many recent improvements to airport security in Athens and that all the passengers boarding the flight to New York had been searched twice, first by the Greek authorities, and then by TWA security personnel.

The Greek authorities put forward a convincing argument. How then had a

bomb, if indeed it was a bomb, been smuggled aboard the aircraft? Another theory was advanced which suggested that a terrorist had flown to New York from Athens and hidden a bomb on board, priming it during the flight, and then disembarked empty-handed. This was considered unlikely. During the turnaround period, the airliner would have been thoroughly searched and any items of baggage would have been removed before reembarkation.

MORE SPECULATION
So could the bomb have been taken aboard at JFK? Unless this was a suicide bombing, that would have been virtually impossible. No item of baggage can be stowed in the hold without its owner boarding the plane. The bomber could have conned some other passenger to carry a piece of baggage for him or her, but again this was deemed very unlikely. All passengers are asked at check-in whether they packed their own bags and if anyone had asked them to take anything on board the plane for them.

TWA's security procedures are as good as any airline's in the world, and their personnel screening is extremely thorough. Despite this, the FBI investigated more than 50 ground and cabin crew who might have had access to Flight 800 while it was on the ground in New York. They also checked out freight

shippers who had consignments on the flight. They came up with nothing.

Another theory put forward was that a bomber could have used what security experts call the "Ramzi Yousef Technique." Yousef, who was arrested by US agents in February, 1995, boarded a Philippine Airlines shuttle flight to Japan. Hidden in various parts of his carry-on bag, Yousef had the components for making a bomb: gun cotton, nitroglycerine solution, and a micro-detonator and timer, both of which were concealed in a contact lens bottle. Airport security staff failed to identify these potentially lethal items when they X-rayed his bag. Once on board the plane, Yousef retired to the bathroom, assembled the device, returned to his seat, and tucked it under the cushion. He disembarked at the next stop and two hours later, while the plane was airborne, the bomb exploded, killing the passenger who had taken Yousef's vacant seat, and forcing the plane to make an emergency landing.

Security experts thought it might be possible that a terrorist, using Yousef's method, might have boarded the aircraft in Athens, assembled the bomb in mid-flight, hidden it, and disembarked in New York. He or she would have had to have found a more subtle hiding place than under a seat cushion—they are routinely checked—perhaps behind a panel

CHIEF INVESTIGATORS: FBI Assistant Director James Kallstrom (left), and National Transport Safety Board Vice-chairman Robert Francis on their way to meet the families of crash victims.

in the bathroom where he or she assembled the bomb.

The bomber could have used a relatively simple timer, set to detonate once Flight 800 was airborne and en route for Paris. If this was the case, why had he or she set it to go off so soon after take-off? This resulted in the aircraft crashing into relatively shallow water. Wouldn't the bomber have set it to detonate over the mid-Atlantic, where there would have been no possibility of investigators recovering the wreckage together with the incriminating evidence it held? Perhaps, after all, it was something as simple as a technical malfunction.

THE JIGSAW

While the FBI were speculating about the bomber, Tom Thurman, head of the FBI's explosives unit, was trying to establish whether there had been a bomb on board Flight 800 in the first place. Thurman was already a legend in his field. It was he who solved the riddle of Pan Am Flight 103 which exploded over Lockerbie, Scotland, in 1988. He achieved this, not by instinct but by meticulous observation. The clue was a tiny fragment of a circuit board which he recognized as identical to one employed in an unexploded bomb, seized by the CIA in Togo in 1986. Thurman knew that

the circuit board had originated in Zurich, Switzerland, and, when put under pressure, the manufacturers admitted having sold 20 such boards to Colonel Gaddafi's Libya.

Six days had elapsed since the crash and the Coast Guard divers had only

recovered a fraction of the wrecked plane. Every fragment the divers found was shipped to the FBI forensic laboratory where Thurman and his team subjected them to microscopic scrutiny, in their search for evidence of bomb damage. A member of the team described what they were looking for. "An explosion generates temperatures far greater than those in a crash scenario," he explained. "You get torturing, feathering, pitting, and tearing in the metal that's entirely different from the damage inflicted by a fire or a fall."

On Wednesday, July 24, exactly a week after the crash, investigators got their first break. Navy divers finally located and recovered the two "black boxes" from Flight 800. The boxes were immediately flown to the National Transportation Safety Board's laboratory in Washington DC for analysis. The flight data recorder, which monitors the aircraft's mechanical and navigational activities, had suffered some damage from saltwater corrosion having spent a week at the bottom of the Atlantic. The cockpit recorder, however, was undamaged and provided a single, vital clue. It had recorded a typical crew conversation at takeoff and for the first 11 minutes of the flight. Nothing in that conversation suggested that anything was wrong. Then there was silence, but just before the silence there was what Robert Francis, vice-chairman of the National Transportation Safety Board,

THE BLACK BOX: The flight data recorder from TWA Flight 800 was eventually discovered by divers. The recorder was damaged but still held important information.

ONE OF MANY: The coffin containing the body of TWA flight attendant Jill Ziemkiewicz is carried into St Patrick's Cathedral, New York.

called a "fraction-of-a-second sound." That sound was the same instantaneous crack which had been heard on the flight recorder of Pan Am Flight 103.

There now seemed little doubt that Flight 800 had been downed by a bomb, but agent James Kallstrom, head of the FBI investigating team, wanted absolute proof. "We need forensic evidence," he said, "before deciding that the crash was the result of a criminal act." Until he had that evidence, he went on to say, he could not rule out the possibility of a catastrophic mechanical malfunction in the aircraft as the cause of its demise.

CIA ACTION

For its part, the CIA appears to have been in little doubt about the cause of the TWA Flight 800 disaster from the outset. Within hours of the crash, the agency had contacted every one of its stations in the world, ordering case officers to hit the streets and put "ultimate pressure" on their contacts for information. The CIA is not given to making public pronouncements, but it appears that the agents came up with nothing.

Ten days after the crash, the salvage team had still only recovered about 1 percent of the wreckage. There was a buzz of excitement when the National Transportation Safety Board announced that one of the fragments had been tested by a mobile vapor detector and had shown a positive reading for explosive residue. This statement was almost immediately contradicted by the FBI forensic laboratory in Washington DC. A similar story emerged a couple of days later, claiming that National Transportation Safety Board investigators had found pitting on one of the metal fragments, but again the FBI contradicted this claim, saying that the pitting could easily have been caused by parts of the aircraft colliding as they fell.

What is certain is that the various agencies investigating the crash, rather than pooling resources and presenting a united front, appeared to be pulling in different directions and issuing wildly contradictory statements. This infuriated the relatives of the crash victims, as well as the media and the White House. At a press conference on August 1, President Clinton made it clear that he was unhappy about the way the investigation was proceeding. On a more positive note, however, he went on to announce that he had ordered tighter security measures at United States airports.

He had sent instructions to all airlines to be more thorough about screening passengers and their baggage, and to insure that all aircraft were meticulously searched when arriving in or leaving the United States. He also announced that he had charged his Vice-President, Al Gore, to head a committee to prepare a plan to install explosive-detection devices in all American airports. The

VITAL CLUES: US Army National Guard soldiers watch as the cockpit from TWA Flight 800 is winched onto a trailer in Hampton Bays, New York.

President accepted that this would mean more delays and inconvenience for passengers, and would probably add to the cost of air travel, but he felt this was a small price to pay if it could prevent another terrorist outrage.

Toward the end of August, investigators made what appeared to be a major breakthrough. For once the FBI and the National Transportation Safety Board spoke with one voice as they announced they had recovered fragments of the aircraft which bore minute traces of a chemical explosive. The bomb scenario appeared to have been proved beyond reasonable doubt.

HOPES DASHED

Two days after the announcement, however, investigators had to admit they had been hasty in their conclusions. Apparently, a month before the disaster, Boeing 747 #N93119, later allocated to Flight 800, had been used by police at

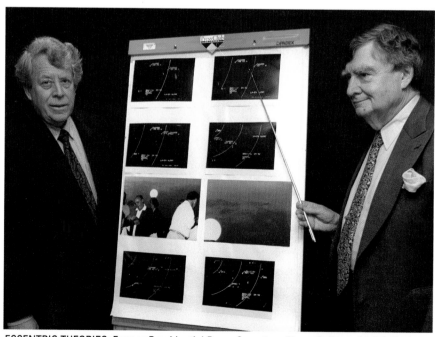

ECCENTRIC THEORIES: Former Presidential Press Secretary Pierre Salinger (right) displays radar photographs which, he claimed, proved Flight 800 was downed by a US Navy missile.

St. Louis airport for a security exercise. This had involved hiding test packages of PETN and RDX, both explosive ingredients, in the plane so that police dogs could hone their skills. The packages had been removed after the exercise but the FBI was forced to admit that traces could have been left behind and that these traces could, in their words, "possibly relate to the trace residues previously identified." Indeed, the PETN found on the floor of the passenger section of the plane, and the RDX found on a piece of the rear cargo compartment, had been puzzling investigators because neither section had showed any other evidence of bomb damage.

FRIENDLY FIRE
This revelation was extremely disheartening for the investigators. While there was no proof that the chemicals had resulted from the police dog exercise, it did introduce an element of doubt. "This discovery definitely hurts any attempt to build a circumstantial case for a bomb," said one FBI man. "Now we definitely need pitting or blast damage to prove that a bomb was placed on board."

The investigation into the downing of TWA Flight 800 wore on, producing nothing promising, let alone conclusive, in the way of evidence. The US public was beginning to lose interest. Then, in mid-November, Pierre Salinger, an ex-ABC news correspondent and former press secretary to John F. Kennedy, appeared on French television and announced that he had evidence which explained the fate of Flight 800.

He claimed to have documentation, given to him by an unnamed French intelligence officer, which offered "very, very, strong proof" that the aircraft had been destroyed accidentally by a missile fired from a US Navy warship during a training exercise. He claimed that, on the evening of the crash, an Air France pilot flying south of Long Island had been forced to make a sudden in-flight maneuver to avoid an incoming missile. Salinger gave his source as a passenger on the Air France flight, but declined to identify him.

WHISTLING IN THE DARK
The FBI interviewed the aircrews and passengers of all Air France flights that had been operating in that area on the night in question. They failed to find anyone who could corroborate Salinger's story. They also checked Navy records to see what activity there had been in the

THE AFTERMATH: A mourner grieves after attending the memorial service for the victims of Flight 800, which was held at hangar 208 at JFK International Airport.

area. They found that, at the time of the crash, their nearest ship had been 150 miles (241km) from the crash site, way out of missile range. Dismissing Salinger's friendly fire theory, investigators pointed out that a massive cover-up would have required a conspiracy of silence by hundreds of sailors, their officers, and an untold number of government officials. The investigators simply weren't buying it.

Salinger's theory was not the last idea to be advanced. One particularly eccentric possibility, fed into the Internet, was

that Flight 800 had been sabotaged in an attempt to assassinate an ex-Secretary of State, Henry Kissinger. As further investigation showed, however, not only was Kissinger not booked on that particular flight, he wasn't even in the United States on the night in question.

As conspiracy rumors continue to circulate, the crash investigators of TWA Flight 800 are persevering in their attempts to find forensic evidence that will answer the crucial question once and for all: "Was TWA Flight 800 pushed or did it fall?"

Death of a Princess

On December 26, 1996, JonBenet Ramsey's body was found in the basement of her parents' home in Boulder, Colorado. She had been bound, gagged, sexually assaulted, and then battered to death. JonBenet was a celebrity in Boulder and far beyond. With her blonde hair and ruby lips, she was a beauty queen. But she was a beauty queen with one major difference. JonBenet Ramsey was just six years old.

In the past 20 years, child beauty pageants have grown from a bizarre sideshow of the American South to a billion-dollar national industry. Every year, tens of thousands of prepubescent children, from California to New York, compete in more than 500 pageants for prizes in excess of $100,000. The lengths to which parents are prepared to go in the quest for victory in these events defy description. An entry fee can run to $500 and specially designed costumes about the same. More disturbing are reports that children as young as five often have their baby teeth removed and replaced by temporary dental plates. Some have even been subjected to extensive and painful plastic surgery to improve their chances of impressing the judges.

PRIZE WINNER

This was the world which John and Patsy Ramsey chose for their daughter JonBenet—pronounced "Shaunbernay." In the space of two years, she managed to win over 50 titles, including Little Miss Charlevoix and National Tiny Miss Beauty. Bedecked in furs, made up to the nines, the six-year-old pranced, danced, and pouted better than any of her peers. The question is, why did the Ramseys indulge in this pastime? They certainly didn't need the prize money. Fifty-three-year-old John Ramsey is a multimillionaire industrialist. His wife, Patsy, a former Miss West Virginia, might just provide the answer. Like many parents, she perhaps saw in JonBenet the answer to her own unfulfilled ambitions in the world of beauty pageants.

Whether little JonBenet's death is directly connected to the pageant world is still open to question, but there is no doubt that the 20 or more publications devoted to children's beauty pageants have become staple fodder for pedophiles. The temptation to make a link between that fact and the nature of JonBenet's death is irresistible.

RANSOM NOTE

It was Patsy Ramsey who went downstairs in the early hours of December 26, 1996, to find a three-page, hand-written note at the bottom of the staircase. The note started ominously: "We have your

LOST BEAUTY: Tragic murder victim JonBenet Ramsey decked out in one of the lavish and expensive costumes she wore to compete in beauty pageants.

HAPPY FAMILY: A Ramsey family portrait. JonBenet (seated on left) with her parents, brothers, and sister.

daughter . . ." It went on to demand a ransom of $118,000 for the child's safe release and contained threats about the consequences of the Ramseys contacting the police or the FBI.

According to Mrs. Ramsey, she immediately ran upstairs and checked her children's bedrooms. Her nine-year-old son Burke was sound asleep, but there was no sign of JonBenet. She then woke her husband and, despite the dire warnings in the ransom note against doing so, they immediately contacted the Boulder Police. Officers arrived in a matter of minutes, but not before John Ramsey had contacted his bank manager at home and arranged for the ransom money to be delivered.

Kidnap and murder are not a common occurrence in Boulder, Colorado. In fact, until December 26, there had not been a single killing in the city for more than a year. Despite their lack of experience in these matters, the local police handled the situation as best they could, while they waited for assistance from the Denver Police Department and the FBI. Officers searched the 15-room, mock-Tudor house and its two-acre (0.8ha) garden. They found nothing. They questioned the Ramseys at length and sat with them as they waited for a call from the kidnapper. None came. At about 1:30 p.m., the officers left, suggesting that John Ramsey search the house one last time.

According to John Ramsey, he conducted the search as the police had suggested and, after about 15 minutes, he entered a small windowless basement room. It was there, he claims, that he discovered the body of his youngest daughter, bound and gagged.

Upstairs, in the living room, Mrs. Ramsey and a neighbor, who had come over to comfort her, heard a scream and seconds later, John Ramsey burst into the room cradling JonBenet's body in his arms. He laid her under the Christmas tree and he and his wife made a frantic if futile attempt to revive her. Meanwhile the neighbor called 911.

FORENSIC NIGHTMARE

John Ramsey's actions in moving his daughter's body and attempting to revive her, understandable though they were, effectively destroyed the crime scene and made the forensic team's job virtually impossible. One of the investigating officers from the scene said later: "We arrived and the mother's hysterical, the father's hysterical; the minister's there; neighbors are running in and out. So there really wasn't a crime scene."

The police removed JonBenet's body from the family home and later that night a preliminary autopsy was conducted by the Boulder County Coroner's Office. The following morning, December 27, pathologist, Dr. Charles Wecht, an expert on crimes against children, told the court that JonBenet had died at approximately 10:00 p.m. on Christmas night. Pending a full autopsy, he stated that she had been asphyxiated, beaten over the head, and sexually assaulted. In his summing up, Wecht was as unambiguous in his disgust about the whole concept of child beauty pageants as he was about the crime itself.

He told the court that he was certain that the perpetrator of the crime was someone whom JonBenet knew and trusted, and that her death was directly

THE SEARCH WIDENS: Boulder detective Steve Thomas (center) leaves a house in Roswell, Georgia after searching it for clues into the murder of JonBenet Ramsey.

TINY CASKET: JonBenet Ramsay's pitifully small flower-bedecked casket is wheeled out of Peachtree Presbyterian Church in Atlanta.

might ask about." The disturbing feature about Dr. Wecht's testimony is that, despite his obviously genuine disgust at the crime committed, he appeared to have lost sight that the victim was only six years old and tacitly suggested that she might have been a willing participant in a sex game that led to her death.

PRIME SUSPECTS

In all murder cases, the police's initial reaction is to suspect a member of the immediate family or a close family friend. The Ramseys were no exception. The day after the coroner's report they were questioned at length at Boulder police station and gave hair, blood, and handwriting samples.

John and Patsy Ramsey told the police that the whole family had gone to bed early on Christmas night because they were planning to fly up to their holiday home in Minneapolis the following morning. They had put JonBenet to bed at about 8:00 p.m. There had not been any sort of disturbance during the night, and the first suspicion they had that something was amiss was when Mrs. Ramsey found the ransom note on the staircase.

The Ramseys were, according to police sources, rational, composed, and astonishingly unemotional considering the circumstances. The police, with no evidence against the Ramseys, gave them permission to leave.

The following morning, December 29,

linked to the lifestyle to which she had been subjected.

"Look at the pictures of herself," he said, "dressed like a young woman. She was six going on twenty-three. I don't think the person who did this ever had the intention of killing her. It was a sex game that went hideously wrong."

Dr. Wecht continued with his evidence. "She was restrained. She was held captive on the floor in a position for someone to sexually molest her . . . Her wrists were bound and a garrote was wrapped around her neck to torture her, not to kill her. The piece of wood was tightened so she couldn't move without inflicting pain. When she moved, it shut off the air . . . The intention was not to strangle and kill, but to gradually cause pain. It was a game and the game went very bad . . . That cord binding her wrists and looped over the sleeves of her night-dress, is also a key clue. When you bind someone in a sex game, you don't want to leave embarrassing marks people

HUNTING FOR CLUES: A detective dusts a window for fingerprints at the Ramsey family home in Boulder, Colorado.

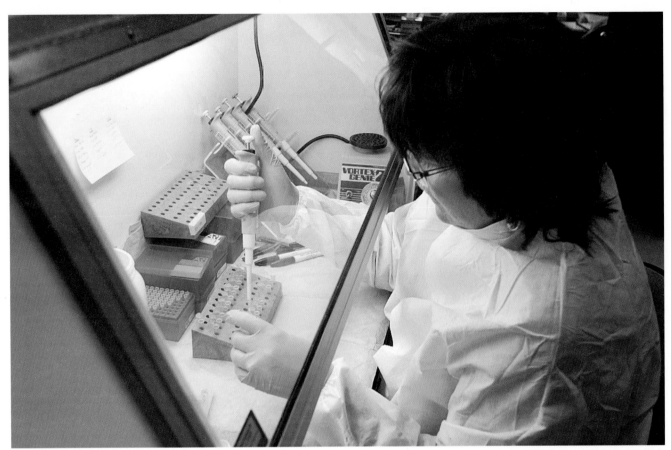

DNA TESTS: Laboratory technician Kathy Dressel works on DNA evidence in the Colorado Bureau of Investigation's headquarters.

after a private memorial service at St. John's Episcopal Church in Boulder, the family flew JonBenet's body to Atlanta, Georgia, their former home, and a funeral service was held with more than 200 mourners. JonBenet Ramsey was buried in one of her many pageant dresses, accompanied by her teddy bear.

Meanwhile the police concentrated their investigation on the Ramseys. Within a few days, they had come up with a number of clues, all of which suggested that either John Ramsey or Patsy Ramsey or both, might well be implicated in JonBenet's murder. Their house in Boulder revealed the most damning evidence. The police found a "practice" ransom note on a note pad which also carried imprints of the real note. Investigators found it strange that any kidnapper would arrive at the scene of the crime without having prepared such a note ahead of time. Would he or she really sit in the victim's house writing out a three-page letter by hand, let alone do it twice? Police also found Polaroid photographs of JonBenet partly clothed, some of which showed bruises on her upper arms. Had she been the victim of prolonged sexual abuse, either by her parents or someone close to the family?

In the Ramseys' vacation home in Minneapolis, police officers found a length of cord identical to the one used to garrote JonBenet. Questions as to how it had it got there were asked.

There were other questions too. From the outset, the $118,000 specified in the ransom note struck the investigators as a relatively modest sum to demand from a multimillionaire for the life of his daughter. Why not a million? Why not two million? Even more intriguing, it emerged that $118,000 was the exact amount John Ramsey had recently received as an annual performance bonus by his company. It seemed very unlikely that this could be a coincidence. The supposition was that if the Ramseys themselves had not killed their daughter, the real killer must have been someone very close to them with an intimate knowledge of their financial affairs.

There was no sign of forced entry at the Ramsey home. Why had the elaborate security system been switched off? There were numerous other anomalies, but the most puzzling question of all was why JonBenet Ramsey had been killed at all. It was clear that she had died several hours before her parents could possibly have discovered the ransom note, and

her body had been left where it was bound to be discovered. What possible incentive would the Ramseys have had to pay the kidnapper when they knew that JonBenet was already dead?

SELF-PRESERVATION

While not actually accused of, let alone charged with the murder of their daughter, the Ramseys were obviously in no doubt that they were under suspicion. Their reaction was, to say the least, proactive. Rather than throwing in their lot with the investigators, they immediately retained the services of a team of top criminal attorneys and a public relations consultant, Pat Korten.

On January 1, less than a week after JonBenet's death, John and Patsy Ramsey flew to Atlanta with their team of advisors. There they appeared on CNN not only to appeal for information which might lead to the arrest and conviction of their daughter's killer, but also to protest their own innocence. John Ramsey said he was "nauseated beyond belief" by suggestions in the press that he and his wife might be connected with the crime. "We are a deeply religious family," he said, "and our involvement is not within the realms of possibility." He went on to say that he was putting up a reward of $50,000 for information which led to the capture of JonBenet's killer. He added that he had retained the services of ex-FBI investigator John Douglas, the legendary pioneer of "personality profiling" and inspiration for the character Agent Jack Douglas in the film *Silence of the Lambs*.

During the interview, an immaculately groomed Patsy Ramsey remained silent save for periodically whimpering: "There's a killer on the loose."

The Boulder police were less than happy about the Ramseys' antics and, the following day, Boulder Mayor Leslie Durgin and senior police officers held their own press conference, during which they dismissed Patsy Ramsey's assertion that there was a "killer on the loose," insisting that the murder of JonBenet Ramsey was a one-off, and that the residents of Boulder could sleep easy in their beds. This could only be taken as a thinly veiled hint to the press that the police knew who killed JonBenet Ramsey and it was only a matter of time before they proved it.

LETTERS AND CALLS

For a while, the police's attention switched from John and Patsy Ramsey and focused on John's two children from his first marriage, Melinda and John Andrew Ramsey. Despite persistent rumors that they had been seen in Boulder over the Christmas holiday, both claimed to have spent the entire time in Atlanta, and that, on December 26, had left that city for Minneapolis where they had planned to meet their father and stepfamily at their vacation home. When they reached Minneapolis, however, a family friend had called them with the news that JonBenet had been kidnapped—her body had not yet been discovered—they had flown immediately to Denver and had taken a cab to Boulder. The police soon corroborated their story, and the spotlight immediately returned to John and Patsy, who were now staying in a variety of supposedly secret locations. Not that they were keeping a particularly low profile.

On February 8, Boulder Crime Stoppers announced that the Ramsey family had made $100,000 available to them as a reward for information leading to JonBenet's killer's arrest and conviction. Larry Wieda, president of Crime Stoppers International, explained the situation: "All we're doing is acting as a vehicle for any information that may come in." Explaining that his organization's rewards were usually in the region of $1,000, he added, "I can't remember any cases that were solved based on offering huge rewards." Despite Mr. Wieda's expert opinion, however, the Ramsey offer certainly generated a massive public response. Within a matter of days, Crime Stoppers had logged more than 1,500 phone calls from citizens claiming to have information relevant to the JonBenet murder.

CLOAK OF SECRECY

The police meanwhile were also inundated with unsolicited calls and letters offering information and help. By the middle of February, they had received more than 1,000 letters and 3,000 phone calls. Speaking for the Boulder police, Detective Steve Thomas told the press: "Only 5 percent of these have warranted some sort of follow-up." He appealed to the public not to waste police time with trivial or malicious calls. He made a special emphasis on calls and letters from ·people claiming psychic powers. Detective Thomas, however, did go on to express particular interest in one anonymous, handwritten letter which had been mailed from Shreveport, Louisiana. The writer claimed to be a parent whose own daughter had competed with JonBenet in a recent child beauty pageant. Detective Thomas said that author might have valuable information and appealed to him or her to come forward. They got no response.

John and Patsy Ramsey's press guru, Pat Korten, was quick to react to news of the mystery letter. He told the press that his clients knew nobody in Shreveport and had no idea who might have written the letter.

Whether it was genuine or not, there must have been something fairly startling in the letter for the Boulder police even to acknowledge its existence. Up to this time, the department had been extraordinarily tight-lipped about their ongoing investigation and had released virtually no information to the press at all. In fact the whole case seemed to be cloaked in secrecy. When John Meyer, the Boulder County Coroner, finished his autopsy on JonBenet Ramsey on February 11, he took the unusual step of refusing to release any details to the press, claiming that he had been told by Boulder detectives and prosecutors in the case that to do so would seriously jeopardize the search for the killer. A spokeswoman for the coroner said that, among the many details of the case that the police and District Attorney's office wished to keep secret, was how many wounds had been inflicted on the victim, the amount and nature of forensic evidence, and details of the *modus operandi* of the killer.

Similarly, two police affidavits and a report from the District Attorney's

CLAMORING FOR RESULTS: Leslie Durgin, Mayor of Boulder, is pressed by journalists for information about the murder of JonBenet Ramsey.

LUCRATIVE REWARD: The Ramseys announce a $100,000 reward for information leading to the arrest and conviction of their daughter's killer.

office, submitted to Boulder District Court, were deemed confidential and were delivered "under seal." The decision to suppress these documents, particularly the autopsy, was challenged in the District Court by Tom Kelly, an attorney working for the *Denver Post*, who claimed that 1,200 autopsies had been performed by the Boulder County Coroner's Office in the previous 10 years, and on no occasion had an objection been raised to release. District Judge Carol Glowinski, presiding, said she would consider the matter and deliver her decision within 48 hours. Her decision turned out to be a compromise. Judge Glowinski ordered that an edited, seven-page version of the report should be released and that remainder should remain "sealed" until 90 days had elapsed or the killer had been arrested, whichever came first.

The censored report contained very little information that had not already-been revealed at the original court hearing on December 27. The one grim new fact to emerge was that, at the time of

her death, JonBenet Ramsey was suffering from chronic inflammation of the vagina. The report went on to describe this condition as a possible indication of long-term sexual abuse.

PR man Pat Korten, speaking on behalf of the Ramsey family, was quick to respond to the implied allegation. He sought out JonBenet's pediatrician, Dr. Francesco Beuf, who made a statement claiming that he had never found any evidence of prior physical or sexual abuse to his patient.

MEDIA FRENZY

As February wore on, relationships between the police and the Ramseys continued to deteriorate. On February 12, the police requested that John and Patsy Ramsey come down to police headquarters to give a second set of handwriting samples. An indignant Pat Korten told the intrigued press that his clients had refused to comply with this request, saying that they had already given handwriting samples, along with blood and hair samples.

The District Attorney's office responded by threatening to seek a court order, which would compel the Ramseys to comply with the request. Denver

PHOTO OPPORTUNIST: Brett Allen Sawyer was arrested for selling photographs of the autopsy of JonBenet Ramsey.

BOYCOTT: The *Globe*, which bought the banned photos of JonBenet, was taken off sale at a number of Colorado supermarkets.

prosecutor Mike Little explained to the press that such an order, known as a 41.1, could only be sought if the authorities have "more than a hunch" that the person cited has committed a crime. "They have to have an articulable suspicion."

Faced with the threat of a 41.1, the Ramseys relented and cooperated with the police. Less than a week later, however, the police were back in contact with the Ramseys, requesting yet another set of handwriting samples. Pat Korten was soon back in front of the microphones. He told the press: "They made a verbal request to us, something like 'we're going to ask you for another handwriting sample, would you agree.' We said, give us something a little more substantial than that. Both parents have been very cooperative in the past in providing samples and things. Each of them twice went willingly. I think the minimum we'd be interested in having is a specific rationale why they need yet

SLOW PROGRESS: Boulder District Attorney Alex Hunter answers questions from reporters about the investigation into the JonBenet murder.

another one. We won't rule out being cooperative, I think, but I'm not sure."

Needless to say, all the publicity surrounding John and Patsy's regular visits to Boulder police headquarters reinforced press speculations that they were prime suspects in the murder.

The Ramseys were hounded by the press, day and night, and moved from one supposedly secret location to another, trying to stay one step ahead of the news crews. On February 12, Patsy Ramsey called the Boulder Sheriff's Department, complaining that she was being "stalked by the media." She and her husband, were staying at the home of a friend, Jay Elowsky, and she claimed that: "Vehicles used by reporters are parked up and down the street outside the house and they appear be studying the house through cameras and binoculars."

REVEALING PICTURES
There were apparently no depths to which the press would not sink in their competitive fight to get fresh material. On February 20, Brett Sawyer, a private

investigator, and Lawrence Smith, a lab technician, were found guilty in Boulder County Court of selling autopsy pictures of JonBenet to the *Globe*, a supermarket tabloid. Sawyer admitted receiving $5,500 for the pictures and said that he had given $200 of that money to Smith for obtaining the negatives. Sentencing the men to three days in jail and four days of community service, Judge Lael Montgomery ordered that the money should be given to the Boulder District Attorney's restitution fund, and that both men should write letters of apology to the Ramsey family. "This case has hardly even begun," said the judge, "and people are already acting crazy. You two made that child an object, a thing for people across the country to ogle and gape at."

Despite the state of near-hysteria which now prevailed, the police were still playing things very close to their chests, and refused to be drawn when faced with a barrage of questions at daily press conferences. Asked if John and Patsy were indeed suspects in the murder of their daughter, they declined to

comment, but assured their audience that they were making good headway with their investigations.

When pressed, Boulder District Attorney Alex Hunter was a little more forthcoming. On February 24, he filed a brief with the Boulder County Court in which he stated that John and Patsy Ramsey had definitely not been eliminated as suspects in their daughter's murder. That was about as far as Hunter could go without actually accusing them of the crime, a point which was not lost on Pat Korten. In a press statement, issued on February 25, he said: "All you have to do is to listen to what the police and District Attorney's office have been saying publicly over the past few weeks to recognize that they consider the Ramseys to be at the top of their list of potential suspects." As spring moved into summer, the police invited Patsy Ramsey to submit to further handwriting samples. Without witnesses or forensic material to support their case, however, it became obvious that they had insufficient evidence to press charges.

IN LOVING MEMORY: A simple wooden cross with a poignant message stands as a reminder of the tragic death of a six-year-old child.

Sex Crimes in the Military

When Private Jessica Bleckley, an army recruit, lodged a complaint against her drill sergeant for sexual assault, the floodgates opened, and the US Army found itself embroiled in the worst scandal in living memory.

The United States armed forces are no strangers to scandal. With more than a million and a half men and women in the services at any one time, it would be unrealistic to expect otherwise. The forces hold their image dear and guard it jealously, and, in the interests of public relations, prefer to deal with their own crimes and misdemeanors internally and, if possible, discreetly. Recent sex scandals that have struck the military, however, are of such gravity and are on so large a scale that they could not possibly avoid the glare of media attention.

The scandals are centered on, but by no means confined to, the Aberdeen Proving Ground in Maryland, home to the 143rd Ordnance Battalion. On November 7, 1996, a senior officer with the battalion announced that three male officers had been charged with rape, assault, and sexual harassment against recruits under their command, and that 17 other cases were currently under investigation. It promised to be the most serious sex scandal to hit the forces since the 1991 "Tailhook Incident," when dozens of women claimed to have been sexually assaulted by Navy aviators. No one was ever convicted in that case and there were screams of "cover up" and "whitewash."

The Army, anxious to avoid a repeat of Tailhook, announced that they would be launching an in-depth investigation into claims of sexual assault, not only at Aberdeen, but at bases throughout the United States and overseas. They promised that each and every case would be thoroughly investigated by the Army Criminal Investigation Command.

To this end, a confidential hot line was established at Aberdeen. Senior officers at the base were shocked when, in the space of two weeks, they received over 4,000 calls; some of the incidents dated back to World War II. More than a

SEX SCANDAL: The Aberdeen Proving Ground where officers were charged with offenses ranging from inappropriate conduct to rape.

COURTROOM SKETCH: Staff Sergeant Delmar Simpson was ultimately sentenced to 25 years for multiple rape.

Aberdeen itself. Captain Paul Goodwin, one of the officers manning the hot line, was appalled: "When you hear how sincere they are, it just breaks your heart."

IMPROPER CONDUCT
The majority of the calls were not accusations of rape or assault, but allegations of sexual relationships between officers and trainees under their command. The Army has an absolute code of conduct that forbids even consensual sex between a superior and subordinate in the same chain of command. In cases involving relationships between higher ranking officers, such misconduct may be treated leniently, but when it occurs between a drill sergeant and a raw recruit, it is viewed with the utmost seriousness. In the eyes of the Army such a relationship constitutes an abuse of power and a breach of trust.

The trouble at Aberdeen first surfaced in September 1996 when a recruit, Private Jessica Bleckley, lodged a complaint against Staff Sergeant Nathanael Beach, claiming that he had sexually assaulted her. Private Bleckley's courage in coming forward inspired other recruits, resulting in a deluge of accusations, alleging a variety of sexual acts to which women soldiers had been subjected. The majority of these accusations were leveled at one man, 30-year-old Staff Sergeant Delmar Simpson. Asked why they had not come forward earlier, many of the trainees claimed that Simpson had

FALL FROM GRACE: Captain Derrick Robertson was promptly discharged from the army after admitting sexual misconduct.

threatened to kill them if they lodged complaints against him. After a short investigation, Simpson was arrested and jailed, pending a court-martial.

The complaints were not solely restricted to drill instructors. One recruit claimed that she had been raped and assaulted by Simpson's commanding officer, Captain Derrick Robertson. Robertson was questioned by the Army Criminal Investigation Command and admitted having consensual sex with the young woman trainee, but denied raping her.

The decision by the Army to go public with these arrests was courageous. Not only did it put the military in a terrible light, it also invited accusations of racial discrimination, since 90 percent of the accused were black and the same percentage of the alleged victims were white. The investigators insisted, however, that they had found absolutely no evidence of discrimination and pointed out that the majority of drill sergeants at Aberdeen happened to be black.

It became clear that incidents of sexual misconduct at Aberdeen and other military bases had been going on for years. How, the press asked, could this have been happening without the knowledge of senior officers? It was suggested that, at best, there had been a serious breakdown in the chain of command and, at worst, there had been a level of tolerance toward such activities.

One female officer, who says she was subjected to sexual harassment during her training, agreed: "I'll bet you a million dollars some leaders knew what was going on a long time ago. When you've got multiple assaults, it's obvious

TOUGH REGIME: Drill Sergeant Eric Fitch supervises a demanding punishment drill at the Aberdeen Proving Ground in Maryland.

that some of them are looking the other way." Another female officer with 10 years' service goes further in her criticism. She claims that her career prospects were seriously damaged when she filed assault charges against a senior officer. "The trouble," she said, "is that the people who are investigating complaints are often the abusers."

When questioned, most soldiers were shocked and horrified by the rape and sexual assault allegations, but in the cases of consensual sex, people were far less surprised and were not particularly disapproving. "Sure it goes on," said Private David Smyth, of the 143rd Battalion. "We eat, sleep, and work together; attractions are bound to happen, not that I approve, mind you. It kinda messes things up. Girls that are getting it on with their sergeant tend to get preferential treatment and that leads to bad feelings with the other recruits."

Other drill sergeants at Aberdeen do not take such a liberal attitude, however. Sergeant Philip Cook talked about a class of trainees who arrived at the base

shortly after the sex allegations were made public. He saw fear in their eyes. "This thing took a lot of the power base away from my hat [referring to the wide-brimmed hat traditionally worn by drill sergeants]. It used to be that when they saw this hat, they knew that I was a straight-and-narrow type of person, and that I knew exactly what to do. But now there's a question in their minds."

For their part, the Army officials have made it clear that they have adopted a "zero tolerance" stance both on sexual abuse and fraternization. Parties guilty of the former will be court-martialed and jailed if found guilty, and those in the latter category will be dismissed from the force. The Army announced that they have taken various steps to combat the problems since the Aberdeen scandal broke. They have recently introduced rape-prevention classes for all new recruits, and drill sergeants are to be given training to avoid sexual-harassment. They have also reinforced the current "buddy system," whereby recruits are encouraged to

operate in pairs. Sergeant Cook believes this is a step in the right direction. "I never talk to soldiers alone," he said, "to protect both them and me."

THE RACE CARD

By the beginning of March 1997, more than 50 women had lodged official complaints of sexual abuse at Aberdeen, including 27 accusations of rape. Eight drill sergeants and one officer had been charged, and another 20 were under investigation. The Army took some consolation in the knowledge that, not only was justice being done, it was being seen done. But was it? On March 13, five women recruits, all white, came forward claiming that they had been bullied into making false accusations of rape against their black drill instructors. They claimed that they had been compelled by Army investigators to make false statements, after being offered immunity from prosecution for consensual sex with their officers, and being threatened with retaliation if they failed to cooperate. All five rescinded their original statements and admitted that any sexual contact they had had with officers had been totally voluntary.

"Eventually I agreed to say whatever they wanted to hear in order for them to leave me alone," claimed Private Brandi Knewson. "I just wanted to leave the post and get on with my life. They promised I could do that if I cooperated with them."

Private Knewson's story is corroborated by Kathryn Leming, a former recruit who has since left the army. She said she never claimed to have been raped but had been informed that, under military law, consensual sex with someone in the direct line of command was deemed to be rape. "They pushed me and pushed me until they basically tried to get me to say rape. But I wouldn't do it. It wasn't the truth," she said.

The other three women—Privates Toni Moreland, Kelly Wagner, and Darla Hornberger—all claim to have been subjected to verbal intimidation during their interviews with investigators. Private Hornberger, married with five children, said, "I could have kept my mouth shut and this would all blow over, but something really wrong has happened."

The five women are sponsored by the NAACP (National Association for the Advancement of Colored People), which claims that the whole investigation was aimed at implicating black, non-commissioned officers in cases of sexual abuse. Kweisi Mfume, president of the NAACP, considers the inquiry is totally discredited. "These statements [by the five woman who recanted] were not even written by them," he said at a press conference. "They were told they would be shipped to Korea, that they would not see their children if they did not sign these statements."

Lieutenant Colonel Gabriel Riesco, Chief of Staff at Aberdeen, strenuously denied that the five women had been coerced into making false statements. He reported that no rape charges had resulted from interviews conducted by any of his officers. "Race has never been an issue in this investigation at all," he avers, "It is an investigation about sin, not skin."

In March and April 1997, the two ringleaders in the sex scandal faced courts marshal. Sergeant Delmar Simpson was found guilty of 18 charges of rape and an assortment of lesser charges and was sentenced to 32 years in prison and a dishonourable discharge from the army.

FALSE STORY: Toni Moreland recanted her statement that she had consensual sex with Staff Sergeant Marvin Kelly.

Captain Derrick Robertson faired rather better. He admitted having sex with a female trainee but denied rape. In a plea bargain he was sentenced to four years in prison.

INTIMIDATED: Privates Kelly Wagner, Darla Hornberger, and Kathryn Leming claimed they had been pressured into lodging false claims.

Hitching a Ride to Death

Every year thousands of young people hitchhike on the roads of Great Britain. Many see it as a cheap and easy way of getting around the country, although it is one that has always been frowned upon by the police. The sudden disappearance of French teenager Celine Figard over Christmas 1995, sparking one of the country's biggest manhunts, showed a shocked nation exactly why.

On December 18, 1995, Celine, a 19-year-old accountancy student, set out from her family home in the small village of Ferrières-lés-Scey in eastern France to travel to southern England, where she planned to spend Christmas with a cousin. She had spent the previous summer in England, and wanted to improve her grasp of the language.

Wary of having their daughter hitchhike, Celine's parents had arranged for truck driver Guy Maillot, a family friend who was also traveling to England, to give Celine a lift through the Channel tunnel. Celine and Maillot spent most of the day on the road—stopping only to visit a vineyard on the way—before spending the night in Maillot's cab on the French side of the tunnel. The following morning they traveled through to England. Celine was then picked up by another French truck driver, Roger Bouvier, with whom she traveled as far as Chieveley, Berkshire—where Bouvier dropped her at an expressway service station. The plan was for Celine to call her cousin to arrange to be picked up from there.

REPORTED MISSING

However, having apparently dialed the wrong number, Celine was unable to get through to her cousin at the Southampton hotel where he worked. So instead she decided to try to hitch a lift with another driver who was going in that direction. Minutes after saying goodbye to Bouvier, she climbed into a white Mercedes-Benz truck driven by a man with a ginger beard. It was the last time she was seen alive.

On Wednesday, December 27, seven days after Celine's disappearance, her father Bernard traveled to England to appeal for help from the public in the search for his missing daughter. At a press conference he asked for anyone with any information on his daughter's whereabouts to come forward. He also pleaded: "Celine, if you can hear us, if you can see us, please show yourself."

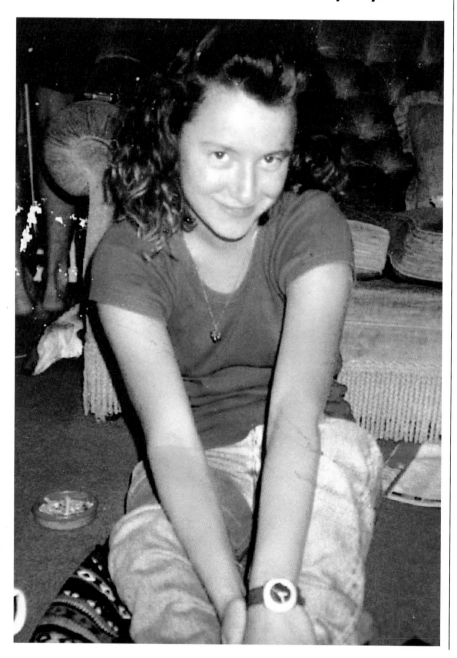

MISSING: Celine had planned to spend Christmas in England with a cousin. Her parents warned her against hitchhiking.

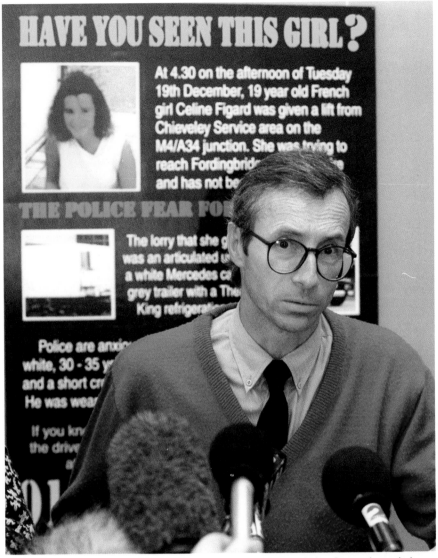

HAVE YOU SEEN THIS GIRL?

At 4.30 on the afternoon of Tuesday 19th December, 19 year old French girl Celine Figard was given a lift from Chieveley Service area on the M4/A34 junction. She was trying to reach Fordingbrid...

THE POLICE FEAR FO...

The lorry that she g... was an articulated u... a white Mercedes ca... grey trailer with a The... King refrigeration...

Police are anxio... white, 30 - 35 y... and a short cr... He was wea...

If you kn... the driv...

PUBLIC APPEAL: Seven days after Celine's disappearance, her father Bernard traveled to England to appeal to the British public for information about his missing daughter.

clothes or of any of her possessions, which suggested that she had been murdered elsewhere—and perhaps some days earlier—before her body was dumped. No attempt had been made to hide the body, which had been discovered by a passing motorist who had stopped to fix a windshield wiper.

Within hours, a full-scale murder investigation was launched. Stuart Morgan, a 37-year-old self-employed truck driver, was first questioned by police in connection with Celine's death on December 31, two days after her body was discovered. He was one of the 1,200 registered owners of white Mercedes trucks in Britain that were interviewed. He denied having seen Celine or having been in the Chieveley area at the time of her abduction.

SUSPICIOUSLY SIMILAR

But what the detectives questioning Morgan did not know at the time was that, as well as owning a white Mercedes truck, he had, until recently, also had a ginger beard—just like the driver identified by Roger Bouvier. He had shaved it off over Christmas, soon after hearing the description of the man wanted in connection with Celine's disappearance. His wife, Glynda, later told reporters that Morgan had spent the whole of the Christmas period in a very anxious state.

On January 21, 1996, Celine was buried close to her family's home in France. Six schoolfriends carried her coffin, and over 1,000 people packed into the eighteenth-century village church for her funeral. Thousands of

The only clue that police investigating Celine's disappearance had to go on was the white Mercedes truck that Roger Bouvier had seen Celine getting into. But so far the driver had failed to come forward, and inquiries soon revealed that hundreds of trucks of the same type that Bouvier had identified were currently on Britain's roads.

Nevertheless, Detective Chief Superintendent Des Thomas, leading the investigation, told reporters: "I have no doubt at all we will find this truck driver. My great concern is we will not find him in time to recover Celine."

Two days later, Thomas' fears were proved correct. Celine's naked body was found near a rest stop on the A449, less than 90 miles (144km) from the spot where she disappeared. She had been raped, beaten, and then strangled to death. There were no signs of her

VITAL CLUE: Celine had been carrying two bottles of rare champagne when she disappeared. Police hoped this clue would help in the search for the killer.

others listened outside to the service over a loudspeaker. Flowers and donations were sent from all over Britain.

On the same day Stuart Morgan was again picked up by police for questioning. Once again, he denied ever having met Celine. However, this time he was asked to provide a DNA sample for comparison with that which forensic scientists had obtained from Celine's body, and which they believed belonged to her attacker. Detectives planned to take samples from all the white Mercedes truck owners they had questioned—the first time DNA testing had been carried out on a nationwide basis in Britain—as well as tacograph records, which would show the vehicles' movements around the time that Celine was abducted. However, Morgan, who at this stage was under no legal obligation, refused to hand over either a DNA sample or his truck's tacograph records.

Over the next three weeks Morgan was stopped and questioned regularly at police road blocks looking for the Mercedes truck throughout southern England. He even told a neighbor that on one particular day he had spoken to police officers 14 times. But it wasn't until a suspicious co-worker tipped off police that Morgan had shaved off his beard over Christmas that he was finally arrested, on February 17, 1996.

That day police searching Morgan's house in Poole, Dorset, found photographs and letters belonging to Celine hidden in a gap between Morgan's garage and garden walls. They also found the mattress from Morgan's truck hidden in his garage. It was covered in blood. There were also spots of blood in Morgan's cab which, when tested, matched that of Celine.

Morgan was then picked out of a police line-up by Roger Bouvier, who identified him as the man he had seen pick Celine up at the Chieveley service station on December 19.

RARE EVIDENCE

And then there were the two bottles of rare Pascal Chrétien champagne—not available in Britain—which Celine had with her when she was abducted. She had been given them by the owner of the vineyard she and Guy Maillot had visited, and had planned to give them to her cousin for Christmas. Soon after Celine's disappearance, police discovered, Morgan had given two bottles of exactly the same champagne to two women who worked at the garage opposite his house, where he often parked his truck. When questioned, Morgan claimed to have bought the bottles from a man "on the M6 motorway." This time he was charged with Celine's murder.

At Morgan's trial on October 1996 the jury heard how, soon after picking up Celine at the Chieveley service station on December 19, Morgan forced her into having sex with him in his truck. He had then beaten and strangled her to death. It was, claimed prosecutor David Farrer: "An act of calculating and unmitigated wickedness."

For the next 10 days Morgan had driven around with Celine's dead body lying in the back of his truck while he tried to decide how to dispose of it. He

GRUESOME DISCOVERY: Police vehicles surround the spot where Celine's naked body was found. She had been raped and then strangled.

INDELIBLE EVIDENCE: The bloodstained mattress from Stuart Morgan's truck was carried into court during his trial. Morgan claimed the blood came from another truck driver.

Figard, and sentenced to life imprisonment. Justice Latham, prosecuting, told him: "What you did caused revulsion in the minds of all right-thinking people." Detectives then announced that they planned to question Morgan about a number of other unsolved murders of young women that had taken place in similar circumstances. It had already become clear that Morgan had been leading a double life for seven years, having set up homes with a wife and a lover at opposite ends of the country. Morgan's wife, Glynda, with whom he had a son, maintained that she would stand by her husband.

Bernard Figard, who, with Celine's mother Martine, had sat through the whole trial of his daughter's killer, nodded approval as Morgan's sentence was passed. Speaking through an interpreter he said: "This man will never pay enough for what he did. I hope he spends the rest of his days rotting in jail."

Monsieur Figard denied wanting revenge for his daughter's death, arguing: "Nothing will bring her back and I am against capital punishment because I think it is too easy." However, he expressed anger that Roger Bouvier—who had told police that Morgan had "a strange look in his eye" when Celine climbed into his truck—had not done more to dissuade Celine from going with him, saying: "If he didn't trust this man, why the hell didn't he do anything to stop her?"

When asked how he and his wife were coming to terms with Celine's death, he said: "We survive more than we live. We have a duty to cope . . . for Celine and for our three other children."

had celebrated Christmas with his family while the truck was parked yards from his house.

At one point Morgan even bought a hacksaw and a spade with which, the prosecution suggested, he planned to dismember and bury the body. It wasn't until December 29, in the early hours of the morning, that he dumped it in woods alongside the A449, where it was found soon afterward.

In his defense Morgan admitted to having picked Celine up at the Chieveley service station on December 19, but denied murder. He claimed that Celine had consented to sex with him in his truck after he had offered her a cup of tea and told her: "This will cost you a kiss for Christmas." A half hour later, Morgan claimed, he had dropped her off safely near her destination.

When asked how Celine's possessions

came to be hidden at his home, he claimed that she had "forgotten" her bag —containing the champagne, letters, and photographs—when he had dropped her off. He had, he said, then "panicked" when hearing of her disappearance, and, not wanting his wife to know he had had sex with another woman, tried to get rid of the evidence. When asked if he often had sex with hitchhikers, he replied: "Yes. I am of the character. I often flirt with women." When questioned about the bloodstained mattress, he claimed that the blood belonged to another truck driver who had "cut his leg."

On October 16, 1996 Morgan was found guilty of the murder of Celine

THE ACCUSED: Stuart Morgan admitted to having picked up Celine Figard at a service station, but denied her murder.

Massacre of the Innocents

Dunblane was a peaceful little town in central Scotland, a place from which middle-class families commute to work in Edinburgh and Glasgow. On March 13, 1996, the serenity of Dunblane was shattered by the grotesque actions of one man, Thomas Hamilton, who barged into the grade school and, in a few brief minutes, systematically slaughtered 16 small children and their teacher.

THE KILLER: Thomas Hamilton was a textbook mass murderer—socially inept, sexually frustrated, and obsessed with firearms.

At about 9:00 a.m. on Wednesday, March 13, 1996, Thomas Hamilton, a small, moon-faced man of 43, walked out of his shabby bachelor apartment in the central Scottish town of Stirling. As he got into his car, he waved to his neighbor, 77-year-old Kathleen Kerr. "He seemed cheerful and happy," she was to tell the police later. She had no way of knowing that Hamilton's top coat concealed two Browning 9mm automatic pistols and two .357in Magnum revolvers. A half hour later, Hamilton pulled up outside the primary school in Dunblane, a small dormitory town some 15 miles (24km) from Stirling.

He got out of his car and headed toward the school entrance, pulling one of his handguns out of his pocket as he went. "The incident started in the playground," Chief Superintendent Louis Munn said later. "Several people saw him, but I don't think they had the opportunity to challenge him." Hamilton fired several shots through classroom windows from the playground, then marched through the front door and past the administrative office, shooting randomly into classrooms as he made his way toward the school gymnasium.

HAIL OF BULLETS

His first victim was a teacher, Mary Blake, who survived despite being struck with a bullet behind the ear. Needless to say, the children were terrified. Eleven-year-old Laura Bryce described how she and her classmates cowered on the floor, trying to shield themselves behind their desks. "The bullets came through the windows and the door. One went straight through my friend's chair. I thought we weren't going to see one another again."

Seconds later, Hamilton burst into the gymnasium where 29 children from the first grade, aged between five and six, were attending a physical education class under the instruction of Eileen Harrild and Gwenne Mayor. Eileen Harrild was the first to be shot, taking a bullet in the chest. She too was destined to survive.

Then the carnage began in earnest. Hamilton stood in the corner of the room and shot Gwenne Mayor dead as she tried to shield some of her pupils. Then he walked around the room, methodically shooting the screaming children at point-blank range, pumping up to three bullets into each little body. Finally sated, he retired into the corner and fired one bullet into his own head.

SHATTERED WORLD: Ron Taylor, the headmaster of Dunblane Primary School, at a press conference following the tragedy.

In the space of less than five minutes, Thomas Hamilton had killed 16 children, one teacher, and himself. He had also wounded 12 other children, some criti-cally. Only one child, six-year-old Robbie Hurst, escaped uninjured. He was found buried beneath the bodies of his school friends, soaked with their blood and shocked into silence.

BLOODBATH

Teachers and school staff arrived at the gym seconds after Hamilton shot him-self. The sight that greeted them was one of unspeakable horror. The school's headmaster, Ron Taylor was one of the first to arrive. "The scene that met us was just utterly appalling," he said. "I just cannot get the images out of my mind. We did what we could. We tried to stop the blood. The survivors were all traumatized."

A few minutes later, paramedic John McEwan entered the gym. He had never seen anything like it in his years with the ambulance service. "There were little bodies in piles and items of bloodstained children's clothing," he said. "One boy was sitting on the floor looking shocked and confused, pointing at a bullet wound in his arm. He looked up at me in bewil-derment as if he was pleading for an explanation. Other children were just sitting there in total shock, their little bodies oozing blood, unable to cry or speak out. I can only describe what I saw as a medieval vision of hell."

Dunblane is a small town and word of the massacre spread like wildfire. There was hardly a family in the town who did not have a relative or friend with a child at the school. Homes and offices were abandoned as anxious parents hurried to the school to check on the well-being of their loved ones. By the time they reached the gates to the playground, however, they found the entrance blocked by police who were only admit-ting emergency vehicles. Finally, they allowed anguished parents through the barricade but not inside the school. No one, they reasoned rightly, should be subjected to the horrific spectacle that lay within.

The atmosphere in the school yard was a mixture of confusion and terror, punctuated briefly by relief as parents of children in the second to sixth grades were asked to collect their children. It was now clear that the victims of the

TERRIBLE REMINDER: Teacher Gwenne Mayor and her pupils. Mrs. Mayor and sixteen of her class died at the hands of Thomas Hamilton.

shooting were in the first grade, which contained almost 100 five and six year olds and was split into three streams. Police and counselors from the Stirling Department of Social Services were on hand to comfort distraught parents.

"The wait was agony," said one woman who accompanied the mother of one first-grader. "We stood in the cold for two hours. Finally, she was called forward and was told her child was unhurt. The police apologized for the delay and explained that they had informed the parents of the dead and injured kids first. That's why we had to wait." Another mother who was not so fortunate was Beverly Birnie. Her five-year-old daughter was injured and undergoing surgery at Stirling Royal Infirmary: "When I heard it was my daughter's class, numbness set in. But now I think of all those parents who were not as lucky as we were."

The accident and emergency department at the Infirmary was under colossal pressure trying to cope with all the victims. One of the doctors on duty, Kathryn Morton, was treating a little girl when she was called away by another staff member and informed that her own daughter, Emily, had been killed in the massacre. She was led down to the hospital morgue where, with other parents, she had to endure the experience of identifying her child's corpse. Jim Benson, the hospital chaplain, was on hand to comfort the bereaved. "There is a likeness even in death," he said, "and parents had no difficulty in recognizing their own. They all looked peaceful. They looked as though they were asleep."

WORLDWIDE OUTRAGE

The sense of horror and outrage at the slaughter in Dunblane spread far beyond the town itself. Messages of sympathy poured in from heads of state and ordinary citizens from all over the world. Two days after the attack, the then British Prime Minister John Major visited the school. He stood in the gym and, close to tears, said, "They must tear this down."

The burning question remained. Who was Thomas Hamilton and what drove him to commit this dreadful crime? Bit by bit, a picture of the killer emerged.

Thomas Hamilton came from a broken home and was raised by his maternal grandparents. Until he was a teenager, he was under the impression that his mother, Agnes, was his older sister. His father, Thomas Watt, now a retired bus driver, never laid eyes on his son after he was 18 months old and showed no interest in him until that dreadful day in Dunblane. "I can't live with his," he said. "I can't take it. I brought this monster into the world."

After leaving school, where he had proved a mediocre student, Thomas Hamilton embarked upon a career as a youth leader. Those who knew him in this capacity are agreed that he was at best incompetent, and at worst a pedophile. Certainly he was sacked from his post as a Dunblane Boy Scout leader in 1974 for what was euphemistically described as "unsuitable behavior." This did not appear to deter Hamilton from his avowed ambition, but further attempts to establish and run youth clubs always ended in failure as parents became aware that he took an unhealthy interest in their children's bodies. He was never actually charged with sexual molestation, but all the signs were there. Gerry Fitzpatrick, now 27, remembered attending one of his clubs years earlier. "He was very weird," he said. "He would make us take off our shirts all the time.

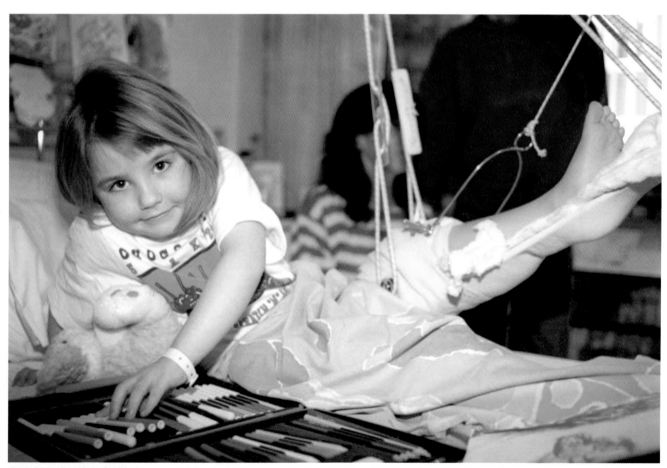

ONE OF THE LUCKY ONES: Six-year-old Amy Hutchinson survived the shooting. What mental scars she carries can only be guessed at.

OUTPOURING OF GRIEF: A police officer lays a wreath among hundreds of others placed at the entrance to Dunblane Primary School.

He liked looking at us. There was something creepy about him."

One of Hamilton's neighbors in Stirling, Grace Ogilvie, remembered being asked up to Hamilton's apartment in 1994: "He played a video of 20 or 30 young boys in swimming trunks, parading around like a fashion show. It wasn't indecent, but I felt uncomfortable."

People in authority were getting suspicious about Hamilton's motives too. Anne Dixon, a Dunblane councillor, told how Hamilton had once been allowed to hold club events at the local school, but that the facility was withdrawn because: "Alarm bells were ringing . . . We knew there were problems there, but nobody could ever prove it."

As one boys' club after another failed and licenses were either refused or rescinded, Hamilton became seriously paranoid, convinced there was a national conspiracy against him and his endeavors. He wrote scores of letters to Members of Parliament, councillors, and other figures of authority, including Scottish Secretary Michael Forsyth, claiming to be the victim of "witch hunts and whispering campaigns."

Five days before the massacre, he went so far as to write a letter to Queen Elizabeth. In it he claimed the campaign which was being waged against him had resulted in "personal distress and loss of standing, and loss of business and ability to earn a living. Indeed," he added, "I cannot even walk the streets for fear of embarrassment and ridicule."

Hamilton almost certainly did have pedophilic tendencies but this does not explain what drove him to murder 16 defenseless children. There are, however, some clues. Hamilton, like many serial killers, was socially inept, a failure in his chosen profession, friendless, and alone. No one knew or cared about his existence. Nobody noticed him. Perhaps it was as simple as that. Thomas Hamilton had an intense ambition to be noticed, to be someone of consequence, and he chose a particularly appalling method of achieving that goal.

GUN CRAZY

Hamilton shared another characteristic with many other serial killers, an obsession with firearms. Handgun controls in Scotland are extremely rigorous yet, despite his dubious mental state, Hamilton had licenses for the four handguns he used in the slaughter in Dunblane. These permits dated back to 1977 and had been renewed every three years since that date.

British law stipulates that no one with a criminal record or a history of mental disorder can own a firearm of any description. The trouble is that this law fails to cope with borderline cases. Thomas Hamilton's pedophilic tendencies were well known but never proved, and his mental instability was never subject to professional assessment. Whatever their misgivings, and some local police officers had expressed them openly, they would have found it hard to justify

removing Hamilton's permits within the framework of the law as it existed in March, 1996.

When it became widely known that Hamilton had held a firearms permit, the public outcry was instant and vociferous. Members of Parliament from all parties demanded radical changes in firearms legislation. The Conservative Government set up an inquiry and in October, 1996, Home Secretary Michael Howard announced: "A package of measures which will give this country the toughest gun-control laws in the world. The country expects nothing less." He went on to say that the Government was preparing legislation which would effectively rid British homes of handguns entirely. High-powered, automatic, and semi-automatic guns would be destroyed, some 200,000 in all. Only single-shot .22in caliber target rifles would be licensed and even these would have to be stored in safes at one of the country's 2,000 gun clubs.

The new law, which would be considered draconian in most parts of the world, did not satisfy a vociferous minority who demanded a total ban on handguns of all types, and reminded Mr. Howard that it was a .22 caliber rifle that was used to assassinate Robert Kennedy.

Nancy McLaren, whose five-year-old granddaughter died at Dunblane, spoke for all the relatives of the victims: "If you had seen little Megan in the morgue, you would fight to have every gun banned."

NATION SHOCKED: Queen Elizabeth talks to a shocked and grieving crowd outside Dunblane Cathedral.

The Killing Fields

It was a story worthy of a Hollywood movie: A young Cambodian doctor, escaping torture and starvation in a country torn apart by civil war, went on to win an Oscar for his role in a movie portraying the horrors that he and his countrymen endured under the Khmer Rouge regime. But the story was brought to a tragic end when Dr. Haing S. Ngor, star of *The Killing Fields*, was brutally gunned down outside his Los Angeles home.

IN MEMORIAM: Known for his courage and dedication to the welfare of others, the killing of Haing Ngor shocked humanitarians around the world.

Ngor's body was discovered at 8:45 p.m. on February 25, 1996, just yards from the two-room Chinatown apartment in which he had lived since coming to the United States in 1980 as a refugee. He had apparently just stepped out of his Mercedes when he was shot twice at point-blank range. A shy, private man, who was unaffected by his fame, Ngor had spent the day relaxing with Cambodian friends in nearby Long Beach. He died within minutes, having lost so much blood that he seemed to police at the scene to be clothed in red.

Ngor's death shocked not only LA's Cambodian community but also people in the movie industry and humanitarian workers around the world. The quiet, inconspicuous doctor always impressed everyone he met—not just with his acting talent, but with his dedication to helping others and the amazing courage he had shown in surviving the atrocities of Cambodia.

He had been a wealthy young doctor when the radical Khmer Rouge regime took over Cambodia in 1975. During the next four years almost two million Cambodians died from starvation, disease, and execution as the Khmer Rouge attempted to impose their vision of a pure Marxist society on the country.

TRAGIC LOSSES

During that time, Ngor lost most of his family. His wife Huoy died in his arms while in labor. He was then forced to pretend to be a taxi driver, knowing that he would be executed if the Khmer Rouge discovered that he was an educated professional. He was once caught scavenging, and was hung from a tree for four days with a fire lit under his feet. On another occasion, his torturers cut off one of his fingers, but he never revealed his true identity.

When Vietnam invaded Cambodia in 1979, Ngor escaped to the United States, arriving in Los Angeles with only $4 in his pocket. It was while he was working as a counselor for other refugees that he was spotted by a casting director and offered the role of the Cambodian photojournalist Dith Pran in *The Killing Fields*. He had never acted before, but knew he could play the part. Like Ngor, Pran was a survivor of the Khmer Rouge, and the two men had shared the same terrifying experiences; as Ngor said: "All of us from that time have the same story." It was for so courageously reliving that story that Ngor was awarded the Oscar for best supporting actor in 1984.

MURDER SUSPECTS: Jason Chan, Indra Lim, and Tak Sun Tan at their arraignment in Los Angeles. All three were accused of Ngor's murder.

Rather than rest on his laurels, Ngor was determined to use his new-found fame to help other survivors of the Khmer Rouge's reign of terror. He became the patron of two refugee organizations, and made frequent trips to Cambodia to campaign against the return of the Khmer Rouge.

Close friends have suggested that Ngor threw himself into his work because he was haunted by the memories of those he had left behind. In his 1989 autobiography, *A Cambodian Odyssey*, he wrote: "Please, in my next life, don't let me separate from my wife and family again. Do you want to be famous and have lost your whole family?"

In the days immediately after Ngor's murder, many commentators drew attention to his outspoken opposition to the Khmer Rouge. It had at first been suspected that Ngor had been killed for money, until police revealed that he still had over $3,000 in his wallet when his body was found.

As homicide Detective John Garcia of the Los Angeles Police Department (LAPD) told reporters: "Robbery does not seem to be the motive." Rumors then began to circulate through the Cambodian community in the United States that Ngor had been assassinated.

It was pointed out that not long before his murder Ngor had declared his willingness to be a witness at the trials of former Khmer Rouge leaders in his homeland. Ngor's nephew, Pich Dom, a Long Beach real estate broker, confirmed that the Khmer Rouge "still have people all over the world." During a visit to Cambodia in 1989 Ngor himself had told reporters: "If the Khmer Rouge want to kill me, they can go ahead. I'm very available." When asked why the Khmer Rouge might have waited so long to carry out the assassination, Dom suggested that they might simply have been waiting for the right opportunity. "If they cannot do it today," he said, "they do it another day." Even the Cambodian Prime Minister voiced a suspicion that the Khmer Rouge had somehow been involved in Ngor's murder.

MISSING ROLEX

In April 1996, two months after Haing Ngor's death, LAPD detectives revealed to the press that on the night of his murder Ngor had been wearing a $6,000 Rolex watch and a gold locket which contained a photograph of his wife. Both items had apparently been missing from the murder scene. The LAPD then announced the arrest of three Asian teenagers—Tak Sun Tan and Indra Lim, both 19, and Jason Chan, 18—on suspicion of the robbery and murder of Haing Ngor. The three were alleged to be members of the Oriental Lazyboys, a Chinatown street gang who were notorious for carjacking and robbing people in their homes. Although they maintained their innocence, Tan, Chan and Lim, under questioning admitted to having been in the area at the time of Ngor's murder, and to have been under the influence of narcotics. Within days they were charged with Ngor's murder.

However, the LAPD's case began to unravel soon after preliminary hearings. Despite their confidence that they had their culprits, detectives proved unable to recover either a murder weapon or the missing Rolex watch and gold locket upon which they had built their case. Then the prosecution's star witness, who had originally claimed to have seen Tak Sun Tan, Indra Lim, and Jason Chan running from the scene of the crime, changed his story. He claimed that detectives had pressured him into identifying the three men and denied having even been in the area at the time of the murder. Craig Hum, prosecuting attorney, suggested that his witness was being intimidated by other gang members. As a result of this confusion, the trial date was postponed.

At the time of writing, no one has so far been found guilty of Haing Ngor's murder. His loss is still mourned by California's Cambodian community, which remembers the slightly built, soft-spoken doctor as "an inspiration."

AFTERMATH: Two of Ngor's neighbors look in horror at the spot where he died.

The End of Peace

For almost 18 months Northern Ireland had enjoyed a life of comparative normality. The Irish Republican Army's cease-fire was holding; armored cars were off the streets, and the peace process, while slow, appeared to be making headway. Then, on the evening of February 9, 1996, a nation's dreams were shattered, when a massive bomb ripped through London's Docklands. The IRA was back.

Shortly after 7:00 p.m. on Friday, February 9, 1996, at the Blacksmith's Arms in London's Docklands, "Happy Hour" was instantly rendered a grotesque misnomer. There was a thunderous explosion and the door and front window of the bar blew in. Customers, showered with broken glass, dived for cover or stood rooted to the spot in a state of shock.

In a nearby restaurant Lana Spencer was tending bar when the explosion happened. She dived under the bar for cover. She too was shocked but, having previously worked in the Northern Ireland city of Belfast, she was in absolutely no doubt about what had just happened.

CODED MESSAGE

Just 80 minutes before the explosion, RTE, the Republic of Ireland's national television network, had received a coded message from the Provisional IRA. It stated that the cease-fire was at an end and warned that a bomb had been planted at the South Quay railroad station in London's Docklands.

Police were still in the process of evacuating the area when the device was detonated. The target of the attack was Canary Wharf, a vast high-rent business complex dominated by Europe's tallest skyscraper, a legacy of Prime Minister Margaret Thatcher's Britain and a virile symbol of the country's economic ambitions. The IRA clearly wanted to hit Britain hard and hit it where it hurt—in the wallet.

And they succeeded. The bomb, which consisted of more than half a ton of explosives, severely damaged the nearby railroad station and devastated five nearby office blocks. It also injured more than 100 people, 36 of them seriously, and promised to cost insurance companies hundreds of millions of dollars in structural damage and lost business. The only good news to emerge from this truly awful event was that by some miracle apparently nobody had been killed by the blast. The following morning, however, when police rescue teams thoroughly searched the bomb site with thermal imagers, they discovered the bodies of two newspaper sellers, Inan ul-Haq Bashir, aged 29, and

PRIME TARGET: Canada Tower in Canary Wharf is Britain's tallest building. It was seen as a high profile target by the bombers of the IRA.

WRECKAGE: Police show journalists the scene of the devastating IRA bombing that spelt the end of the 18-month cease-fire.

his colleague, 31-year-old John Jeffries.

Politicians of every party were quick to condemn the attack, calling it a "barbaric outrage." Even Queen Elizabeth, not normally given to strong words, described the attack as a "sickening act of violence." From the White House, President Clinton, who had been in Belfast only a few months earlier trying to broker a peace initiative, was virulent in his condemnation of the resumption of violence by the IRA.

Gerry Adams, head of Sinn Fein, the IRA's political wing, seemed genuinely surprised by the attack, although he was unwilling to condemn it outright. "I had no prior knowledge that this was going to happen," he said, looking somewhat bewildered, "My sympathies and my thoughts are with those who were injured and with their families."

Conor Cruise O'Brien, the Irish historian and former Cabinet Minister, was skeptical about Adams' protestations of innocence, however: "This was not entirely unexpected," he said. "It is interesting that Gerry Adams has been unnaturally quiet in recent weeks. He knew perfectly well what was going on."

In Northern Ireland itself, the reaction to the bombing by the security forces was instantaneous. The Royal Ulster Constabulary donned body armor for the first time in almost a year, checkpoints were reestablished, and armored Land Rovers replaced police foot patrols in the housing estates of Belfast and Derry. Within a matter of hours, it was as if there had never been a cease-fire.

"Here we go again," said one housewife from the Falls Road district, "the same old bloody story."

ANSWERS

What the people of Northern Ireland wanted to know was why, after 18 months of peace, 18 months which had fostered an amazing level of social and economic recovery, had the IRA chosen to wreck everything? The answer can be found in the message delivered to RTE at 5:40 p.m. on the night of the bombing. It was classic IRA rhetoric: "Time and time again over the last 18 months, selfish party political and sectional interests in the London Parliament have been placed before the rights of the people of Ireland. The blame for the failure thus far of the Irish peace lies squarely with John Major and his government."

In the streets of Belfast and Derry, while there was little obvious support or sympathy for the actions of the IRA, there was a measure of understanding at their frustration with the British Government which, in their eyes, had deliberately put obstacles in the way of Sinn Fein joining the peace process. With more than 3,000 people dead as a result of political and sectarian violence over the past 25 years, the population of Northern Ireland were furious with both sides of the political divide at the squandered opportunity for lasting normality in their community. In London, the antiterrorist squad was working overtime. In the previous year and a half of relative calm, all its resources had been

focused on intelligence work, and now it was the time to use the information gathered during the cease-fire to identify and apprehend those responsible for the Docklands bombing.

WHAT NEXT?

The authorities hoped fervently that the bombing was an isolated act. Eight days later, however, a powerful bomb ripped apart a double-decker bus in central London, killing one person, an IRA bomber. Fortunately the bus was almost empty and nobody else was injured, but the incident dashed any hopes that the cease-fire could be salvaged. The bus bombing was followed by a massive explosion in Manchester on June 15, which injured 200 people and devastated the city center. A month later, violence returned to Northern Ireland when a hotel in Enniskillen was bombed.

It was more than a year before Scotland Yard tracked down a suspect for the Docklands bombing. On April 10, 1997, 29-year-old James McCardle was arrested along with six other men at a farmhouse in Cullyhanna, County Armagh, Northern Ireland. He was sent back to London where he was charged with two counts of murder and conspiracy to cause the explosion at South Quay on February 9, 1996. While McCardle awaited trial, sporadic IRA violence continued, both in mainland Britain and in Northern Ireland. On July 21, 1997, however, there was yet another glimmer of hope when the IRA announced another indefinite ceasefire.

ROUTINE CHECKS: Security officers still check vehicles entering the London Docklands area as a result of the bombing.

The Unabomber Caught

No one could work out the identity of the bomber who terrorized American universities and hi-tech industry for more than 17 years. Finally, in April 1996, the FBI arrested Theodore Kaczynski, a hermit and ex-university lecturer.

The forest which surrounds Lincoln, Montana, provides a fringe to one of the last great expanses of wilderness in North America. There are no roads, no cars, no electricity, no buildings, except for a handful of wooden shacks, and precious few people. On April 4, 1996, however, these same remote woodlands were teeming with FBI agents, masquerading as lumberjacks, hunters, and mountain men. They were armed to the teeth, and equipped with sensors, microphones, and satellite telephones. In the trees, sharpshooters were hidden, ready to act at a split second's notice. The object of this intense attention was an isolated building among the trees. This apparently simple plywood shack, measuring 10-by-12ft (3-by-3.6m), was home to Ted Kaczynski, a 53-year-old hermit and ex-academic, the man they believed to be the infamous Unabomber.

One of the agents approached the front door of the shack and knocked. Seconds later he found himself staring up at Kaczynski's bearded face, and the longest, most expensive manhunt in United States history was effectively over. Not that the FBI were ready to crow at this stage. Having questioned more than 200 suspects over a 17-year period, they had been wrong too many times to allow themselves the luxury of overconfidence. It was only after they arrested Kaczynski and searched his shack that agents were satisfied that they finally had their man.

The tiny building was a veritable bomb factory. There was one completed bomb and several others in various

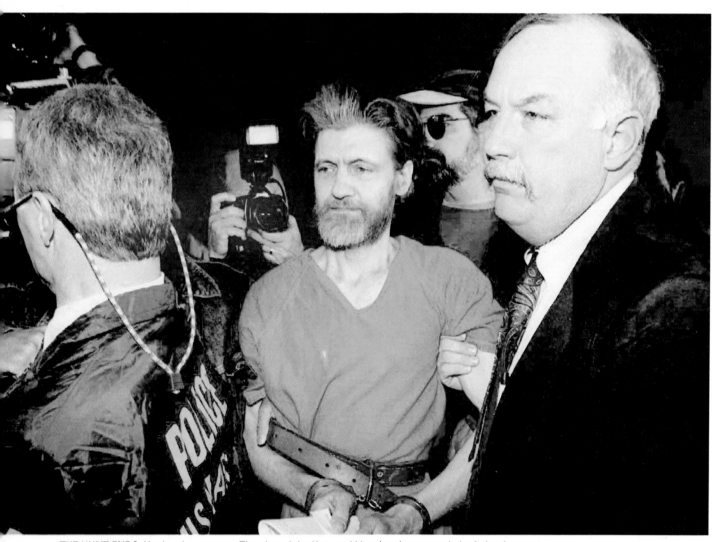

THE HUNT ENDS: Unabomber suspect Theodore John Kaczynski is taken into custody by federal agents.

POOR LIKENESS: A 1994 artist's sketch of the Unabomber. His elusiveness meant that he was to evade capture for 17 years.

stages of manufacture. There were also chemicals, wires, switches, everything a bomb-maker might need. Along with these, agents found 10 ring binders full of bomb diagrams, together with other documentation connecting Kaczynski directly with the Unabomber. As a senior official at the State Department later described it, it was a "slam-dunk."

CAMPAIGN OF TERROR

The saga of the Unabomber dated back to May 25, 1978 when a package was delivered to the University of Illinois, addressed to one of the faculty. The package was sent back to a return address at Northwestern University, where it exploded, injuring a campus policeman. A year later, a second such bomb exploded at Northwestern, injuring the graduate student who opened the package. The bomber's next targets were executives of American and United Airlines. In 1981 and 1982, the bomber turned his attention back to seats of learning, delivering explosive devices to the University of Utah, Vanderbilt University, and to the University of California, Berkeley.

The FBI, who were by now convinced that all the attacks had been the work of one man, dubbed him "Unabomber." A task force was formed in 1982 which was housed in the Federal Building in San Francisco. It comprised agents from the FBI and the Bureau of Alcohol, Tobacco, and Firearms (ATF), together with United States postal inspectors. They had a monumental task ahead of them. The attacks appeared to be geographically random and, despite the assistance of a massive mainframe computer borrowed from the Pentagon, they were unable to find a positive link.

The one thing the task force did know about the Unabomber was that he was clever and methodical. While by no means a sophisticated bomb-maker, he took great care to cover his tracks. He left no fingerprints and scraped the labels off batteries so that they could not be traced. The postage stamps he used were long past their issue date and the wires and switches he employed were out of production.

As the task force toiled away, the bombings suddenly stopped. Investigators hoped that the Unabomber had either sated whatever sick craving he was harboring, or better still, that he had blown himself up. This, however, did nothing to lessen their determination to solve his crimes.

Three years later, in May 1985, the campaign started again with another bombing at the University of California, Berkeley. This was rapidly followed by attacks on Boeing Aircraft at Auburn, Washington, and at the University of Michigan. The Unabomber's next target was a computer store in Sacramento, California. On December 11, the owner of the store opened a package and it exploded, killing him instantly. The bomber had registered his first fatality.

MORE VICTIMS

Between 1987 and 1993, there were three more bombings. Then on December 10, 1994, a package was delivered to an advertising executive in Caldwell, New Jersey. It exploded in his face, and he died in the hospital from massive head injuries. The Unabomber's last victim, a timber lobbyist from Sacramento, died on April 24, 1995, just five days after the Oklahoma bombing. This brought the Unabomber's grisly total to 16 bombs in 17 years, which had caused three deaths and 23 serious injuries. And the FBI were no nearer catching him.

Perhaps the Unabomber felt his activities had been overshadowed by the Oklahoma bombing. The immediacy of the last attack and a radical change in

1958   **1958**   **1959**

1962   **1994**   **1996**

BOMBER'S PROGRESS: Photographs of Theodore Kaczynski show his gradual deterioration from a fresh-faced high school student to a hermit.

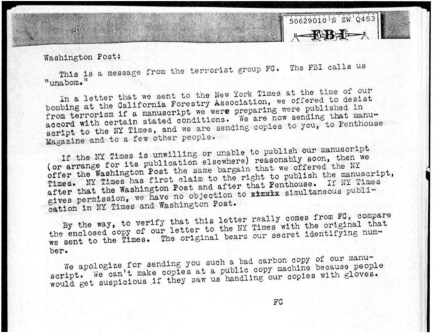

Washington Post:

This is a message from the terrorist group FC. The FBI calls us "unabom."

In a letter that we sent to the New York Times at the time of our bombing at the California Forestry Association, we offered to desist from terrorism if a manuscript we were preparing were published in accord with certain stated conditions. We are now sending that manuscript to the NY Times, and we are sending copies to you, to Penthouse Magazine and to a few other people.

If the NY Times is unwilling or unable to publish our manuscript (or arrange for its publication elsewhere) reasonably soon, then we offer the Washington Post the same bargain that we offered the NY Times. NY Times has first claim to the right to publish the manuscript, after that the Washington Post and after that Penthouse. If NY Times gives permission, we have no objection to ximxix simultaneous publication in NY Times and Washington Post.

By the way, to verify that this letter really comes from FC, compare the enclosed copy of our letter to the NY Times with the original that we sent to the Times. The original bears our secret identifying number.

We apologize for sending you such a bad carbon copy of our manuscript. We can't make copies at a public copy machine because people would get suspicious if they saw us handling our copies with gloves.

FC

WORDS OF WISDOM: Part of the Unabomber's 'Grand Manifesto,' which he insisted be published in full by the *Washington Post*.

his behavior suggest that might be the case. In the past, the bomber had sometimes written notes to his victims, justifying his actions, but in 1995 he went public, writing letters to newspapers, taunting the FBI and the police. He wrote to the *New York Times*: "It doesn't appear the FBI is going to catch us anytime soon." Then, on June 28, 1995, he wrote to the *San Francisco Chronicle*, threatening to blow up an aircraft at Los Angeles International Airport. He promised to abort the mission if the *New York Times* and the *Washington Post* agreed to publish a 35,000-word treatise. It was a rambling diatribe, condemning technology and modern civilization.

Before making a decision whether or not to capitulate to the Unabomber's demand, the editors of the two newspapers approached the FBI and the Attorney General, Janet Reno. There was obviously a powerful argument for not publishing. No one, least of all the government, wanted to appear to be bowing to pressure from a terrorist. On the other hand, a refusal to publish might result in untold loss of life. In addition to this, the FBI argued, such a document must reveal something about the author, and perhaps might strike a chord with someone, an old friend, a teacher, a work colleague.

David Kaczynski, Ted's younger brother, a social worker in New York, had had deep misgivings about his hermit sibling for some years. They were once extremely close but, as Ted became increasingly reclusive and his behavior increasingly bizarre, contact between them had diminished from occasional to virtually nonexistent.

Two months after the publication of the Unabomber's manifesto, David Kaczynski helped his mother move from the family home in Chicago. While sorting through old papers, he came across journals and letters written by his brother many years earlier. There was something eerily familiar about the prose style and the bizarre philosophy demonstrated in the documents. They could have been lifted straight out of the Unabomber's treatise.

MORAL OBLIGATION
David Kaczynski found the idea that his brother might be a serial killer fantastic and dreadful. However, he was a deeply moral man, and despite his reservations, he felt obliged to turn the documents he had found over to the authorities. David got in touch with the FBI through an attorney friend of his in New York. When the FBI agents searched the house in Chicago, they found bomb-making equipment hidden in a small shed in the yard. This, together with Ted's letters and journals, convinced the FBI that they might at last be on the trail of the elusive Unabomber. Asked about Ted's whereabouts, David readily directed them to his brother's shack in Montana. The rest is history.

So, just who is Ted Kaczynski and what drove him to commit his awful crimes? Born in Chicago in 1942 to a Polish immigrant family, he displayed a brilliant mind from the outset. He galloped through Evergreen Park High School, graduating a year early. He showed interest in the school's extracurricular activities, and was a member of several high-school clubs. He had one abiding passion, however, as his contemporary Dale Eickelman recalls: "I remember Ted had the know-how of putting together things like batteries, wire leads, potassium nitrate, and whatever created explosions." Eickelman went on to describe how they would go out to the countryside together and detonate homemade bombs, manufactured from lengths of pipe or old cans.

BRILLIANT LONER
At the age of 16 Kaczynski won a place at Harvard. Here again he is best remembered for two things: academic excellence and social isolation. He graduated just after his twentieth birthday and headed off for the University of Michigan from which he was awarded a masters degree and a Ph.D. He was immediately offered a post as an assistant professor in mathematics at the University of California, Berkeley.

This was in the mid-sixties when student radicalism was at its height, yet Kaczynski showed no interest in leftist politics, the very politics he would espouse in his manifesto 25 years later. In fact, he is remembered as something of a conformist, dressing in a suit and tie while his peers were wearing flowers in their hair. After only two years at Berkeley, Kaczynski suddenly resigned his teaching post. He gave no reason for leaving and his professor, John W. Addison, remembers trying unsuccessfully to dissuade him from throwing away a promising teaching career.

In 1971, Kaczynski bought a plot of land in Montana and built himself a tiny plywood shack in which to live. It had no running water or electricity, and a bucket served as a makeshift bathroom. He did a few odd jobs for neighboring farmers but, for the most part, lived in total isolation, surviving by hunting rabbits and deer. He spent his days reading the works of British writers such as Thackeray, Shakespeare, and an assortment of scientific journals.

In 1978 Kaczynski decided to rejoin society. He moved back to Chicago and got a job at a rubber factory, where both

FAMILY INVOLVEMENT: David Kaczynski's lawyer addresses journalists outside the family home in Schenectady, NY.

his father and brother worked. After a few months, Ted had an affair with a female colleague who dumped him. Kaczynski retaliated by writing obscene limericks about her and pinning them up on the factory notice board. His brother David, who was also his supervisor, reprimanded him, and Ted responded by sticking one of his poems on the machine which David was operating. David fired his brother on the spot. Within weeks of Ted Kaczynski's rejection and dismissal from the factory, the first Unabomber package exploded at Northwestern University. The Unabomber was born.

After seemingly interminable delays, submissions, objections, and the hiring and firing of attorneys, the trial of Ted Kaczynski finally got under way in January 1998, only to be interrupted once again by a suicide attempt by the defendant. The saga continues.

HIGH PROFILE: Leslie Stahl and Mike Wallace, hosts of the television news program *60 Minutes* interview members of the Kaczynski family shortly after Theodore's arrest.

Slaughter Down Under

To the casual observer, Martin Bryant seemed every inch the archetypal Australian beach bum, complete with his surfboard and bleach-blond, shoulder-length hair. But Bryant was a loner, a man without any friends, and that made him very, very angry. On Sunday, April 28, 1996, he decided to punish the society that had rejected him. The revenge he took manifested itself as one of the most horrific crimes in living memory.

THE MISFIT: Martin Bryant lived a solitary life. He was obsessed with firearms and enjoyed killing wild animals.

Port Arthur, situated on the southeast coast of the Australian island of Tasmania, has a grim past. From 1830 to 1877 it was perhaps the most viciously run penal colony in the British Empire. The ruins of the old prison still stand and have become a major tourist attraction. More than a quarter of a million people from all around the world flock there every year and few fail to be shaken by the chill of the place. But the horror of Port Arthur was strictly confined to the past until Sunday, April 28, 1996 when death on a terrible scale visited the prison town again.

RANDOM SHOTS

It was lunchtime at the Broad Arrow Café and a young man with blond hair was sitting alone on the deck outside the café quietly eating his lunch. Parked nearby was his beat-up yellow Volvo with a surfboard strapped to the roof. Martin Bryant, 28, finished his meal and then calmly bent down and unzipped a sports bag which was lying by his feet. He removed an Armalite AR-15 semi-automatic rifle and strolled inside the café. Then, without warning, he started shooting at random, laughing hysterically as customers were gunned down where they sat. Some made a run for it and were shot in the back; others dived under tables, but Bryant sauntered over and shot them where they lay. At least 20 people—men, women, and children—died in this merciless onslaught, which lasted less than five minutes.

Satisfied that he had killed everyone in the café, Bryant wandered outside and proceeded to shoot fleeing tourists in the back. He then climbed into his car and drove out of the prison complex, shooting out of the window as he went. He had only traveled a few hundred yards when he saw Nanette Mikac running down the road. She was carrying her three-year-old daughter Madeline and her six-year-old daughter Allanah was running alongside. He shot and killed Nanette and Madeline. Allanah ran a further 60 feet (18m) and hid behind a

DEEP SHOCK: Walter Mikac is shattered by the loss of his wife and two daughters at the hands of Martin Bryant.

hour, Martin Bryant had killed 32 people and wounded countless others. It was the worst act ever perpetrated by a single gunman.

Within minutes, heavily armed police officers had surrounded the guest house. Bryant kept them at bay by firing at them and threatening to kill his hostages if his demands for a helicopter and safe passage were not met. The police decided to play a waiting game and the siege was destined to last through the night.

While that standoff was under way, people were beginning to learn a bit more about the young man who had committed this outrage. He was raised in Hobart, the capital of Tasmania, and had left school at the age of 15. He was described by his peers as an imbecile. Even the most charitable of his acquaintances described him as "slow." Martin Bryant's background was to say the least

gum tree. Bryant got out of his car, stalked the child, shot her in the head, and then drove off.

Five minutes later Bryant walked into the Fox and Hounds Hotel which, like the Broad Arrow Café, was crowded with tourists. Again Bryant started shooting at random. Two young girls were shot in the head and killed and several other customers were critically wounded. Bryant strolled out into the street and in a reprise of the scenario at the café, started to shoot fleeing tourists in the back. "It was horrifying," one survivor said, "I saw this guy. One minute he was running down the sidewalk, the next his head exploded."

Bryant got back into his car and drove away, slowing occasionally to fire out of the window. He had traveled about 20 miles (32km) when he reached a Mobil gas station. Here he intercepted a Toyota Corolla driven by Sydney lawyer Zoe Anne Hall, who was on her way to Port Arthur with a colleague, Glen Pears. Bryant ordered Pears out of the car and forced him to get into the trunk. He then shot Ms. Hall in the head, threw her body into the road, and drove off with his hostage.

Two miles (3.2km) down the road, the gunman reached the Seascape Guest House. He broke into the hotel and, with Pears in tow, apparently took hostage the elderly owners, David and Sally Martin. He took up a position at a top-floor window and amused himself for a while by firing at helicopters which were ferrying the dead and wounded to the hospital. In the space of less than a half

LAID TO REST: Archdeacon Legg leads the procession to Hobart Regonial Cemetery for the burial of 59-year-old Royce Thompson.

odd. In 1990, he and his father Maurice had moved into the house of Helen Harvey, an elderly and eccentric gambling heiress. There were rumors that Martin Bryant soon became the old woman's boy-toy. She took him everywhere with her and showered him with expensive gifts. In 1993 Maurice Bryant died in suspicious circumstances. His body was found at the bottom of a well, weighted down and riddled with bullets. An inquest jury brought in a verdict of suicide, but in light of the massacre, police have now reopened the case.

FREAK ACCIDENT?

Less than a year after Maurice's death, Helen Harvey was killed in a freak automobile accident in which Martin Bryant was a passenger. At the time, this was judged to be an accidental death but again the police are taking a long, hard look at the case file. Bryant inherited Helen Harvey's house and almost half a million dollars in cash, meaning that he had little or no need even to work.

Despite his comparative wealth and good looks, however, he found difficulty in establishing relationships. He spent most of his time alone, was obsessed with firearms, and took great pleasure in annoying his neighbors by firing his automatic rifle at squirrels. Some neighbors had gone as far as to lodge complaints with the local police, saying that they considered Bryant to be a potential danger, but no action was ever taken against him. It is an all too familiar profile for a random mass murderer. Consider Thomas Hamilton who, a mere six weeks earlier, slaughtered 16 schoolchildren in Dunblane, Scotland, or James Huberty who shot 21 people in a McDonalds in San Diego in 1984, or Michael Ryan who killed 16 people in Hungerford, England, in 1987. All of them were dysfunctional loners. All of them had a fixation with firearms.

Dawn broke on the morning of April 29 and the Seascape Guest House was still surrounded with armed police officers. They had heard nothing from Bryant for several hours. Then they saw smoke billowing out of one of the first-floor windows. Soon the timber building was an inferno. The only person to emerge was Bryant, his clothes ablaze. Police extinguished the flames, placed him under arrest, and took him off to the burn unit at the Royal Hobart Hospital, where he was initially charged with one count of murder. The bodies of Glen Pears and the Martins were found in the burned-out wreckage of the guest house later that day. They had all been shot. These deaths brought the total of Bryant's victims up to 35, which was more than all the homicides committed in Tasmania in the previous five years.

A memorial service was held for the victims of the massacre at St. David's Cathedral, Hobart. The service was attended by Australia's Governor General Sir William Deane and Prime Minister John Howard. Messages of sympathy flooded in from all over the world, from President Clinton, Queen Elizabeth, and British Prime Minister John Major, all of whom had witnessed human carnage in their own countries in recent years.

ANGRY DEMANDS

The whole of Australia was in a state of mourning but, as the weeks passed, grief was replaced by anger. There were demands for the restoration of the death penalty and the banning of automatic weapons. These demands did not fall on deaf ears. While the Government was reluctant to consider the reintroduction of capital punishment, they quickly introduced legislation which severely restricts the ownership of firearms.

Martin Bryant's trial opened on November 7, 1996, in the Supreme Court of Tasmania. He faced 72 charges, including 35 of murder and 20 of attempted murder. As each charge was read out, Bryant merely smiled and said: "not guilty." Toward the end of the seemingly endless recital of charges, however, he burst out laughing and changed his plea to guilty on all counts. So, in fact, there was no trial. All that remained for court to decide was the sentence.

In a rare case of cross-court coopera-

BRYANT'S LAST STAND: Firefighters gather at the Seascape guest house where Martin Bryant holed up after his killing spree.

MOURNERS: Prime Minister John Howard, his wife, and opposition leader Kim Beazley attend the memorial service for victims of the massacre.

tion, the prosecution and the defense agreed that Bryant should be jailed for life without the possibility of parole. John Avery, Bryant's counsel, told the judge: "My client is clearly a distressed and disturbed young man. Although he is not mentally ill, he has become increasingly unhappy and angry at having no friends and has contemplated suicide, but this anger changed into a plan of murderous revenge. He told me that he wasn't worried about losing his property. It was just in his mind to go down to Port Arthur and kill a lot of people."

The prosecution psychiatrist in a moment of compassion said: "We should see him as some freak of nature, a natural disaster, rather than a malicious human being."

It was then up to Chief Justice William Cox to pass sentence. In his preamble he said that Bryant "having had a murderous plan in contemplation and active preparation for some time, deliberately killed two people against

RETRIBUTION: The public demand the reintroduction of capital punishment.

whom he held a grudge [the Martins— the reason for Bryant's resentment is unknown] and then embarked upon a trail of devastation which took the lives of a further 33 human beings who were total strangers to him."

Throughout the judge's address, Bryant snickered inanely and at one stage even interrupted him by asking for a recess so that he could get a soda. Judge Cox was not amused and went on to sentence Bryant to imprisonment for the term of his natural life. This included 35 life sentences for murder, and a further 21 years in prison for each of 37 other offenses. Bryant was still giggling as he was led away to prison.

A month after the trial and conviction of Martin Bryant, Tasmanian MPs voted unanimously that he should be stripped of all his assets, estimated at between $400,000 and $500,000, and that the proceeds should be distributed among the bereaved families and survivors of his appalling crime.

Carnage in Saudi

United States' soldiers serving overseas have always been a target for terrorist organizations, especially in an area as politically delicate as the Middle East. For the most part servicemen and their families consider the risk as just another aspect of their job. But when a huge terrorist bomb ripped through the King Abdul Aziz Air Base in Saudi Arabia on the night of June 25, 1996, the whole of the US military was thrown into shock.

The King Abdul Aziz Air Base had been the Middle East home of the US Air Force's 4404th Air Wing ever since the Gulf War, when a multinational military force had been assembled in Saudi Arabia to drive Iraqi forces from neighboring Kuwait. Since the end of the war it had been the 4404th's F16 and F18 fighter pilots' job to patrol and enforce the UN no-fly zone imposed on defeated Iraq. Two thousand US servicemen were stationed at the base, located close to the city of Dhahran—the site of an Iraqi Scud missile attack which killed 28 US soldiers during the war. They shared their base with a handful of British, French, and Saudi troops.

Although relations between the United States and the Saudi government was officially good, in the months before

TOTAL DESTRUCTION: Stunned US servicemen survey the results of the bomb that killed 16 of their comrades.

JUST IN TIME: Staff Sergeant Alfredo Guerrero—seen here at a press conference after the blast—had only seconds to raise the alarm.

cover up a larger problem, despite its assurances that all Americans in the country were now safe. Although Saudi Arabia was still the richest nation in the Middle East, recent economic problems had led to public discontent with the Saudi ruling elite's opulent lifestyle. Support for the country's extremist Shiite Muslim minority, which advocated the removal of all Western influences from Saudi Arabia, was growing. The ailing Saudi leader, King Fahd had suffered a stroke in 1995 and, although back in charge after briefly handing over power to his half-brother Crown Prince Abdullah, had lost much of his authority.

The situation was becoming increasingly volatile, and for months US establishments across Saudi Arabia had been receiving threats of imminent terrorist attacks.

So when a fuel tanker was spotted slowly circling a parking lot close to the apartment buildings on the King Abdul

June, 1996, the 5,000 American military personnel in Saudi Arabia had been issued with warnings to be extra security-conscious. Despite the Saudi government's support for US concerns in the Middle East—and the United States' support for the Saudi regime—anti-American feeling in the region had been growing since the Gulf War. Objections to the United States military presence were particularly strong.

PUBLIC EXECUTION

In November 1995, five American servicemen were killed when a car bomb tore apart a US military training base in the Saudi Arabian capital of Riyadh. More than 60 others had been seriously injured. Two separate terrorist organizations claimed responsibility for the blast, and demanded the eviction of all US forces from the country. The following May—after demands by President Clinton that those responsible be "brought to justice"—four Saudis were publicly executed for the crime. The whole nation had watched them confess on Saudi Arabian television.

However, despite repeated requests to the Saudi authorities, US intelligence officers had not been allowed to interview any of the accused before their execution. This had led to concern that the Saudi Government was attempting to

PICKING UP THE PIECES: Investigators lay out the remains of the truck bomb so they can search for clues.

"WE THOUGHT IT WAS THE END OF THE WORLD": The 5,000lb (2,268kg) bomb left a crater 35 feet (10.6m) deep and 85 feet (25.9m) wide.

Aziz Air Base on the night of June 25, 1996, suspicions were raised. The US serviceman on patrol that evening watched as the tanker reversed up to the concrete security barriers that surrounded Building 131—the Khobar Towers apartment block. It was just after 10:00 p.m. As far as the watchman knew, no fuel truck was scheduled to be in the area at that time.

In any case, there was certainly no reason for the driver to park so close to apartment buildings that late at night. Then he noticed a second vehicle, a white Chevrolet Caprice Classic, which was also slowly circling the parking lot. Concerned, he decided to alert Saudi security guards posted close by.

However, before the guards could approach the vehicles, two men jumped from the cab of the fuel truck. They ran to the waiting Chevrolet and jumped in. The car sped away into the night.

Staff Sergeant Alfredo Guerrero saw the whole thing from an observation post, and watched the car racing away. He later told reporters: "That was the kicker. They were in a hurry. I felt something was going to happen very soon."

Guerrero immediately raised the alarm, and with two other men he began trying to evacuate the residential apartment blocks below. At the same time guards in other nearby buildings attempted to do the same.

But it was already too late. Seconds later the fuel tanker exploded, lighting up the night sky and tearing the front off an apartment block used by 125 American, British, and French troops.

DEVASTATING BLAST

Master Sergeant William Sine was walking down a corridor in the Khobar Towers apartment block when the bomb exploded. He was thrown to the ground by the blast, which plunged the building into darkness. He later told reporters that he knew right away that "there were some people dead." Although no one yet knew what had happened, he said: "I could feel a lot of blood on my hands and I knew it couldn't be sweat because it was too thick." He was later treated for cuts to his face and arms caused by flying glass.

Another serviceman caught in the blast, Staff Sergeant Tyler Christie said:

"I heard a deafening noise and then the windows shattered and the walls fell in. People were running everywhere."

Out in the street, according to one Saudi eyewitness: "There were hundreds of people. Some were crying. Some just sat on the ground and covered their ears. We thought it was the end of the world." The 5,000lb (2,268kg) truck bomb—more than twice the size of the one which destroyed the Federal building in Oklahoma City—had ripped through the eight-story Khobar Towers apartment block and nearby buildings sending glass and masonry flying through the air. Windows were blown out across the compound. The explosion left a crater 35 feet (10.6m) deep and 85 feet (25.9m) wide where the fuel truck had been. As the emergency services started pulling people out of the rubble, the dazed survivors began to count the casualties. Nineteen US Servicemen were killed in the blast and over 200 were injured, all in a few seconds.

It was the worst terrorist attack on US soldiers overseas since the 1983 bombing of the US Marine headquarters in Beirut. That assault had left 241 men dead and led President Ronald Reagan to pull the US military out of the Lebanon. This time it was President Clinton who was faced with the unseen enemy. Within hours of the Dhahran bombing he declared: "The cowards who committed this murderous act must not go unpunished. America takes care of its own."

THE INVESTIGATION

On July 31, an emotional memorial service was held at Eglin Air Force base in Florida. It was from there that 12 of the 19 servicemen who lost their lives in the Khobar Towers apartment block explosion had come. Men who had been wounded in the blast and relatives of those killed, were joined by President Clinton, who told them during the service: "We stand with you in sorrow and outrage that they were taken before their time, felled by the hands of hatred." He called the bombing "an act of savagery matched only by its cowardice." A second service, also attended by the President, was held at Patrick Air Force base later that same day.

In the meantime the investigation into the attack by US and Saudi intelligence agents had begun, and was already exposing serious cracks in the alliance between the two countries.

The first question asked after the attack was: why was security at the base so lax? Critics demanded to know why the so-called "buffer zone" between the Khobar Towers apartment block and the concrete security barriers which separated it from a public road was only 105 feet (32m) wide. This, as had been proved by the massive destruction wreaked by the bomb, was woefully inadequate. In fact, as Brigadier General Terry Schwalier, commander of the base, revealed, only three months before the attack permission had been sought from the Saudis to move the perimeter back

DIVIDED LEADERSHIP: Saudi Arabia's ailing King Fahd (above), shared power with his half-brother Crown Prince Abdullah.

390 feet (119m). However, Schwalier's concerns for the security of his men had been dismissed, and he had been told: "No, not at this time."

It was also soon revealed that in the six months before the blast, six separate security alerts had been issued at the base. On each occasion unidentified cars had been seen driving up to the perimeter fence, stopping, and then driving away. A US intelligence report issued days before the bombing had noted this as warranting "improved security efforts." Again, little had been done to act on these findings.

GREATER SECURITY

In the light of this information, the first demand the US authorities made in the wake of the bombing was for the 4404th Air Wing to be moved to a more secure base. This caused immediate friction with the Saudi Government. Having put up a $2.7 million reward for information leading to the capture of the bombers, it was now insisting that the Dhahran base was secure. Then there was the question of who would pay the cost of the relocation—some $200 million. US Defense Secretary William Perry was pressing for the Saudi Government to foot half of the bill.

Eventually a compromise was arrived at, and the 4404th Air Wing were moved to the al-Kharj air base, which was situated in the desert 60 miles (96km) south of the Saudi capital, Riyadh. From there, it was hoped, any attack coming from miles away would be spotted. A bonus was that there was no nearby city into which terrorists could disappear in the way they had done after the attack on Khobar Towers.

UNITED IN GRIEF: President Clinton leads a memorial service for those lost in the blast. He told mourners: "We stand with you in sorrow and outrage."

SURVIVOR: Master Sergeant William Sine, who was injured in the Khobar Towers blast, meets the press.

were attempting to overthrow the Saudi royal family. With the weak leadership of King Fahd and the collapse of the Saudi economy, they had the perfect breeding ground for popular support. Another possibility was the involvement of the United States' old enemy in the Middle East, Iran.

In August 1996 US Defense Secretary William Perry had announced that the United States suspected Iran of links to both the bombing of Khobar Towers and the explosion of TWA Flight 800. However, Iran had demanded that the United States produce evidence to back up this claim, and Perry had been forced to backtrack under pressure from the White House.

Either way, the US Government was in no mood for taking further chances with American lives. A month after the bombing, the State Department announced that it would pay for civil servants and the families of servicemen stationed in Saudi Arabia to return to

It then became clear that US intelligence officers were being frustrated in their investigations into the bombing by Saudi officials who were refusing them access to vital evidence and witnesses. Although intelligence reports had revealed that other attacks on US installations were being planned, FBI and CIA officials in Saudi Arabia were facing a wall of silence. They were informed that a number of suspects in the bombing had been arrested, but were not told who they were or how many of them there were. FBI director Louis Freeh traveled to Riyadh to plead for cooperation from the Saudi secret police, but achieved little.

The US Attorney General Janet Reno became involved, criticizing Saudi investigators for failing to keep the promise of full cooperation made by King Fahd. Asked to justify this reluctance to involve the United States in the case, Prince Bandar bin Sultan, the Saudi Ambassador in Washington, would only say that there were "important and sensitive" security concerns.

What the US Government feared was that the Saudis were covering up a much more widespread problem than had at first been suspected. One rumor suggested that a group of disenchanted Saudi veterans of the war in Afghanistan

GETAWAY DRIVER?: Hani Abdel Rahim al-Sayegh was at last arrested in Canada after a huge surveillance operation.

FLY PAST: US aircraft fly in "missing man" formation during a memorial service at Eglin airforce base for those killed by the bombing.

the United States. This was a measure usually reserved for countries on the brink of civil war.

Then, in the fall of 1996, the Saudi Government announced the results of a three-month undercover operation carried out by its intelligence agents. It claimed to have arrested some 40 suspects in the Khobar Towers bombing, including the drivers of both the fuel truck and the getaway car. Tape recordings taken from wiretaps and transcripts of interviews with suspects were passed onto the FBI and the CIA.

SUSPECTS TRACED

The Saudi evidence seemed to suggest that Iran was indeed behind the bombing. The 40 suspects held by the Saudi secret police were all, it was claimed, members of Saudi Arabia's extremist Shiite Muslim minority. The Saudi authorities alleged that they had been trained and supplied with explosives by

Hezbollah, the radical Islamic terrorist group backed by Iran. According to the Saudis, key members of the team which had been assembled for the attack on Khobar Towers had traveled to the Iranian capital, Tehran, before carrying out their mission. After the attack, it was alleged, they had been supplied with fake passports in order to flee the country. The Saudi Government claimed that the passports had been supplied by the Iranian embassy in Syria—another state frequently accused by the United States of sponsoring terrorism.

The question now was: would the United States act? The US Republican House Speaker, Newt Gingrich, called for air strikes to be carried out against Iran if the information from Saudi Arabia proved correct. He said: "We have to take the indirect killing of Americans as an act of war . . . and consider very seriously certain very high-value targets in Iran."

His calls for action were lent further

weight when US and Saudi agents linked Hani Abdel Rahim al-Sayegh, the suspected driver of the getaway car used in the bombing, with a senior Iranian intelligence officer. Sayegh had been arrested in Canada after a huge surveillance operation. He had been taped making telephone calls to relatives back home in which he implicated himself and others as members of Hezbollah. According to intelligence sources, he had been in regular contact with Brigadier Ahmad Sherifi—an Iranian Hezbollah organizer—for two years before the bombing. According to the Saudis, Sherifi had been instrumental in the supply of components for the bomb which destroyed Khobar Towers.

If this were true, it would prove that Iran had directly sponsored the murder of 19 US servicemen. Six years after the end of the Gulf War, it seemed that the stage was once again being set for a showdown in the Middle East.

Fatal Investigation

In her short career, Veronica Guerin established herself as Ireland's foremost investigative journalist. Her avowed aim was to expose Dublin's underworld. Fearlessly, and some would say recklessly, she confronted gangsters and drug barons head on. It was a crusade that ultimately would cost her her life.

Veronica Guerin was in good spirits as she headed down the courthouse steps in Naas, a suburb 20 miles (32km) south of Dublin on 26 June, 1996. The 36-year-old investigative journalist had just been fined $200 for her second speeding offense; she had expected to be banned from driving for at least three months.

She drove her red Opel out of the parking lot and headed up the dual highway toward the capital. She spent the first 10 minutes of her journey on her mobile phone informing family, friends, and employers of her good fortune.

When she stopped at a set of traffic signals on the outskirts of Dublin, she called a friend—a policeman friend. Her call was picked up by his answering machine. "Ha, ha," her message started, "you didn't get me . . . "

While she was talking, she did not notice a motorcycle pull up alongside her at the signals. Nor did she see the helmeted passenger jump off the motorcycle, take two steps toward her car, and fire five shots through the window. But there was a horrifying record of the killing on the answering machine. One minute Veronica Guerin was alive and laughing, then there were five flat bangs, and then silence. She was dead.

The motorcycle roared off toward Dublin. The whole incident had lasted no more than a few seconds, and the drivers of the other vehicles waiting at the signals had no idea what was going on.

OUTRAGE

The level of public outrage at the assassination of Veronica Guerin was unprecedented in the Irish Republic. In a country which has witnessed, and is still witnessing, more than its share of bloodshed, nonpolitical murder is extremely rare, and the slaying of a young mother, who had dedicated her life to exposing the drug gangs of Dublin, was totally unacceptable.

There was absolutely no doubt in anyone's mind that the murder had been executed or commissioned by the very criminals that Guerin had been investigating. The Irish Prime Minister, John Bruton, suspended all parliamentary business for the day and summed up the universal feeling of outrage, saying: "Veronica Guerin's murder is a direct attack on one of the pillars of our democracy—the freedom of the press. The murder of a journalist in the course of her work is sinister in the extreme. Someone, somewhere, decided to take her life and almost certainly did so to

AVID INVESTIGATOR: Veronica Guerin was a journalist who was not afraid of chasing after a difficult story—whatever the consequences.

CAR CLUES: Irish police examine the red Opel in which Veronica Guerin was shot.

for a story even then. She supplemented her income, writing about stocks and shares and corporate take-overs, by freelancing for other newspapers and the British Broadcasting Corporation (BBC). In 1993, however, she got the scoop of which every journalist dreams.

It became known that Eamonn Casey, the Roman Catholic Bishop of Galway, was the father of a teenage son in the United States. Father Casey promptly resigned and disappeared. Veronica Guerin somehow tracked him down to South America and persuaded the errant bishop to grant her an exclusive interview. Her story was syndicated all over the world and Veronica Guerin was suddenly a household name.

LOOSE CANNON
A few months after the Casey exclusive, Guerin was headhunted by the prestigious Irish newspaper, the Sunday Independent. Her special assignment was to investigate Dublin's underworld, and more specifically the drug barons who controlled the city. Although a daunting task, she did not hesitate in accepting the offer. It suited her personality perfectly—ambitious, feisty, tenacious, and utterly fearless—but it also unleashed her as a journalistic loose cannon which the Dublin underworld ultimately could not tolerate.

prevent information coming into the public arena." Opposition leader Bertie Ahern responded by describing it as: "One of the worst murders in the history of the state."

Tributes to Veronica Guerin poured in. Aengus Fanning, editor of the Sunday Independent and Guerin's boss, said: "She was probably the most remarkable journalist I have ever met in my life. She was a woman working alone, among some of the darkest and most unappealing people in society." He went on to announce that the newspaper would be offering a reward of $150,000 for information leading to the apprehension and conviction of her killer.

NATIONAL HERO
Veronica Guerin's funeral was held on June 29, 1996, at the Church of Our Lady Queen of Heaven, three days after her murder. The service, conducted by the Archbishop of Dublin, was attended by more than 1,000 mourners, including the Irish President, the Prime Minister, and countless other dignitaries.

Two days later the whole country observed a minute's silence in Guerin's memory, a gesture usually extended only to heads of state or national heroes. The fact was, despite her comparative youth and journalistic inexperience, Veronica Guerin had become just that, a national hero.

To get some idea of why Veronica Guerin was murdered and by whom, the police had to take a close look at her

journalistic career. They quickly found that there was no shortage of candidates for the killing.

Guerin entered journalism in 1990 as a 30-year-old mother of an infant son. Her early years as a business correspondent for the Sunday Tribune were not particularly distinguished, but colleagues remember her as having a nose

FINAL FAREWELL: Seven-year-old Cathal Guerin watches as his mother's coffin is lowered into the ground. Veronica Guerin had received threats that her child could be kidnapped.

Guerin's first target was Martin Cahill, nicknamed "the General," a notorious Dublin crime boss. He had a reputation as a vicious psychopath who had once nailed a police informer to the floor of his house, and on another occasion had literally skinned an adversary alive. None of this apparently intimidated Guerin, who pestered him for months until he finally agreed to give her an interview. It proved to be a futile exercise. When they finally met, "the General" refused to speak on the record and stoutly denied any involvement in criminal activities.

REVEALING ARTICLE

A few months after the interview, in August 1994, "the General" was assassinated by IRA hitmen, apparently for his drug dealings with Protestant paramilitaries in Northern Ireland. Guerin leaped into print, claiming that, while the IRA had ordered the assassination, the actual murder had been carried out by one of the victim's underworld cronies. She did not name the killer, but to those in the know, there was little doubt about the identity of the alleged killer.

A couple of weeks after the article was published, a gunman attacked Guerin's cottage. One bullet shattered the living room window, seconds after Guerin had left the room with her four-year-old son; a second lodged in the guttering. It is doubtful whether the attack constituted a serious attempt on Guerin's life; it was more likely a very unsubtle warning. Guerin admitted the attack frightened her, but added that she had no intention of abandoning her crusade against organized crime. "I thought, what was the point of giving in to them," she wrote. "That's just what they want. Then they'll think they can just continue doing it to everyone else."

Guerin's next move was to cultivate one of "the General's" close associates, John Traynor, known as "the Coach." Traynor was a big-time con man and police informant. He was also the man police believed to be responsible for the attack on Guerin's cottage. Ignoring their warnings, Guerin conducted several interviews with Traynor during December, 1994. He proved far more forthcoming than "the General," relishing the publicity that his association with Guerin might afford him. In January, 1995, Guerin published a piece in which she described Traynor as "the true master of his criminal craft." She went on to describe some outrageous,

if unlikely, escapades undertaken by Traynor in his criminal past. Police dismissed most of the stories as idle boasts and it is a measure of Guerin's nativity that she printed everything Traynor told her without checking her facts.

A week after the article was published in the Sunday Independent, Guerin was at home alone when a masked man burst in, brandishing a handgun. He ordered her to her knees, pointed the gun at the back of her head, hesitated for a moment, adjusted his aim, and shot her in the leg. After the gunman fled, Guerin managed to drag herself to the telephone and call the police.

Typically, Guerin discharged herself from hospital against doctor's orders and, unable to drive, persuaded her husband, Graham Tuley, to take her on a tour of the homes of gangsters whom she suspected might have been responsible for the attack. In her own words, she wanted to "let the bastards see they didn't get me."

Guerin was back at her desk within a week of the shooting and, in the following edition of the Sunday Independent, served defiant notice on her adversaries: "I have said and I will say again now, that I have no intention of stopping my work . . . My employers have offered alternatives, but I somehow cannot see myself reporting from catwalks or preparing a gardening column."

ENEMIES INCREASE

For the next nine months, it was business as usual for Veronica Guerin, as she investigated and exposed corruption and crime in and around Dublin. In the process she had acquired for herself an impressive list of enemies of the worst possible type.

In September, 1995, she decided that it was John Gilligan's turn to answer a few questions. Gilligan, a career criminal with a reputation for violence, had been released from prison less than three years earlier yet had inexplicably amassed a considerable fortune, and had just opened a multimillion dollar equestrian center in County Kildare. Guerin wanted to know how he had done it.

She called at Gilligan's house unannounced and, according to her version of events, was greeted on the doorstep by Gilligan dressed in a silk robe. When she introduced herself and explained why she was there, Gilligan allegedly became aggressive. Hitting her in the face and chest, he screamed, "If you write one word about me, I'll kill you, your

IRISH GANGLAND BOSS: John Gilligan was one of the people confronted by Veronica Guerin. He allegedly punched her and threatened to kill her family.

HAPPY FAMILY: Veronica Guerin, together with husband Graham and young son Cathal, enjoys a respite from her dangerous job.

husband, your son, your family, everyone belonging to you." Guerin said that he then pushed her back toward her car, hitting her as she went, and tore at her clothes to ensure that she wasn't wearing a "wire." Finally, according to Guerin, Gilligan pushed her into the car and told her to get off his property.

Perhaps because it was a face-to-face confrontation, this assault appears to have shaken Guerin far more than the two preceding gun attacks. She consulted the newspaper's lawyer and, after some coercion, agreed to press assault charges against Gilligan.

After the previous attacks, Guerin had stated, or at least hinted, that she would seriously consider abandoning investigative journalism if her family came into jeopardy but, despite the overt threats made by Gilligan and pleas from members of her family, she opted to continue.

MASSIVE MANHUNT
On Tuesday, June 25, 1996, John Gilligan was in court in Dublin charged with assault on Veronica Guerin. Gilligan denied the charge and was granted bail pending a full hearing on July 9. That hearing never took place. Immediately

after leaving the court, Gilligan drove to the airport and took a flight to Amsterdam on what he described as a "business trip." The following day, June 26, Guerin herself left court and took that fateful drive up the Naas dual highway.

Gilligan, knowing that he must be a suspect, vehemently denied any connection with the killing. Contacted by phone by a Daily Mail reporter, he responded: "I didn't do anything wrong. I have nothing to prove to anyone. I had a run-in with her, that's all. I have been set up."

While Gilligan was an obvious suspect, the Irish police embarked on a massive investigation of the Dublin criminal underworld. In the next few months, the 50 detectives assigned to the case questioned more than 1,000 people and arrested 60, none of whom were charged with Guerin's murder. During the operation, however, police did seize over $200,000 in cash and more than a hundred illegal weapons.

On October 8, Gilligan entered the picture again. He was arrested by customs officers at London's Heathrow airport as he was about to board a plane to Amsterdam. He was found to be carrying approximately $500,000 in cash and was promptly charged, under Section 49 of

the Drugs Trafficking Act, with laundering narcotics money. He was remanded in custody in Belmarsh high security prison pending trial. Irish police officers have since interviewed him at Belmarsh, but he still maintains his innocence in the Guerin killing.

Ten days after Gilligan was picked up at Heathrow, Paul Ward, a 32-year-old Dubliner, was arrested and charged with conspiracy to murder "Veronica Guerin with other persons not yet charged, and with harboring persons known to have murdered Ms. Guerin." Police opposed bail on the grounds that Ward was likely to interfere with other witnesses. He was remanded in custody at Dublin's Mountjoy prison, pending trial.

By this time police had long been convinced that the murder was a conspiracy involving up to a dozen underworld figures. Helped by Interpol, they had already spent months trying to trace known criminals who had left Ireland immediately after the Guerin killing. Among them is the so-called "Tosser," who police believe drove the motorcycle that carried the gunman. Several other suspects involved in hiding the killers and disposing of the motorcycle and gun are also still at large.

Terror in Atlanta

In July 1996 athletes, coaches, and spectators from no fewer than 197 nations converged on Atlanta, Georgia, for the Centennial Olympics, the ultimate gesture of peace and harmony in a fractured world. The games were deemed an unqualified success until, in the early hours of July 27, that peace and harmony was shattered by a pipe bomb exploding in Centennial Olympic Park.

SHAKEN TO THE CORE: A flash from a big explosion can be seen in this image taken from a video shot in Centennial Park at the time the bomb went off.

When it comes to choreographing a spectacular, America has no equal. From rock concerts to presidential elections, the country has a capacity for meticulous organization, combined with unabashed razzmatazz, a marriage which both impresses and astonishes the rest of the world. The 1996 Centennial Olympics in Atlanta were designed to be the spectacular to end all spectaculars, and for the first seven days, everything seemed to be going according to plan. Then disaster struck.

At 1:21 a.m. on Saturday, July 27, a terrorist bomb exploded in the Centennial Olympic Park, where many thousands of revelers had gathered for a free rock concert. The explosion left two people dead and more than 100 injured. It was an act of wanton and random barbarity which sent shock waves around the world.

The first hint that anything might be amiss came about 20 minutes before the explosion, when the FBI received a 911 call warning that there was a bomb in the park. About the same time, a park security guard, Richard Jewell, noticed an olive-green knapsack lying unattended on the ground at the base of the AT&T tower, about 164ft (50m) from a stage where "Jack Mack and the Heart Attack" were performing. Jewell immediately alerted the Georgia Bureau of Investigation and, within minutes, agent Tom Davis was on the scene. Davis followed standard procedure and, after calling the bomb ordnance squad, began to evacuate the area. It was a slow job. Many of the audience were drunk and

uncooperative; others simply didn't see what all the fuss was about. Minutes after the evacuation started, there was a flash of light, a loud bang, and the smell of cordite filled the air.

Initially, few of the revelers in Centennial Olympic Park realized what had happened. Many of them thought the explosion was some pyrotechnic spectacular, augmenting the rock concert, and actually applauded. It was not long, however, before the true horror of the situation sank in. Panic broke out and people stampeded away from the bomb site. Sultan Muhammad, a resident of Atlanta, described the scene: "I saw five or six police officers go down. A lot of people had blood on them."

There were two fatalities. Alice Hawthorne, aged 44, was killed by flying shrapnel and Melih Uzunyol, a 37-year-old Turkish cameraman, died of a heart attack as he rushed to the scene of the explosion. Agent Davis had a miraculous escape. He was just feet away from the bomb when it was detonated. He was thrown into the air by the blast. When he landed, he realized that a chunk of metal had hit him in the rear, but its passage had been stopped by the police badge, in his back pocket.

CONFUSION REIGNS

Everywhere people were wandering around dazed and wounded. Jennifer Ellis, an Olympics volunteer, described how she tended to a man who had been standing near the stage: "'What happened? What happened?' he kept saying. He had a gash in his neck and I kept putting pressure on his neck. I was afraid he was going to bleed to death."

Farther away from the scene of the bombing, Jeff Mitchell described how he heard "a muffled explosion, like it was inside something. Then a man in front of me dropped to his knees and fell to the ground. I thought, I don't even want to know what's going on over there." Mary Deckert of Atlanta described how she felt something whiz past her head and turned around to see a man being hit. Her husband saw another man "with shrapnel all across his face and chest."

Within minutes of the explosion, fleets of ambulances arrived at the park to ferry the injured to local hospitals. Tens of thousands of concertgoers flooded out onto the streets, only to find that the surrounding area was blocked by a police security cordon. As a result many people were unable to reach their homes or hotels and were forced to spend the

HELPING HANDS: Citizens act in a responsible way and administer first aid to the some of the victims of the bombing in Centennial Park.

night lying on the sidewalk as police helicopters roared overhead.

A reception center was set up at the Grady Memorial hospital, where relatives and friends of the wounded waited anxiously for news of their loved ones. Mercifully, the news was for the most part good. With a few exceptions, the wounds were superficial and many of the hundreds rushed to hospital were released after treatment in the accident and emergency department.

TERRORIST ATTACK?

The explosion at the Centennial Olympic Park happened a mere eight days after the downing of TWA Flight 800 and America had terrorism on its mind. The White House and the law enforcement agencies were well aware that the Olympics were an obvious potential target for terrorist activity, and no expense or trouble had been spared to ensure that they went off without incident. Vice-President Al Gore took personal responsibility for reviewing security arrangements for the Games, and by any standard they were impressive.

More than 30,000 law enforcement officers had been deployed to protect the 10,000 athletes and two million spectators. In addition to this, 11,000

National Guard and military personnel were assigned to the Games, including 500 commandos from Delta Force and the Navy SEAL. Many of these, armed with concealed weapons, had been patrolling the various Olympic sites in plain clothes. There was also an FBI hostage team on hand, along with bomb disposal experts and specialists in biological and chemical weapons. There were even scientists from the Nuclear Emergency Search Team ready to deal with any nuclear threat. There were metal detectors at the entrance of all the sports venues and manhole covers in the city had been welded down.

Despite all these precautions, a man was apprehended at the opening ceremonies carrying a handgun, and whoever planted the bomb at the Centennial Olympic Park had obviously walked through the security cordon without undue difficulty.

As for the bomb itself, it was a crude device, a pipe bomb measuring 2-by-10-ins (5-by-25cm) and packed tightly with nails, chunks of metal, and "black powder" explosive. Within a matter of hours of the attack, the FBI pronounced it to be a terrorist act and expressed the opinion that the device was domestic in origin. "There is no

evidence of foreign involvement," declared a senior FBI spokesman.

Daylight broke and the Centennial Olympic Park was deserted except for hundreds of police and law enforcement officials from a dozen different agencies. The investigation was conducted under the direction of the FBI. Tapes from the surveillance cameras were studied along with amateur video surrendered to police by concertgoers. The nearby telephone booth, from which the 911 warning call had been made, was closely examined for fingerprints and footprints. Fragments of the bomb and its charge, including pieces of shrapnel removed from the bodies of the victims, were flown to the FBI crime laboratory in Washington, D.C.

The FBI were particularly optimistic about the bomb fragments providing them with clues to its origins. One explosive expert explained that pipe bombs generally leave good forensic evidence, in the form of both chemical residue and fragments of casing, unlike more sophisticated devices which often burn completely. On the down side, however, he pointed out that the materials employed —a length of plumbing pipe, some black powder, and a few bits of metal—are so commonplace that they are virtually

HUNTING FOR CLUES: Investigators inspect the scene of the bomb explosion which killed two and injured more than a hundred others.

Internet," he said, "nor on the hate lines linked to the Olympics."

So who would want to bomb the Olympics? State-sponsored terrorism seems highly unlikely. There were 197 teams present including those notorious for terrorism, such as Iraq, Iran, Palestine, North Korea, and Libya. The indiscriminate nature of the attack could as well have resulted in the death of one of their own as anyone else. Perhaps terrorism expert William Waugh, was right when he said sadly: "Sometimes it's just a lone nut or even a kid."

THE GAMES GO ON

At 5:30 a.m. on the day of the bombing, Francois Carrard, director general of the International Olympic Committee, made a defiant speech. "The Games will go on," he said. President Bill Clinton backed Carrard all the way as he described the bombing as "an evil act of terror, an act of cowardice that stands in sharp contrast to the courage of Olympic athletes."

The mood in the Olympic village was somber, but the athletes and coaches were united in their determination to continue. "We've got to get on with what we're here to do," said Robert Norris, track-and-field coach for the South African team. "We're too busy to worry." United States hammer thrower Kevin McMahon was more philosophical about the situation as he said, "This is just a reminder that sport is the ideal, not the reality. It would be nice to do nothing but practice and compete, but that would be living life with blinders on."

impossible to trace. "The less sophisticated the bomb," he said, "the less it tells you about the maker."

As to who might have been responsible for the bombing, Joe Roy, director of the Southern Poverty Law Center's Militia Task Force, had his own definite theories. He explained that pipe bombs are commonly used by militia extremists and that the Olympic Games were derided by the ultra-right. "The movement perceives the Olympics as a showcase for the new world order," he said. "It's all the nations of the world coming together in the spirit of peace and harmony. They hate that." Noah Chandler of the Center for Democratic Renewal, an organization that closely monitors right-wing groups in the South, was less forthright on this angle, saying that he had not noticed local fascists taking much interest in the games. "I've seen very little on the

VICTIM ONE: Alice Hawthorne was killed in the explosion.

VICTIM TWO: Cameraman Melih Uzunyol died of a heart attack en route to the scene.

FORENSIC EVIDENCE: Agents examine the phone booth outside Centennial Park from which the bomb warning came.

So, hours after the explosion, with the Olympic flag at half-mast, the Games continued. The mood was subdued as spectators sat under a gray and drizzly sky, but at least they did come. Attendances were over 90 percent of the forecast, as members of the public embraced the Olympic spirit and refused to be cowed by threats of violence. And they were rewarded for their courage. They saw Donovan Bailey set a new world record in the 100 meters, and Gail Devers win her second gold medal in the women's 100 meters. "It's time for me to be joyous about what I did," said Gail, "but it's also a time for sadness."

A SUSPECT

Most disasters produce a familiar cast of characters—victims, villains, and heroes. The Atlanta bombing was no exception. One of the heroes was Tom Davis, the Georgia Bureau of Investigation agent who helped clear the area, and undoubtedly saved scores of lives. The other was Richard Jewell, the security guard who first spotted the knapsack, and alerted Davis. Jewell, a portly, 33-year-old Atlantan, was feted by the press and television. He reacted to his new celebrity status with appropriate humility. "I was just in the right place at the right time," he told Katie Couric of NBC.

Jewell was understandably flattered when, two days after the bombing, the FBI invited him down to their Atlanta headquarters to help them with a training video about bomb-prevention. Little did he know that they had a quite different and more sinister motive for issuing the invitation.

On July 30, just three days after the bombing, it became clear that the FBI were considering Richard Jewell as a possible suspect in the crime. An unnamed agent told Newsweek magazine that Jewell's statements after the bombing were not consistent with surveillance camera videos of the AT&T tower where he was stationed. The source also said that Jewell fitted what is known as the "wanna-be" profile. This describes a frustrated individual with a military or law enforcement background who plans a disaster with the sole intention of coming to the rescue and making himself a hero.

The FBI had started to investigate Jewell's background after they received a call from Piedmont College, where, until recently, he had been a security guard until he was dismissed for "over zealous behavior." When he left that job, he allegedly told colleagues, "If anything happens at the Olympics, I want to be in the middle of it."

As they delved deeper into Jewell's past, they discovered that he had had a

NO SURRENDER: Crowds pour into the park one day after the blast. Despite the circumstances, attendance was only fractionally down.

checkered career on the fringes of law enforcement, but had never really made the grade. His first job out of high school in 1982 was working as a "private detective" for an Atlanta security firm. After several jobs working as a security guard, Jewell left Atlanta and took a job in north Georgia as a jailer for the Habersham County sheriff's department.

In 1990, while working as a jailer, he had moonlighted as a security guard and displayed his zealousness by arresting a couple for making a noise in a hot tub. He had no authority to make the arrest and he ended up in court, charged with disorderly conduct. He pleaded guilty and was sentenced to probation.

Two years later, Jewell finally got his foot in the door of the real world of law enforcement, when he was appointed deputy sheriff. To say he was keen would be a masterpiece of understatement. "He'd work 12-hour shifts, go home, shower, then come back, and ride with the day deputy," said former deputy sheriff Randy Bowden. "That's how much he liked being in a patrol car."

SHOW OF RESPECT: The Olympic flag flies at half mast.

In 1995, Jewell wrecked his own patrol car after a high-speed chase with a "suspicious" vehicle. The sheriff of Habersham County had had enough of Jewell's gung-ho behavior and demoted him to his old job as a jailer. Jewell promptly quit the department.

SEARCH WARRANT
Jewell certainly fitted the FBI's "wannabe" profile, but the fact was that they didn't have a single shred of evidence against him, and it was amazing that they managed to obtain a search warrant for his home. On August 2, dozens of FBI officers descended on the two-bedroom apartment which Richard Jewell shared with his mother. Jewell sat on the steps of the apartment block for 12 hours as officers ransacked the apartment and removed dozens of boxes of books, videos, and other personal belongings. The street outside the block was thronged with press, and overhead helicopters and a blimp provided reporters and cameramen with an aerial vantage point to monitor the event. Any pretense

that Richard Jewell was not a suspect in the Atlanta bombing was very much a thing of the past.

Over the next few days, Richard Jewell was subjected to trial by media. He responded by threatening to sue the FBI, NBC, the Atlanta Journal-Constitution, and Piedmont College. His attorneys went to court to obtain an order forcing the FBI to hand over affidavits that justified the search warrant for Jewell's apartment—the point being that it was the responsibility of the FBI to show "probable cause," before obtaining a warrant. Under United States law suspicion does not in itself constitute probable cause. Suspicion means that the suspect could have committed a crime; probable cause means he or she more than likely did commit the crime. When Jewell's lawyer finally got sight of the affidavits, they were flimsy to say the least, based on circumstantial evidence and hearsay.

The FBI backpedaled furiously. They returned all Jewell's belongings, albeit without an apology, then they held a press conference in which they claimed to be following up several leads and stated that Richard Jewell was no longer on their list of suspects.

OFFENSIVE BEHAVIOR

The FBI's conduct toward Jewell aroused widespread criticism in the media and with civil liberties organizations. One of his attorneys summed up the public disquiet when he said: "In pursuing Jewell without one whit of evidence, and thus without probable cause, the FBI offended the respect for civil rights and personal liberty that every American should hold dear. Now, in soft-pedaling their actions, in lying about them, they insult our very intelligence."

The tirade against the FBI was such that its director, Louis Freeh, stepped into the fray. He announced from his Washington headquarters that he had ordered two separate investigations. One would attempt to identify the agent or agents responsible for leaking Jewell's name to the press. The other would look into the "interview" with Jewell at the Atlanta headquarters of the FBI two days after the bombing.

The second of these investigations had an ominous ring to it. It was alleged that, under pressure from Washington, Atlanta agents lured Jewell to the local headquarters under the pretense of seeking his help with a video. What they really wanted to do, according to

PRIME SUSPECT: Richard Jewell, a security guard at Centennial Park, was questioned by the FBI about the bombing, but was later released without being charged with any offense.

Jewell's attorney, was to interrogate him without legal representation.

What became clear was that Freeh himself had a hands-on role in the entire Jewell investigation. It also emerged that top FBI agents monitored the phoney interview with Jewell from their Hoover Building headquarters in Washington, and even funneled questions to the Atlanta agents who were conducting the operation. No one openly accused Freeh of being involved in this plan to trick Richard Jewell out of his constitutional rights, let alone being involved in the interview itself, but it is unlikely that he didn't know what was going on. In the words of one senior FBI agent: "This was a significant case, and Freeh keeps close tabs on all significant cases."

Meanwhile, Richard Jewell and his attorneys were seeking retribution. NBC quickly settled out of court for an alleged $500,000 for slanderous comments made by their anchorman Tom Brokaw. In a broadcast about a week after the bombing, Brokaw said: "Look, they probably got enough to arrest him [Jewell]. They probably have got enough to try him." The trouble for Brokaw and NBC was that the FBI had absolutely nothing on him.

As for the investigation itself, the FBI battles on, but the trail is cold and it is highly unlikely that we will ever know who committed the outrage at the Centennial Olympic Park.

A Nation Under Scrutiny

When two young girls were rescued from a makeshift dungeon in the house of Belgian pedophile Marc Dutroux, there was relief mixed with disgust. Within days, the scale and horror of Dutroux's activities became clear, together with evidence of police and judicial incompetence, and corruption. The scandal that unfolded shook the nation.

On the afternoon of August 9, 1996, 14-year-old Laetitia Delhez was walking home from the swimming pool in the Belgian town of Bertrix. She never arrived. Laetitia's anxious parents alerted the police, who in turn appealed to the public for information. Of the dozens of calls they received over the next two days, one was from a 15-year-old boy who said he had seen a battered white truck parked outside the pool on the afternoon of Laetitia's disappearance. The driver of the truck had seemed suspicious to the boy, and so he had made a point of memorizing the vehicle registration plate

The truck turned out to be registered to one Marc Dutroux, a 40-year-old convicted rapist and pedophile. Police raided Dutroux's dilapidated home in Marcinelle, near the French border. They searched the building, but found no sign of the missing girl. Dutroux and his wife, Michelle, were taken in for questioning. After two days, Dutroux cracked. "I'm going to take you to the girls," he said.

Back at the house, which the police had supposedly searched 48 hours earlier, Dutroux guided the investigators to his "dungeon," a concrete cell, measuring 9.8-by-6.5-feet (3-by-2m), concealed by sliding doors behind a basement cabinet. Inside they found not only Laetitia, but also 12-year-old Sabine Dardenne, who had vanished three months earlier while riding her bicycle in the Belgian village of Kain. The girls were in an appalling state, terrified and malnourished. They had both been sexually abused. In the same room, police also found pornographic videos and photographs, many of which featured Dutroux raping young children, including Laetitia and Sabine.

THE HORROR UNFOLDS

There were more horrors to come. Dutroux proceeded to lead police to a country house which he also owned, and showed them where to find the bodies of two eight year olds, Melissa Russo and Julie Lejeune, who had disappeared in June 1995. Dutroux admitted kidnapping and assaulting the two girls, but denied

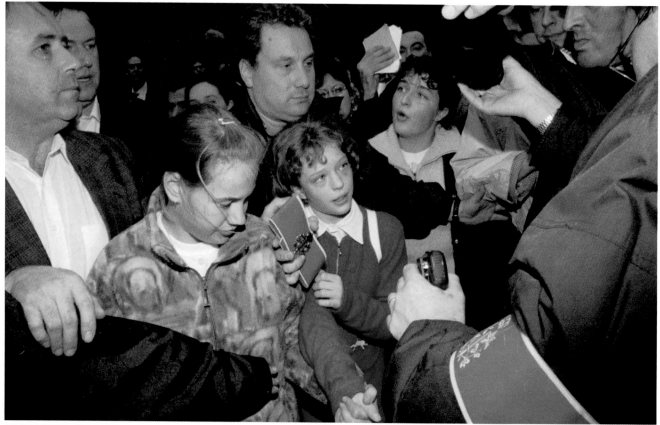

LUCKY SURVIVOR: Sabine Dardenne (center, wearing red) at a demonstration held to remember those children killed by the sex gang.

YOUNG VICTIMS: This poster of Julie Lejeune and Melissa Russo was issued shortly after their disappearance. Their bodies were found a year later, buried in Dutroux's garden.

In prison, Dutroux bragged openly about his "business empire." He claimed that the actual abductions had been carried out by two associates, who were paid $1,600 for each child they delivered to him. Dutroux himself had devised the kidnap method: "You just put your hand over their mouth. Once they're in the car, they cannot get out because of the child-proof locks." Dutroux claimed that he received between $3,200 and $4,800 for each child he sold on to pedophile rings around Europe.

As a sideline, Dutroux produced pornographic videos, 300 of which police found in his various properties. They featured Dutroux himself and other men performing sex acts with children. Prosecutor Michel Boulet, who had the unenviable task of viewing some of the tapes, declared: "All those who can be identified on these videos will be prosecuted."

PUBLIC OUTCRY

As details of Marc Dutroux's past came to light, the level of public anger against him intensified. In 1989, convicted of kidnapping and raping five girls, aged between 12 and 19, Dutroux had been sentenced to 13 years in prison. His wife Michelle had also been jailed for three years for aiding and abetting him. Astonishingly, Dutroux was paroled in 1992, a mere three years after his conviction. The grounds for his early release, against the advice of the prison psychiatrist, was "good behavior."

News of this apparent laxity was greeted with rage and disbelief. The heaviest criticism was leveled at the

killing them. According to him, they had starved to death while he was serving a four-month prison sentence for car theft. He claimed to have paid an associate $1,500 to feed them while he was away. The man apparently did his job for six weeks and then took off with the money. When Dutroux was released from jail, Melissa was already dead and Julie died in his arms hours later.

Two weeks later, the picture got even grimmer as police uncovered other graves at one of Dutroux's properties. They were those of An Marchal and Eefje Lambreks, two teenage friends who had disappeared in August, 1995.

Photographs, videos, and other documentation left police in no doubt that Marc Dutroux was part of, if not the leader, of an extensive and lucrative pedophile ring.

THOROUGH SEARCH: Police search everywhere for clues at the house of Bernard Weinstein, an associate of Dutroux's and part of his stolen car ring.

PAST HISTORY: Marc Dutroux had already been convicted once of raping several young girls, but this did not prevent him from abducting many more on his release.

had received tips about Dutroux's designs on young children within months of his release. As early as 1993, a police informant had told authorities that Dutroux was in the process of building a basement cell to hold kidnapped girls before shipping them overseas. The following year, they had received a tip that Dutroux was quoting prices for abducted girls. In December 1995, the police actually visited the house where Melissa and Julie were being held, to question Dutroux on an unrelated matter. They had heard a child crying, but Michelle had persuaded them that it was one of her own children who was at home from school with the flu.

Things were to get even worse. Rumors began to circulate that, not only had the police bungled the case, there was also a strong suspicion that corrupt officers might actually have been protecting Dutroux and other people in "high places" who were customers for his grim trade. These suspicions were given new weight when, in October, 1996, the Examining Magistrate, Jean Marc Connerotte, was dismissed from then Justice Minister, Melchior Wathelet. In his own defense, Wathelet pointed out that, having served three years on remand before his trial, Dutroux had actually served almost half his sentence, and that he had only approved the release based on the recommendation of a committee of correction officials and social workers. He added that he had appended a note to Dutroux's file: "Follow very closely."

NORMAL LIFE

Social service agencies appear to have paid little attention to this instruction. Their last visit to his home, dated July 27, 1996, noted nothing unusual, save for a degree of marital friction between Dutroux and his ex-schoolteacher wife. It is one of the horrific aspects of the Dutroux saga that he and his wife managed to give the appearance of leading a relatively stable family life with their three children, while beneath their feet was a dungeon where other children were being brutally raped. Another incredible oversight by the so-called "caring agencies" is that they overlooked Dutroux's lifestyle. He and his wife were on welfare, yet owned seven houses and at least three cars.

Soon the police found themselves in the firing line too. Documents leaked to the press disclosed that the investigators

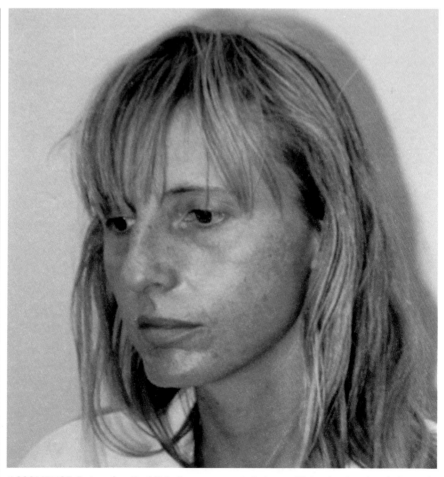

ACCOMPLICE: Dutroux's wife, Michelle, was arrested along with her husband and charged with the kidnap and murder of Julie Lejeune and Melissa Russo.

DAWN RAID: Police search the grounds of Dutroux's house in Sart-la-Buissiere. Although unemployed, Dutroux owned seven properties.

the case by the Supreme Court of Justice for alleged lack of impartiality.

Connerotte, nicknamed the "little judge," was a nationally respected figure who had worked tirelessly to crush the pedophile ring, and had been instrumental in securing the release of Sabine and Laetitia. In the months since Dutroux's arrest, aggressive tactics had won wide acclaim and had resulted in the arrest of about 20 other alleged pedophiles.

Connerotte's crime was having accepted a plate of spaghetti and a fountain pen at a fund-raising dinner for the families of victims of child abuse, an event which happened to be attended by relatives of two of Marc Dutroux's victims. It might have been unwise for Connerotte to accept the invitation, but it certainly did not warrant his dismissal from the case. The public outcry was immediate and vociferous. Overnight, "the little judge" became a national hero, a champion against political and judicial corruption and incompetence.

This often divided, small country was united in its outrage. In Brussels, Antwerp, Ghent, and dozens of smaller cities throughout Belgium, thousands of workers abandoned their tools and took to the streets in protest. Railroad and bus services were shut down; freeway intersections were blocked; government offices were picketed; and firemen hosed down the courthouse in Liège to the cry of "clean up justice."

Gino Russo, Melissa's father, spoke for many of them when he said: "It's the equivalent to spitting on their tomb," referring to the burial place of his daughter and Julie Lejeune.

The Belgian government was caught off guard. The Prime Minister, Jean-Luc Dehaene, quickly announced that he was to introduce measures to ensure more openness in the judiciary and government. He also promised a full inquiry into the way in which the Dutroux case had been handled.

Long before the results of the inquiry were published, another scandal hit the Charleroi district police force. On September 10, investigators raided police headquarters and arrested 11 of its officers, including Chief Inspector Georges Zicot, who headed the car-theft squad for the region. Zicot was charged with providing stolen vehicles to Marc Dutroux for a car-theft operation he was running in conjunction with his pedophile ring.

German authorities claimed that they had alerted Zicot and other Belgian officers that scores of stolen cars—mainly BMWs and Porsches—were flooding into the country from Belgium, but that their leads were never followed up. Whether this was a result of staggering incompetence or outright complicity is as yet unproven, but the very fact that Zicot was under investigation diminished the public's faith in the efficiency and integrity of their country's police force and judiciary.

COOLS CONNECTION

As if all that was not bad enough, two days after the swoop on the Charleroi police headquarters, a case concerning Andre Cools reared its ugly head again, further eroding Belgian public confidence in the judicial system.

Cools, a leading member of the French-speaking Socialist Party and former Deputy Prime Minister, was gunned down in 1991. No one had ever been arrested for his murder and the case had blighted the Belgian political scene for more than five years. It was widely rumored that Cools's death was directly linked to a corruption scandal that had

THE 'LITTLE JUDGE': Jean-Marc Connerotte became a national hero for helping uncover the pedophile ring. There was public outrage when he was dismissed from the case.

occurred in the late 1980s in which bribes were alleged to have been paid to Belgian politicians by Augusta, the Italian helicopter manufacturer. Augusta had always emphatically denied the charges, but in 1994–95 the scandal led to the resignation of four Belgian government ministers, a general's suicide, and the resignation of Willy Claes, the Belgian Secretary General to NATO, lending them some credibility.

On September 12, 1997, as the Belgian public struggled to cope with the horrors of the Dutroux case, the police in Liège finally announced that they had arrested Alain van der Biest, along with five other men, including a policeman, and had charged them with the murder of Andre Cools. Van der Biest, a flamboyant novelist, ex-government minister, and one-time protégé of Cools, had reportedly confessed to having hired two Sicilian hitmen to carry out the assassination, a confession he was later to retract.

According to the police, van de Biest

MISTAKES: Members of the Dutroux investigation outline police and judicial blunders in their report to parliament.

had ordered Cools to be killed as part of a political vendetta within the Socialist Party. It appears that he was about to blow the whistle on some of his colleagues. Shortly before he died, Cools had revealed that he was about to make public "shocking revelations" of corruption in the party and promised to dismiss and prosecute those responsible.

MANY ENEMIES

Cools's determination to end political corruption in his district earned him more than his share of enemies. One mourner at his funeral cracked: "If everyone who had trouble with Andre was implicated in his murder, half of Liège would be under suspicion." Cools's son, Marcel, confirmed this in a more sober fashion when he said: "It was common knowledge that among the mourners round my father's grave, there were those who would sleep easier in their beds for his passing." Even at this stage, Marcel was convinced that van der Biest, his own godfather, was somehow implicated in the killing. "He could not look me in the eye at the funeral," he said.

Others in the Socialist Party were not convinced, however. "He was too much of a wimp to lead a gang of killers," said one ex-colleague. "Besides, he was usually too drunk to tie his own shoelaces."

The investigation into the murder of Andre Cools was scandalously slow and sloppy. Shortly after the shooting, the police received an anonymous letter naming van de Biest and others as possible culprits. The tip-off received scant attention. The following year, one of the suspects, arrested for an unrelated offense, confessed to the killing and

gave the police a detailed description of how it had been executed. He was released without charge.

Prosecutors were reluctant to cite a direct link between the Dutroux and Cools cases, but a connection was there, not just as a matter of supposition, but as a matter of fact. Both cases point to a cozy relationship among politicians, police, and organized crime in French-speaking south-east Belgium. More specifically, both cases involve Jean-Marc Connerotte. He was appointed investigating magistrate in the Cools murder and, as in the Dutroux case, he was dismissed mid-investigation. Perhaps he ruffled too many feathers by writing to the Belgian king, saying that he knew who had killed Andre Cools and naming van der Biest as the ringleader.

As details of the investigation became known, there was yet another public outcry against the police and the judiciary, who were seen as corrupt or inept, or both. The first casualty of this uproar was the police superintendent in charge of coordinating the Cools investigation since 1992. Hours after van de Biest's arrest, he tendered his resignation.

DAMNING INDICTMENT

When the parliamentary report into the Dutroux investigation was finally published on April 15, 1997, it vindicated the public's scepticism. The damning 300-page document pulled no punches as it condemned breathtaking failures of communication and initiatives between various agencies, and the failure of some 30 individual police and judicial investigators to fulfill their duties.

The report exposed fierce competition between the gendarmerie and the other branches of the police force, and, in particular, the gendarmerie's willful refusal to submit to judicial supervision. This unacceptable level of interinstitutional rivalry was found to be more than matched by personal rivalry and bitterness between individual officers within the same service. In addition, the document suggested that: "There were strong signs of protection," based on the fact that the committee had uncovered failings so bizarre that they could not simply be explained away by incompetence or a fundamental lack of communication.

The report went on to criticize individual members of the judiciary for failing to communicate with colleagues working on the same investigation. The Chief Prosecutor for Brussels came in

MASS DEMONSTRATION: Almost half a million Belgians took to the streets to demonstrate their rage against the Dutroux scandal.

for particular vilification. "Monsieur Dejemeppe does not fulfill the requirements to direct his team," the report said, and argued his plea that he had trusted his subordinates did not absolve him from responsibility.

The Chief of Police in Charleroi, René Michaux, was chastised for failing to conduct the Dutroux case systematically or to follow up important leads. His superiors, the Ministry of Justice and the instructing judge, Martine Doutrewe, were also criticized for failing to take up

the Ministry's offer to provide extra resources for the investigation.

Renaat Landuyt, one of the report's compilers, summed it up for everyone involved when he said: "If police had acted on the information they had received from an informer in 1993, that Dutroux was building rooms off his cellar to hide kidnapped children, the kidnappings could have been prevented. Later disregarded information could have led to their rescue alive. Instead, four were to die."

A Deadly Eccentric

John Du Pont was a legend in Newton Square, Philadelphia. One of the heirs to the Du Pont chemical empire, he was a multimillionaire and well-known for his extravagant philanthropy. He was equally popular for his eccentricity, but was generally considered to be a harmless man. On January 27, 1996, however, he proved himself to be anything but harmless.

On the afternoon of January 27, police were called to the Foxhunter estate in Newton Square, 18 miles (30km) from the city of Philadelphia. A man had been shot in the grounds of the estate, home to chemicals heir John Du Pont. They arrived to find the victim was 36-year-old David Schultz, an Olympic Gold Medalist, who lived on the estate where he ran a wrestling school. Schultz had been shot three times and was dead by the time police arrived on the scene.

There was never any doubt about the identity of the killer. Schultz's widow, Nancy, had watched through an upstairs window of the mansion as Du Pont shot her husband at point-blank range with a handgun. If solving the crime was a simple matter, arresting the suspect was not—John Du Pont was a firearms fanatic and marksman and, by the time police arrived at Foxhunter, he had barricaded himself in the house with a massive arsenal of weapons and ammunition.

Du Pont was well-known to the local police, not as a criminal, but as a philanthropist and ally. One of scores of heirs

SPLENDID ISOLATION: An aerial view of the luxury home of John Du Pont. Olympic wrestler Dave Schultz died in the grounds.

BUDDIES: John Du Pont seen wrestling with the bearded Dave Schultz in happier times. An avid fan, Du Pont donated large sums of money to the US Wrestling Association.

fed, and trained Olympic hopefuls and paid them $300 a week pocket money. He also donated $500,000 a year to the US Wrestling Association. David Schultz became an integral part of this project. Not only did he train young wrestlers, his status as an Olympian lent credibility to the Foxhunter Team.

INDECENT ADVANCES

The training camp which started with such promise soon ran into trouble, however, mainly as a direct result of John Du Pont's increasingly bizarre behavior. Rumors started to circulate that, despite having been married and fathered two children, he was in fact a homosexual and had made indecent advances toward the young men who were living and training on the estate. Certainly many of them left Foxhunter and its luxury rather than be subjected to their benefactor's conduct. Du Pont and Schultz were known to have a fiery relationship. They argued constantly and Schultz was fired on several occasions. However, there was never any suggestion that Du Pont harbored murderous thoughts toward him.

The police SWAT team, wearing flack jackets and helmets, surrounded the house and prepared for an assault but it soon became clear that Du Pont was not alone in the building. Three of his employees were barricaded inside with him and this presented the police with a potential hostage situation. Police negotiators managed to contact Du Pont on a cellular telephone but his conditions of surrender were so outrageous and incoherent that the negotiations soon broke down. As day turned into night, a police

to the vast Du Pont fortune, his wealth was estimated to be in excess of $50,000,000. Unlike many heirs to great fortunes, Du Pont had not lived the life of the idle rich. He had achieved a great deal in his 57 years. He was a sportsman and biologist of note. Two species of birds he discovered were named after him. He had built the Delaware Museum of Natural History to house his magnificent collection of 66,000 stuffed birds and 2,000,000 seashells.

Du Pont's other great love was sport, especially wrestling and the pentathlon, disciplines which he considered underfunded and generally overlooked by the media. In 1988, he decided to rectify this situation. He spent $600,000 building a 14,000 sq ft (1,300 sq m) training camp on his 800-acre (324 ha) estate. He housed,

MEDIA CIRCUS: A police sergeant waits behind the wheel of his squad car while journalists and photographers block the way into the Du Pont estate.

spokesman said: "We have no idea what motivated Mr. Du Pont to do what he did, but he is a marksman and he has an arsenal in there. We intend to take as long as it takes to resolve this problem without anyone else getting injured."

The standoff was destined to last for 48 hours and the police came in for widespread criticism for the way they conducted themselves during the operation. Police marksmen frequently had Du Pont in the cross hairs of their telescopic sights as he wandered through his 19th-century-style mansion and they were heard to tell their commander, "I've got him," but the order to shoot was never given. At press conferences, the police referred to Du Pont with a tone of respect not usually extended to murder suspects, always addressing him as "Mr. Du Pont." They even allowed him to

get a night's sleep during the raid and provided him with an early morning call. The explanation of the treatment given to Du Pont is simple. Several of the officers who took part in the siege knew him personally. Some of them had even received firearms instruction from him on his rifle range. Some years earlier, Du Pont had become a volunteer police officer and had bought tens of thousands of dollars' worth of equipment for the local police force. "You've got to remember," said retired policeman John Halota, "he trained half these guys."

SUB-ZERO TEMPERATURES

The siege of Foxhunter Manor ran into its second day and there was still no sign of Du Pont giving himself up. The temperature was well below zero, and on the evening of January 28, the police decided

to shut off the house's fuel supply in the hope of flushing out their suspect. The ruse worked and the following morning John Du Pont emerged from the mansion to examine the boiler. He was promptly arrested and charged with the murder of David Schultz.

While Du Pont awaited trial, his family closed ranks. Countless family feuds and corporate infighting were put on hold in view of the greater interest in salvaging something of the family name. Their first move was to try to get him committed to a mental institution, hoping that psychiatrists would find him unfit to stand trial. His sister-in-law, Martha Du Pont, told reporters that the family had been trying to persuade him to get psychiatric help for years. "He was a loaded gun waiting to go off," she said. She went on to explain that John had always been

UNDER ARREST: Du Pont is lead away in handcuffs after a two-day stand-off at his home. He was later charged with the murder of Schultz.

EYE WITNESS: Nancy Schultz, the widow of the victim, saw the shooting from an upstairs window.

eccentric but, after the death of his beloved mother in 1988, his mental state had rapidly deteriorated. He became convinced at different times that he was the Dalai Lama, Jesus Christ, or the Tsar of Russia. He banned all African-American wrestlers from his school because he said that the color black reminded him of death. He charged around the countryside in a tank and had all the geese on his farm slaughtered because he was convinced that they were casting spells on him. He ordered a resident wrestler to remove his cap because he thought it concealed a device which was sending messages to him. He also wandered around his estate in his dressing gown with a machine gun taking potshots at sparrows.

ABUSIVE BEHAVIOR

According to one woman who lived in the next property to Foxhunter, Du Pont had taken his tank for a spin around the estate a few weeks before the shooting. He had overrun several trees, banging his head on branches and the side of the tank turret. Then, streaming with blood, he had parked the vehicle outside her house, banged on the door and asked her if her husband could "come out and play." When she said he couldn't, Du Pont rumbled off in his tank screaming abuse at her as he went.

Another witness came forward to say that Du Pont took cocaine and painkillers and would scratch himself until he bled in an attempt to remove phantom bugs from his skin. In the words of his own defense counsel, Du Pont was "barking mad." Even Schultz's father agreed that Du Pont was insane. "I really think the man is paranoid and deeply in need of medical help," he said.

"David felt the same thing but was able to help him; he was a calming influence. Even when Du Pont sacked him and ordered him off the farm, David had a way of sloughing it off, like he could handle it." Despite this mass of anecdotal evidence, informed opinion, and Du Pont's own bizarre behavior, the Du Pont legal team were unable to convince the courts that Du Pont was insane and he was deemed fit to stand trial.

ABOVE THE LAW

When the trial opened in early March, Du Pont arrived in court in a wheelchair, heavily bearded and sporting shoulder-length hair. Despite the earlier court decision, his defense team stuck with their original defense of insanity and Du Pont did his very best to justify their argument with frequent outbursts and claims to be the Dalai Lama, a god king who was above the law. Neither Judge Patricia Jenkins nor the jury were convinced and after a short recess they found Du Pont guilty of third-degree murder. They added that they also found him to be mentally ill but not insane.

Du Pont received a sentence of 20 years, initially to be served in a secure psychiatric hospital, but he will ultimately be transferred to prison when he is deemed fit to handle it. However, the maximum sentence is seldom imposed and it is quite likely that he will be released on parole in five to ten years.

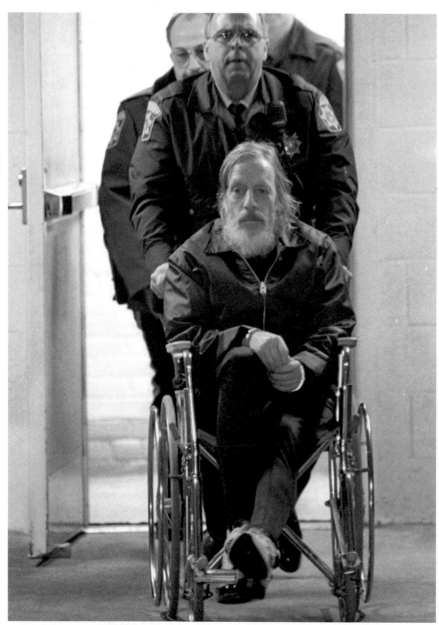

UNRECOGNIZABLE: A bedraggled John Du Pont is wheeled into the Delaware County Courthouse after his lawyers had failed to convince the authorities that he was insane.

Minister of Murder

TV preacher John Nelson Canning had a firm following among the elderly residents of the town of Sebring, Florida. Many were members of the church he had founded, and some even trusted him to look after their finances. But Canning's greed would lead to the deaths of the two members of his congregation who trusted him most.

The first that police in Sebring knew of the murders of Hazel and Leo Gleese was when the Reverend John Nelson Canning walked into the town police station to report their deaths on January 3, 1995. The 59-year-old Canning told the police that he had discovered the bodies of the retired couple after dropping in to visit them at their home. He explained that the Gleeses were long-term members of the "Fountain of Life Church" of which he was founder, and that he had been caring for them in recent years. During that time, he said, the Gleeses had "adopted" him, and he had come to call them "Mom and Dad."

The small town police officers, who sped over the Gleeses' house immediately, found a scene they would never forget. In the kitchen, 90-year-old Hazel Gleese was lying face down in a pool of her own blood. Her husband Leo, also 90, was in the living room, slumped against a wall. They had both been beaten and then strangled to death. Strewn around the house, the investigating officers also found bank statements and other financial documents, soaked in blood. There was also evidence that the Gleeses had put up a fight.

When the Gleeses were buried a few days later, the whole population of Sebring was there. Conducting the service, the Reverend Canning told mourners: "Some of you have been long-time friends of Mom and Dad for many years. But I doubt if any of you has been any closer to them than my wife and I have." He described how it had been his honor to preside over the Gleeses' marriage in 1984. Close to tears, he added: "I'm proud they asked me to be their son. I'm proud I could call them Mom and Dad." With no children of their own, the Gleeses had decided to adopt Canning and his wife Judy in 1994.

SUSPICIONS AROUSED

By the time of the funeral, however, state detectives already suspected Canning of murdering his adoptive parents himself. Their suspicions had been aroused soon after Canning had reported the crime. Having given a detailed statement of how he had discovered the bodies of Hazel and Leo Gleese, Canning announced, almost casually: "By the way, I found them yesterday morning."

HOUSE OF GOD: The Fountain of Life Church, where Reverend John Canning was pastor.

CRIME SCENE: The home of Hazel and Leo Gleese, where the unfortunate elderly couple were found dead.

The detectives were stunned. The bodies of Hazel and Leo Gleese had been lying where they had been killed for over 24 hours. Canning knew about it, and had not reported the crime. When asked why this was, he replied: "I was afraid to report it because there were no witnesses, and someone would think that I did it. I just went in and was shocked out of my senses. I couldn't bring myself to report the deaths until today, for fear that my mere presence would implicate me." Instead, he told the police, he had panicked. Still in a state of shock, he had locked up the Gleeses' house and hurried away from the murder scene. He said he had then spent a whole day trying to decide what he should do before reporting the crime.

But when he was asked where he had spent that terrible day, Canning further amazed the police by telling them that he had gone to the shore with friends and then gone out for a social dinner.

Canning's story was beginning to sound more and more suspicious. Was this really the behavior of a man who had just discovered the brutal murder of two people he thought of as his parents? The detectives started to question Canning more closely. As Detective Phil Ramer told reporters: "When it takes someone a day to report two dead bodies, it doesn't take a rocket scientist to work out who the suspect is." "The more Canning talked," added Detective Sergeant Steve Carr, "the more inconsistencies there were with his story."

CLOSE RELATIONSHIP

The detectives soon learned that residents of the sleepy town considered the Cannings and the Gleeses to be a close family. The Reverend Canning, a former pastor at a church in Maine, had moved to Sebring and founded the Fountain of Life Church in 1980. A multidenominational church, the Fountain of Life had about 50 elderly members in Sebring, and was the pretext for a regular series of television sermons by Canning. It was as members of the church that the Gleeses—Leo, a retired accountant, and Hazel, a former beautician—first met.

It was around the time the Gleeses adopted Canning and his wife that the old couple, by then confined to their home by poor health, had given Canning power of attorney over their financial affairs. It was a mistake that was to cost them their lives. The police investigation revealed that the Gleeses were not the only housebound members of Canning's congregation to turn control of their financial affairs over to the minister. A number of other parishioners were

SAYING GOODBYE: Reverend Canning conducts the funeral service for the Gleeses, who had adopted him.

SUSPECT: At Sebring's police headquarters, detectives noted that the more Canning talked, the more inconsistencies appeared in his story.

entrusting him with their money too. Detectives were also surprised to learn that for the last 15 years the Fountain of Life Church had been operating from an abandoned warehouse. For a number of years Canning had been collecting money for the construction of a new "sanctuary," but it was only now that work had begun on the project. The detectives decided to look into Canning's own financial affairs.

It turned out that within weeks of taking control of the Gleeses' finances, Canning had completely paid off his own mortgage, and then gone on a spending spree. At the same time he had sold one of the Gleeses' two homes, worth $83,000. The money from the sale had disappeared, along with another $16,000 of the Gleeses' savings. Canning, however, had begun work on building an expensive extension to his house.

When friends of the Gleeses were interviewed, they reported that, weeks before her death, Hazel Gleese had become suspicious about Canning's handling of her and her husband's finances. She had told them that she intended to go to their bank in the New Year to discuss the matter with the manager. Then, a week before Leo and Hazel were murdered, the couple had apparently discovered that Canning had been forging their signatures on checks to himself.

The investigating officers immediately tied this to the bank statements that had been found scattered throughout the Gleeses' house after their murder. However, they still had no hard evidence to link Canning to the crime itself. Until, that is, they learned about the dump next to the site of the Fountain of Life's new church. This, explained Chief Robert Glick of the Sebring police department to the press, "more than anything else expedited the case."

VITAL EVIDENCE

Witnesses reported that on the day of the murders the Reverend John Canning had made a number of trips out to the dump. A search of the area yielded several items which were linked to the crime scene by laboratory analysis— including Leo Gleese's walking stick. It was covered in blood.

At the same time officers searching the Canning's home discovered a watch that was also smeared with blood. Tests identified the blood as belonging to Leo Gleese. The detectives had their case. Shortly after he had conducted the Gleeses' funeral service, John Canning was arrested.

In February 1996, the Reverend John Nelson Canning was found guilty of the murder of Hazel and Leo Gleese. At his trial he admitted battering and strangling the couple to death after they had

MONEY ILL SPENT: At the time of his arrest, Canning was working on an extension to his home in Sebring, paid for with the Gleeses' savings.

found out that he had been stealing from them. He described how they had confronted him with the evidence of his treachery on the night of January 3, 1995, showing him their bank statements. He had then killed them both.

Canning was sentenced to life impris-

onment, with no possibility of parole. Detective Phil Ramer told the press: "It's the most despicable thing I have ever heard of. Of all the people in the world you should be able to trust, it's your pastor. They couldn't do it in his case, and he wound up killing them."

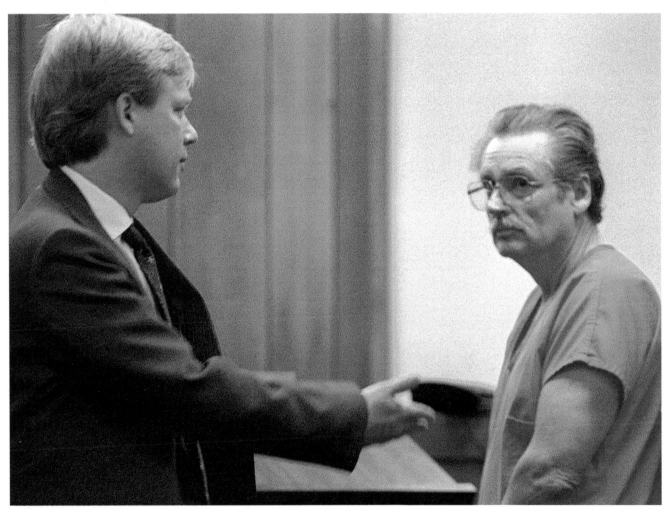

CLOSE QUESTIONING: Canning is grilled in court. He ultimately confessed to both murders.

Real-Life Soap

Sex, glamor, intrigue, and murder have always been regular ingredients in Brazil's hugely popular soap operas. In a country where large numbers of people can neither read nor write—but where almost every household has a television set—steamy TV series like *The Next Victim* and *Exploding Hearts* are the number-one entertainment. But ever since the 1992 murder of soap star Daniella Perez, Brazil has been gripped by a drama that has turned out to be more bizarre than any soap opera plot.

A former professional ballerina, 22-year-old Daniella Perez was the star of Brazil's top-rated soap Corpo e Alma (Body and Soul), a show created and scripted by her mother Gloria Perez, one of Brazil's most renowned scriptwriters. Daniella played Yasmin, a passionate teenage beauty with a tempestuous love life. It was her first major role, and it had made her famous throughout Brazil. She was young, rich, and apparently happily married to fellow actor Raul Gazolla.

Then, on the night of December 28, 1992, hours after she had filmed an episode of Body and Soul in which her character had ended her relationship with her on-screen boyfriend, Perez's body was discovered on a trash dump near to the Rio de Janeiro studios of Globo TV. She had been stabbed to death with a pair of scissors.

DOOMED LOVE: The on-screen affair of *Body and Soul* stars Daniella Perez (center) and Guilherme de Padua (right) was viewed by millions.

SECRET PASSION: Guilherme de Padua was arrested within hours of Daniella's killing. He claimed they had been lovers.

The following day Rio police arrested Perez's co-star Guilherme de Padua and his wife Paula de Thomaz, and charged both with Daniella Perez's murder. For the next four years the Brazilian public were to be enthralled by the twists and turns of a case that involved all the elements of an overheated TV drama—a case that, unfolding live on television, would repeatedly call into question the line between fantasy and reality, and that would eventually threaten to divide Brazilian society.

Soaps are big business in Brazil, making millions each year from companies desperate to associate their products with TV's biggest stars, and Globo TV—the producers of Body and Soul—weren't about to let a story as big as this one get away just because it was real. When Daniella Perez's funeral was attended by thousands of distraught fans, Globo broadcast the whole ceremony live on national television. As every new piece of evidence was turned up in the investigation into Daniella's murder, Globo was there. And, by the time the case eventually came to trial, Globo had already struck a deal to screen the entire proceedings, day by day, live from the courtroom.

It was turning into the biggest soap opera Brazil had ever seen. And the lead role was being played by Guilherme de Padua. A former stripper turned actor, de Padua—then 23—had only recently landed a major part in Body and Soul. He played Bira, the moody and jealous boyfriend of Perez's character, Yasmin. Insiders working on the show claimed that he often carried this behavior over into real life, and seemed to be becoming obsessed with his attractive co-star.

On the night of Daniella's murder, de Padua had apparently appeared to be upset by the filming of the breakup of Yasmin and Bira's relationship—behaving as if it were he rather than his character who was being rejected. The show's director reported seeing him leave the set in tears after shooting was finished. De Padua then left the studios, refusing to speak to fellow cast and crew members. Not long afterward Daniella was murdered.

CHANGE OF MIND

Arrested the following day as chief suspect in Daniella's murder, de Padua initially confessed to the crime. However, within a few hours he had retracted his confession, and instead pointed the finger at his pretty young wife, Paula de Thomaz.

De Thomaz, 25, the child of a well-to-do Rio de Janeiro family, had been married to de Padua for just seven months at the time of the murder. She was also three months pregnant with his child. De Padua claimed that de Thomaz had stabbed Daniella Perez to death "in a jealous rage," after she discovered the truth about the secret affair that he claimed he and Daniella had been having for months. De Thomaz, in turn, denied the allegation—despite confusing matters by having reportedly confessed "informally" to police officers at the time of her own arrest.

It was four years before the truth could be heard in court. During that time, the Daniella Perez murder case became a national spectacle.

In a country where a 1991 study revealed that, out of over 4,000 cases of violence against women by their husbands or lovers, only two led to convictions, Daniella's murder soon became a focus for political and social protest. From 1992, Brazil witnessed regular marches by women's groups demanding justice for Daniella and a change to a legal system which so often saw men escape punishment for such crimes. Daniella's mother, Gloria Perez, soon found herself leading a national campaign to alter the 30-year limit on murder sentences. It garnered over a million signatures of support. People from all levels of society—from campaigners against poverty to the "Maes de Acari," a group made up of mothers of Brazil's missing children—had suddenly found themselves united behind a single cause. Politicians were forced to comment on the case, and to examine the issues it had exposed.

Meanwhile, from his prison cell Guilherme de Padua claimed to have written a book entitled The Story Which Brazil Does Not Know that would prove his innocence and damn his wife. However the book's publication was immediately prohibited until after the completion of the trials of both de Padua and de Thomaz, and has yet to see the light of day. For her part de Thomaz, still maintaining her innocence, obtained a divorce from de Padua in November 1994. The previous year she had given birth to de Padua's son, Felipe, in jail. The baby was taken into the care of his

TRAGIC BEAUTY: Young, rich, and worshipped throughout Brazil, Daniella was just 22 when she was murdered.

grandparents. In an interview with one of Brazil's best-selling magazines, Paula claimed: "Guilherme ended Daniella's life and is now trying to destroy mine, and that of my parents and my son."

Finally, on January 22, 1997—over four years after Daniella Perez's death—the trial of Guilherme de Padua began in a courtroom packed with journalists and film crews. For four days, millions tuned into Globo TV to watch the evidence unfold. Outside the courtroom huge video screens were set up to broadcast the proceedings to the crowds that gathered in the street, while protest groups continued their campaign on the steps of the courthouse. Inside a jury was hearing how the affair between Daniella Perez and de Padua had led to the actress's violent death.

Jose Filho, prosecuting attorney, described how de Padua had developed an intense obsession with his leading lady during the few months that their affair had been going on behind the scenes of Body and Soul. And the more intense their relationship became, the prosecution argued, the more de Padua began to confuse it with the on-screen affair between their characters. He

became jealous of the other members of the cast, as well as of Daniella's own fame and success, feeling that she was stealing the limelight from him in the show. He was also terrified that their affair would be discovered.

All of this, the prosecution alleged, was enough to push de Padua over the edge into murder—a murder triggered by having to act out the breakup of the affair between his character and Daniella's, in a scene that had been written by Daniella's own mother.

ALTERED LICENSE
Soon after filming had been completed on the night of December 28, 1992, the packed courtroom heard, a visibly shaken de Padua had left the Globo TV studios and driven home to the affluent suburb of Copacobana, where he and de Thomaz lived. After altering his car's license plate—from LM 115 to OM 115—using masking tape, de Padua then drove back toward the studios, having arranged to meet Perez at a service station. He was accompanied—at least part of the way—by his wife.

According to the prosecution, de Padua then met up with Perez at the

service station, where she was knocked unconscious by a blow to the head and bundled into de Padua's car. De Padua and de Thomaz, it was alleged, then drove to an isolated spot, where one or both of them stabbed Perez 18 times in the chest and throat with a pair of scissors. Her dead body was then hidden in undergrowth.

The whole crime, the prosecution suggested, had been premeditated. It may even have been part of the bizarre "love pact" that was alleged to have recently been undertaken between de Padua and de Thomaz, which had also involved them having each other's names tattooed on their genitals.

In his defense, de Padua continued to claim that his wife had committed the murder in a fit of jealousy. He admitted to having punched Perez—explaining the blow to her head—but claimed that he had done so while trying to defend his pregnant wife as the two women fought over him. De Thomaz had then stabbed the unconscious Perez to death, de Padua asserted, although he claimed not to have seen the actual crime take place. He failed to provide a reasonable explanation for this. He also denied having

ACCESSORY TO MURDER?: Paula de Thomaz was tried separately for her part in Daniella's death. Did she help her husband kill his co-star?

BLIND JUSTICE: A protestor demonstrates at the trial of Guilherme de Padua. The trial brought women together from all over Brazil to campaign for a change in the law.

abducted Perez, claiming that she had made her own way to the spot where she was murdered. His defense attorney, Paulo Ramalho, argued that his client had "no plausible reason" for murdering Perez. When questioned about his affair with Perez, de Padua denied having been obsessed with the actress, maintaining that he simply wanted to get closer to her mother—Gloria Perez, the scriptwriter of *Body and Soul*—in order to further his career.

MEMORY LOSS

Things were further complicated when a number of witnesses, who had originally claimed to have seen de Padua abduct Perez from the service station, later admitted to being unable to remember exactly what they had seen. One witness, Hugo da Silveira, testified to having seen Paula de Thomaz at the scene of the crime, but when first questioned had only been able to give a very vague description of her. The same witness was unable to identify de Padua's car, despite having supposedly spotted it at the crime scene and written down the number on the license plate.

Paula de Thomaz, meanwhile, continued to maintain that she was shopping at the time of the murder—and for some seven hours afterwards—in the nearby Barra shopping mall, having been dropped off there by her husband. She has always claimed that a number of witnesses who could support her story refused for fear of getting involved in

such a high-profile case. On January 24, 1997, after hearing three days of evidence, the jury in the Perez murder case stayed up all night deliberating. The following day they delivered their verdict.

On Saturday January 25, 1997, Guilherme de Padua was found guilty of the premeditated murder of Daniella Perez. He was sentenced to 19 years in jail, of which he had already served four. Delivering the sentence, Judge Jose Geraldo Antonio described de Padua as "violent, perverse, and cowardly."

At a second trial in May 1997, Paula de Thomaz was found guilty of assisting her husband in Daniella Perez's murder.

Meanwhile Gloria Perez, who said after the murder that she felt as if she had scripted her own daughter's death, has returned to writing soap operas. Her latest project, *Exploding Hearts*, is currently the number-one show in Brazil. It has all the glamor, romance, and intrigue of *Body and Soul*, but with a difference. It focuses on one of Brazil's most pressing social concerns: the plight of its thousands of missing children. For years women whose sons and daughters have disappeared have gathered in the center of Rio de Janeiro to hand out photographs and leaflets in the hope that someone might have seen their children. Since *Exploding Hearts* began showing the pictures of such kids on television—along with telephone numbers to call—a number of children have been reunited with their families.

Gloria Perez herself has always maintained that soap operas can and should provide more than just entertainment. Her daughter's murder proved to the whole country just how powerful a medium television can be.

MOMENT OF TRUTH: Dressed in a white T-shirt, Guilherme de Padua stands as his sentence is read out. He was sentenced to 19 years in jail for Daniella's murder.

Up Against the Moscow Mafia

Paul Tatum was a stranger in a strange land. He was one of hundreds of Western businessmen who, in the late 1980s, had foreseen the collapse of communism and the huge potential that would exist in Russia under a market economy. Initially things went well for Tatum, but they quickly turned sour. The Russian Mafia wanted him out, and he wouldn't go. Tatum's stubbornness cost him his life.

It was a scene straight out of a 1950s gangster movie. On Sunday, November 3, 1996, Paul Tatum, a 41-year-old entrepreneur from Oklahoma, stepped onto the crowded platform of a Moscow subway station and was gunned down by a Mafia hitman armed with a Kalashnikov rifle. It was the gruesome conclusion to a long and complex business war Tatum had been waging with his Russian partners. He thus became the first American to die in what is an all too common fashion in post-Communist Russia.

Tatum was a product of the 1980s, an all-American, Reaganite go-getter who embraced the ideal of free enterprise and the mighty dollar. After graduating from Oklahoma State University, he went into the oil business and, by his mid-twenties, had amassed a modest fortune, and achieved a position of respect in local business circles.

He might well have continued with this successful, if unspectacular, career if he had not joined the 1985 Oklahoma trade mission to what was then the Soviet Union. Despite the fact that the country was still operating under a totally repressive communist regime, Tatum immediately saw the true potential of Russia as a market for Western technology and ingenuity. He was overwhelmed and seduced by the sheer scale of that potential. On his return to the United States, he told a friend: "It was as if I saw myself standing on a mountain top, from which I could see everything, my past, my present, my future. I immediately felt that here [Russia] my life's hopes would come true."

By 1989, the oil business in Oklahoma had gone through a deep recession and Tatum had personally lost more than a million dollars in the collapse of the

CARPETBAGGER: Paul Tatum was confident he could make millions from the Radisson-Slavyanskaya hotel.

LOSING BATTLE: Moscow police question suspects in downtown Moscow. Their fight against organized crime is bordering on hopeless.

Penn Square Bank, which had failed as a direct result of that recession. Tatum decided it was time for a change. He consolidated all his personal assets and, together with a group of other investors, formed Americom, Inc., a service company which installed and ran state-of-the-art business centers in existing hotels. The company was an immediate success in the United States and Tatum felt confident that his concept would have global appeal. In 1990, less than a year after the launch of Americom, Tatum struck a deal with the Soviet Union's state-run tourist agency, Intourist, to create a world-class hotel in central Moscow.

LUXURY INVESTMENT

What he created, on the banks of the River Moskva, was the Radisson-Slavyanskaya hotel. It rapidly became, and remains, one of the most fashionable hotels in the city. It has conference facilities, screening rooms, an American-style steak house, a health spa, and an array of outrageously expensive designer boutiques. In its early days, the Radisson-Slavyanskaya was the sole preserve of visiting businessmen and

wealthy tourists. No ordinary Russian could afford a cup of coffee in the place, let alone stay in one of its luxurious suites. Since the fall of communism,

however, all that has changed. Now the place is teeming with Russian "businessmen" with suspicious bulges under their left armpits, usually accompanied by

HIGH LIFE: Despite his financial problems, Paul Tatum continued to enjoy living ostentatiously. Here he is seen with a group that includes actress Sharon Stone.

dazzling blondes, and throwing money about like confetti.

While the hotel prospered, Tatum personally started to run into trouble. When the Soviet Union collapsed and the true catastrophe of the Russian economy became apparent, Intourist effectively ceased to exist as a business entity and Americom found itself without a Russian partner. Tatum's consortium was severely under-capitalized and was under pressure from the Radisson group to repay a million-dollar loan they had obtained to fund start-up costs. The Moscow city government stepped in and took over Intourist's interest in the business and, while it provided no additional capital, it clearly wanted to take control of the whole operation.

Paul Tatum appears to have been completely unaffected by the financial pressures and corporate acrimony he was facing. He lived ostentatiously. He had a taste for fast cars and expensive suits, and could be seen escorting a succession of beautiful women to Moscow's most expensive restaurants and nightclubs. On one occasion he flew nine members of his family to Moscow from the United States and then chartered a helicopter to show them the countryside. "We landed 46 times in three days," said his brother-in-law, Rick Furmanek.

The question is, where was all the money coming from? What limited capital Tatum had after the Penn Square Bank collapse had been invested in Americom and, apart from his modest salary, all the profits from the hotel were plowed straight back into the corporation. If he was borrowing heavily, it certainly wasn't from the Bank of America. Perhaps it was from one of those Russian "businessmen" with the bulging armpits?

CRISIS GROWS

By the fall of 1994, the situation at the hotel had reached crisis point. Radisson sued Americom for the return of their loan, and dissolved the partnership, and the Russians, unhappy with Tatum's performance, installed their own man at the Radisson hotel as general manager. He was a young Chechen named Umar Dzhabrailov. Fairly or unfairly, the word "Chechen" has become synonymous with "gangster" in post-Communist Russia.

Tatum was furious at having Dzhabrailov foisted on him. He told several friends and associates that he believed the young Chechen was no more than a front man for an organized crime syndicate bent on taking control of the hotel. After Tatum's murder, Dzhabrailov vehemently denied having any involvement in the incident and complained that the only reason he was under suspicion was because of his ethnic background.

He may not have been quite as squeaky clean as he would have people believe. It has recently emerged that US government agencies involved in combating organized crime in Russia had kept Dzhabrailov under surveillance for some considerable time before Paul Tatum's murder, although they admit they have no solid evidence so far to connect him with the Russian Mafia.

The relationship between Tatum and the Russians continued to deteriorate. Eric Knapp, Tatum's deputy, described the situation. "We could no longer hire or fire, execute leases, or even pay employees. Even the phone service to Paul's room was cut off."

In the spring of 1995, Tatum's bodyguard was stabbed, beaten up, and then sent to tell his boss that it was time to

ARMED AND DANGEROUS: Paul Tatum's bodyguards carried guns and accompanied him wherever he went. However, they did not lift a finger to prevent his murder.

LAID TO REST: During his funeral service held in Moscow, Paul Tatum was eulogized as a stubborn idealist who died standing up to danger.

leave Moscow. Paul Tatum was from Oklahoma and came from a tradition that didn't take kindly to threats. He decided to fight back, a decision which almost certainly cost him his life.

Tatum went on the attack. He took out advertisements in the *Moscow Times*, lambasting his Russian "partners" and the Mayor of Moscow, Yuri Luzhov. By this time Tatum was seriously in debt and attempted to cover his legal costs by advertising what he called "freedom bonds."

On a more personal level, he hired a private detective to investigate Umar Dzhabrailov, hoping to prove his connections with organized crime. He even went so far as to contact the Russian internal revenue suggesting it conduct an audit of the young Chechen's accounts.

Rather than being anxious about the consequences of his aggressive behavior, Tatum seemed to be relishing the situation. A few weeks before his death, he told Eric Knapp: "I bet they really turn the heat up on me now." Knapp tried to caution his friend, but to no avail. "I

think he knew he was at risk," he said after the murder, "but I don't think he ever thought it would come to bullets." Tatum's attorney, Raymond Markovich, thought that his client had basically lost touch with reality. "Paul believed in Horatio Alger and rags to riches," he said, "and he believed in Hollywood endings. It was all going to come out okay."

NO WITNESSES

There is probably a great deal of truth in Markovich's analysis of the situation. After six years in Moscow, Tatum was no newcomer, and he must have been more than aware of the escalating lawlessness which surrounded him.

At about 4:30 p.m. he left his beloved Slavyanskaya Hotel, flanked by two armed bodyguards, and took the short walk to the Kievskaya subway station. He was en route to a business meeting at the Starlight Diner, a popular haunt for expatriate businessmen. Neither he nor his guards noticed that they were being followed. Tatum walked down the steps of the station and onto the platform. His pursuer pulled a balaclava over his face,

produced a Kalashnikov rifle from under his coat, and fired 11 bullets into Paul Tatum's body. He died instantly. The killer then put the rifle into a plastic bag and calmly walked away. Nobody, including Tatum's bodyguards, made any attempt to stop him. The station was crowded at the time of the killing, yet investigators could not persuade a solitary witness to come forward.

Organized crime is now rife in Moscow, a city that used to be one of the safest in the world. In 1995, Moscow police reported more than 3,000 murders, an increase of 1,740 percent over the figures for 1987. One government study concluded that virtually every retailer in the city is now paying large sums in protection money to organized crime. As crime levels continue to rise, stores regularly run out of stocks of handguns, flak jackets, and mace. "The crime today knows no limits," says Pavel Gusev, a prominent Russian journalist. "In the United States, the Mafia has already divided up the spheres of business, so the bosses no longer kill each other off. Here we have a wild market."

The Final Reckoning

On June 12, 1994 Nicole Brown Simpson, ex-wife of former American football star, O.J. Simpson, and her friend, Ronald Goldman, were found with their throats slashed outside Nicole's Los Angeles home. On October 3, 1995, the whole world looked on in shock as Simpson was declared "not guilty" in the twentieth-century's most controversial murder case. The victims' families immediately filed a "wrongful death" suit against Simpson and he was put on trial a second time for murder.

When *The People* v. *Orenthal James Simpson* concluded in October 1995, nobody could believe the verdict, particularly the victims' families, who were convinced that Simpson had committed the double murder. As Simpson hugged his lawyer, relatives of the victims broke down into sobs of disbelief. Fred Goldman, whose 25-year-old son Ronald was stabbed to death with 35-year-old Nicole Brown Simpson, was heard shouting: "No, no, no. Murderer, murderer, murderer!" The whole trial had been dominated by the issue of race

CALLED TO ACCOUNT: O.J. Simpson leaves court with defense attorney Daniel Leonard after testifying for the first time.

NO-NONSENSE JUDGE: Superior Court Judge Hiroshi Fujisaki ensured the civil trial did not become a media circus.

rather than by who committed the crime—centering around Simpson's claim: "I was a victim of racist cops." Detective Mark Fuhrman effectively put the Los Angeles Police Department on trial after he allegedly said: "If I had my way, they would take all the niggers, put them together in a big group, and burn them."

The families of the two victims would not let Simpson get away with what they saw as murder. They immediately filed suits against Simpson for wrongful death. They accused Simpson of killing his victims with "vicious and outrageous savagery," which, of course, he denied. Under the rules for civil litigation, Simpson had no constitutional right to remain silent by invoking the Fifth Amendment; the jury, rather than finding him "guilty beyond reasonable doubt," needed only to find "preponderance of evidence" to find him guilty, and only nine out of the 12 jurors need agree.

On September 18, 1996 the jury selection began for the civil trial—the jury was picked from the predominantly white areas of West Los Angeles around the Santa Monica courthouse. Initially, there was one black juror, Rosemary Carraway, but she was promptly dismissed when it was discovered that her daughter worked for the Los Angeles District Attorney's office. She was replaced by an Asian computer programer, picked at random from four alternative jurors. The jury then had six women and six men. Nine were white, one Hispanic, one Asian, and one was Jamaican-born of mixed black and Asian parentage. This jury was in stark contrast to the all-black jury of the previous year's criminal trial.

The civil trial opened on October 23, 1996 and had little of the media fanfare of the previous trial. Superior Court Judge Hiroshi Fujisaki could not be more different from Judge Lance Ito, who courted the media and ended by selling his story. Judge Fujisaki is an efficient, no-nonsense judge who was keen to move the case along in record time, not relishing the prospect of another year-long media circus. At the very start of the proceedings he placed a gagging order on all those involved in the trial and cameras were banned from the courtroom. Fujisaki also ruled that videotapes of former Los Angeles police detective Mark Fuhrman's testimony could not be shown to jurors, making it difficult for the defense to offer arguments of police conspiracy against Simpson——which is what swung the jury in Simpson's favor in the criminal case. Members of the media and legal VIPs were relegated to watching the trial on a screen in the Doubletree Hotel next door to the courthouse.

KEY WITNESS

O.J. Simpson, 50-year-old former football star turned actor, was impeccably dressed for the first day in court. He stopped to sign autographs as he strode confidently to the witness box. Once in the box, a nervous smile slowly appeared on his face—who could blame him? This was the moment the world had waited for, at last Simpson was being called to account for his actions in his own words. The plaintiffs' key attorney was David Petrocelli, who chose Peter Gelblum, Tom Lambert, and Ed Medvene from Mitchell, Silberberg & Knupp. Simpson was up against a formidable team. A medley of lawyers representing the Nicole Brown Simpson estate and Ronald Goldman's mother were all under the supervision of Petrocelli and Gelblum. The defense's key attorney was Robert Baker, assisted by his son Phillip, together with Dan Leonard of F. Lee Bailey and Robert Blasier, who had defended Simpson in the criminal trial.

David Petrocelli, for the plaintiffs, started out determined to discredit Simpson's testimony. It was Simpson's conflicting versions of nearly every aspect of the murder case that Petrocelli wanted to root out. On a huge screen behind Simpson, Petrocelli projected Nicole's cut and bruised face. Petrocelli: "How many times did you strike Nicole?" Simpson: "Never." Petrocelli: "How many times did you slap her?" Simpson: "Never." Petrocelli: "How many times did you kick and beat her?" Simpson: "Never." Petrocelli: "If Nicole said you hit her, she would be lying, is that true?" Simpson: "Yes." Petrocelli described numerous occasions when Nicole had a split lip, a welt over her eye, and red marks around her neck. Simpson replied

MARCHING TO JUSTICE: The Brown family, from left, Tonya, Judith, and Dominique Brown arrive at the Los Angeles Superior Court with one of their many attorneys.

BRUTALLY MURDERED: Nicole Brown Simpson was brutally stabbed to death in her home on June 12, 1994.

FRIEND AND VICTIM: Ron Goldman was a close friend of Nicole's; he was also found stabbed and with his throat slit.

that Nicole tended to pick her pimples. "A lot of this redness was normally there most nights, once she had picked and cleaned her face," he said.

In her diary Nicole noted the times Simpson hit her; she also complained to the police. Simpson discounted the evidence as lies. However, he did admit that he and Nicole had "physical altercations," and that they both repeatedly engaged in what he termed as "rassling." Despite his emphatic denial of ever physically abusing Nicole, he did admit somewhat confusingly that: "I was wrong for everything that led to this." After his first day on the stand Simpson remained calm and collected, seemingly in control of the proceedings. The actor in him maintained the cool exterior in contrast to the previous trial's sudden outbursts of anger. One family member overheard the plaintiffs saying: "We've got to get him angry. The one thing he's doing is keeping his cool."

The civil trial prosecution team learned from the mistakes committed by their counterparts in the criminal trial and rethought their strategy. Marcia Clark and Christopher Darden, leading attorneys for the prosecution in the criminal trial, built their case around a timeline——that the murders were committed between 10:15 and 10:20 p.m. on June 12, 1994. This, they believed, gave Simpson plenty of time to commit the murders and make his way back to his Rockingham estate by 10:45 or 10:50 p.m., which is when Allan Park, the limousine driver who took Simpson to the airport, said he saw a dark figure entering the house. Park had been ringing the bell for some time before Simpson emerged at

CHANGE OF HEART: "Kato" Kaelin, who was uncooperative in the criminal trial, was happy to testify in the civil trial.

10:50 p.m. apologizing, saying he had fallen asleep. Simpson also variously claimed to have been reading, sitting on his bed, or chipping golf balls at the time of the murders.

Petrocelli dispensed with the Los Angeles County Coroner and chose to put Dr. Werner Spitz on the stand, a well known and respected pathologist. Spitz testified that the incriminating cuts on Simpson's hand were caused in the death struggle between Simpson and Ronald Goldman when Goldman apparently gouged Simpson with his fingernails. Simpson was consistently vague on what had caused the cuts, undermining the defense's case. Simpson testified in January that he had cut his left hand as he was getting ready to go to Chicago. "I bleed all the time," he told police. He has also said that he cut his hand on a glass in his Chicago hotel room, and another time that he cut his hand after he returned from Chicago.

KATO TALKS

Brian "Kato" Kaelin was a friend of Simpson and Nicole and a frequent houseguest. In the criminal trial he was not a cooperative witness, yet in the civil trial he was more forthcoming about the events of June 12, 1994. He testified that Simpson was "brooding" the day before the murders over his ex-wife's sexual escapades. Kaelin went on to mention that the three thumps which he heard sounded "like someone falling back against my bedroom wall." So why the sudden change of heart? It is thought that Kaelin feared Simpson and did not want to testify against his "friend." But having distanced himself from Simpson, Kaelin had nothing to lose and perhaps felt guilty about the events that went on in the house. Marcia Clark believes that even now, Kaelin is not revealing all he knows.

In the criminal trial, William Bodziak, the FBI shoe expert, testified that the bloody footprints leading away from grisly crime scene came from a pair of rare size 12, Italian, Bruno Magli shoes. Only 299 pairs were sold in the United States. Simpson denied owning such a pair of "ugly-ass" shoes. Initially, Petrocelli only had one photo of Simpson wearing what looked like the Bruno Magli shoes, taken by freelance photographer Harry Scull. The defense declared that the photo was a fake, claiming that it had been doctored. The defense also demonstrated that Bodziak was unable to identify an assortment of other bloodied shoe prints at the scene of the crime. Then

CAUGHT ON CAMERA: Photographer Brian McCrone with photographs he took of Simpson allegedly wearing the Bruno Magli shoes.

came good news for the prosecution, other photographs of Simpson wearing the shoes had been discovered. Freelance photographer Brian McCrone sent Petrocelli and Gelblum photographs of Simpson allegedly wearing the Bruno

Magli shoes, but most important of all were 30 other photographs showing Simpson at a football game at Rich Stadium, Buffalo, New York, on September 26, 1993, wearing those very same shoes. These photographs were

CRUCIAL EVIDENCE: The prosecution presented the famous white Ford Bronco chase and tape recordings as the nearest Simpson came to admitting his guilt.

taken by freelance photographer E.J. Flammer, who had published one of the photographs in the Buffalo Bills newsletter in November 1993. Flammer also had a dated invoice for the photo assignment and a copy of his sideline pass for the game. There was no danger of this evidence being a fake.

Simpson was finally forced to backpedal, saying: "I know I've had similar shoes." Of all Simpson's conflicting statements, Petrocelli believes that nothing was more important than his denial of owning the Bruno Magli shoes: "There's no question that the shoes were the single most important piece of evidence in the case. And that is because they have nothing to do with the LAPD. The shoes have nothing to do with race."

DAMNING FACTS

The shoe photographs were the most damaging piece of evidence gathered by the prosecution.

Much of the evidence amassed by Petrocelli and his team was not used because they had to select the strongest and most irrefutable facts to bring before the jury. Among the unused evidence were notes of a West Los Angeles therapist who had separately treated Nicole Brown and Ronald Goldman; these contained Nicole's account of being beaten by Simpson in the days just before the murders. The recollections of a Connecticut limousine driver were also revealing. He described how, after a

meeting at the Forschner Group, a knife company, Simpson used a complimentary knife to demonstrate how to kill someone—only a week before the murders.

The prosecution in the criminal trial was worried that introducing Simpson's slow-speed Bronco chase and the associated transcripts could damage their case by presenting him in a sympathetic light as the grief-stricken and suicidal husband. In the civil trial the prosecution decided to present it to the jury—as far as the plaintiffs were concerned, here was the crucial admission of guilt they needed. There was so much information from transcripts to phone records to laboratory analysis to tape recordings that Petrocelli took to listening to the cassettes while he was driving home.

One of the tapes was played in court for the first time. It recorded Simpson talking to the Los Angeles police during the car chase, five days after the killings on June 17. The recording proved to be another damning piece of evidence. Simpson was sitting in the back of the Bronco talking by cell phone to LAPD detective Thomas Lange and holding a gun in his other hand while his friend Al Cowlings led police on a chase. Simpson wanted to use the gun, Lange wanted to prevent him from using it: Lange: "And nobody's going to get hurt." Simpson: "I'm the only one that deserves it . . . I'm going to get hurt." Lange: "Don't do this." Simpson: "All I did was love

Nicole. That's all I did, was love her . . . " Also discovered in the car was a fake goatee beard, a passport, and several thousand dollars in cash.

In his continuing attempt to discredit Simpson, Petrocelli delved further into the tempestuous relationship between O.J. and Nicole, concentrating on the final two months of her life. Here, Petrocelli believes, lies the motive for the murders—the least explored aspect of the trial. He focused on Simpson's friends rather than Nicole's. This made the difference in understanding Simpson and his motives. It was Simpson's former golfing buddies that provided Petrocelli with the most helpful information. Simpson thanked some of these buddies in his supposed "suicide" letter he left in his house before taking off in the Bronco. Initially, many of them were staunch supporters of Simpson, believing him to be innocent. It was not until well into the criminal trial that they began to doubt Simpson and his innocence. Ex-buddies such as Alan Austin and Ron Shipp described Simpson's jealous rages and the obsession with Nicole. They also retold the last two months of Simpson and Nicole's relationship, of the emotional break Nicole made with Simpson at a time when he was considering a reconciliation.

Simpson argues that it was Nicole who was the pursuer, not him, he called her attentions "incessant." However, Nicole's diary documents all the fights between her and Simpson in the last few

VITAL REVELATION: Paula Barbieri, a former girlfriend of Simpson, told of her split with Simpson the day of the murders.

THE WAITING GAME: A crowd gathers outside the court on February 4, 1997, to await the verdict in the civil trial against O.J. Simpson.

weeks, all of which Simpson claims are lies. O.J.'s behavior became more and more threatening. He sent Nicole a letter threatening to report her to the Internal Revenue Service for failing to pay capital-gains taxes. Nicole retaliated by denying Simpson access to their two children. O.J. sought to win her over by giving her a $6,000 diamond and sapphire bracelet for her birthday on May 19, but she returned the gift within two weeks, intensifying Simpson's anger.

What may have tipped the balance was the testimony of Simpson's former girlfriend, Paula Barbieri. She testified that on the day of the murders she left a message for Simpson on his cell phone ending their relationship. Simpson denied learning of the break-up, but Petrocelli put up a display of the phone records that showed Simpson retrieved his messages and made eight calls to Barbieri that day. Petrocelli argued that in these last three weeks Simpson's obsession with Nicole grew to dangerous levels, developing into a rage which led him to kill her and Ronald Goldman.

Rockingham, Simpson's estate, became the central meeting place for the defense team. The property is surrounded by two fences and manned by a security guard. Simpson's mother Eunice, his

sister Shirley Baker, and her husband Benny were staying in the house, with Shirley doing the cooking. To save on expenses, lawyers Robert Blasier and Dan Leonard were living on the estate. Lawyers Robert and Phillip Baker also met and worked with Simpson at Rockingham. It was also where many of the defense witnesses were coached.

The greatest potential resource for the defense was Simpson himself. One source said: "O.J. is intelligent. He knows the case better than anyone else. I can't think of a client who was more active." Yet despite this Simpson did not seem at ease with his lawyers in court. There did not seem to be the chemistry that Fred Goldman and his family had with their lawyers. Having taken on the case, the Bakers encountered social ostracism by some members of Los Angeles' well-heeled society.

EASIER QUESTIONS

After the barrage of questioning from Petrocelli, Simpson had an easier ride with Baker. Baker allowed O.J. to give his version of events and describe his relationship with Nicole. Simpson painted Nicole as a volatile and unstable woman who began to associate with a rather "dangerous" crowd in the final

months of her life. However, Petrocelli through his questioning had highlighted Simpson's backpedaling and contradictions at every turn, so no matter what Simpson said it was hard to believe the answer. In his closing argument Petrocelli displayed a list of 60 people who would have had to lie or be mistaken for Simpson to be innocent.

On January 30, 1997, the jury was sent away to deliberate. Simpson spent his time playing golf. Fred Goldman spent hours alone driving around Los Angeles. Denise Brown, Nicole's sister, was at her parents' house trying to comfort her mother Judith. Judith was worried that Simpson could somehow hurt Denise. At this late stage there were potential problems. Two of the jurors from the criminal trial had sent letters to two jurors of the civil trial offering their help in attaining an agent and what their financial options were——it wasn't just the criminal trial that was big business.

When Judge Fujisaki heard of this, he was furious and launched an immediate investigation. A similar occurrence had happened in the criminal trial when one of the jurors, Francine Florio-Bunten, tried to capitalize on being a juror during the trial. Judge Fujisaki wanted none of these shenanigans in his trial. Whether

JUDGEMENT DAY: Fred Goldman, his daughter Kim, and wife Patti embrace after hearing Simpson has been found liable on all counts for the murder of his son Ron Goldman.

Simpson was held liable for the killings or not, he would not go to prison and, depending on the cleverness of his attorneys, he may not even have to pay the full damages. This case, however, was less about the money involved and more about retribution. As Fred Goldman said: "We don't care about the money. We want a jury in a court of law to hold the killer responsible." None of the Goldman family will speak the name of Simpson; he is simply known as "the killer." Goldman was devastated by the criminal verdict: "I was numb; I was blown away. I thought a hung jury was possible, but I had never imagined an acquittal."

The verdict came in the early evening of February 4, 1997. It was unanimous: Simpson was liable for the murders of Nicole Brown Simpson and Ronald

Goldman. He was ordered to compensate the parents of Ronald Goldman with the sum of $8.5 million for his wrongful death. Petrocelli hugged his wife and son and slumped into a chair, "We couldn't have done better. I didn't think it would be unanimous. Isn't it incredible?" The verdict for the Goldmans and the Browns was bittersweet. Fred Goldman popped the champagne and celebrated, thanking his lawyers and friends. "Finally there is justice for Ron."

Meanwhile, in the Beach Hotel, Judith Brown remained calm as she listened to a broadcast of the verdict being read out in court. Now there were other matters to consider, for having lost the custody battle on December 20 for 11-year-old Sydney and eight-year-old Justin, Simpson and Nicole's daughter and son, they were now in the hands of a man

who had just been found liable for the death of their mother. Yet another twist to this morbid tale is that because the estate of Nicole Brown Simpson had not filed a wrongful death suit, this paves the way for the children to sue their father for their mother's wrongful death.

Despite the verdict, Simpson is still a free man. Yet he stands to lose much of his wealth, his houses, his cars, his social standing, his friends, everything he claims he's worked for over the last 20 years. Simpson's lawyers claimed he was $9 million in debt and had no prospect of earning more. Some of the original defense team have yet to be paid and there are the bills from the custody battle. However, plaintiff lawyers argued that he had the potential wealth of $15.7 million, based on money he could make from commercial deals and selling his story. Simpson has already made $1 million with his book I Want To Tell You and the Star, the supermarket tabloid, paid $450,000 for the picture rights of his homecoming after his acquittal.

MISSING MILLIONS

But where is Simpson getting the resources to maintain his Rockingham estate, his Bentley car and domestic staff? The Goldman family has hired an investigator to find out what Simpson is worth. Anticipating the verdict, Simpson sold much of his property and heavily mortgaged his home, protecting the proceeds in legal and untouchable havens. It is reported that Simpson has around $8 million hidden away in banks in the Caribbean, Switzerland, and Jersey (in the Channel Islands).

On February 10, 1997 the jury returned with the additional punitive damages that Simpson has to pay to the victims' families: $25 million. Each family was awarded half the money, with the jury voting eleven to one in favor of punitive damages and ten to two on the amounts. In the case of Nicole's family, the money will go to the children; for the Goldman family, the money will be split between Fred and his wife. Sadly, these monetary rewards will do little to ease the pain of Fred Goldman who has lost a son, or Judith Brown who has lost a daughter in a most vicious and brutal killing. Simpson has decided to appeal against the verdict. For this he will have to post a bond one and a half times the total amount. The appeal process could take years; this may not yet be the end of the O.J. Simpson murder case.

For many Americans, black and

PUBLIC OUTCRY: The crowd outside the Los Angeles Superior Court reacts to the final verdict on February 4, 1997.

white, the civil trial verdict had one message: that justice is defined by race. In the criminal trial with a predominantly black jury, Simpson was not guilty. In the civil trial with the jury predominately white, Simpson was found liable for the two deaths. This has undermined the confidence anyone might have in either verdict. Despite the civil trial' verdict Simpson is still a free man and has custody of his children. The Browns, however, are appealing against Simpson keeping custody. So Sydney and Justin Simpson remain caught up in the middle of legal battles. The civil trial may be over, but the conflict goes on.

STILL IN CHARGE: Simpson, Sydney, and Justin arrive in the Bahamas for a holiday three months after the verdict.

Oklahoma Verdict

It was widely reported to be the trial of the century. The defendant: Timothy McVeigh. The crime: the bombing of the Alfred P. Murrah Federal Building in Oklahoma City, April 19, 1995, which resulted in the deaths of no fewer than 168 men, women, and children.

The shock waves of the explosion in Oklahoma City rocked the nation to its core. The greatest act of mass-murder in United States history had, it seemed, been committed not by foreign terrorists, but by an American citizen—a former war hero who had been honored for his service to his country. For the two years it had taken to bring the case against Timothy McVeigh to court, the United States had been haunted by stories about secretive, heavily armed militias plotting to overthrow the government. By the time McVeigh was due to stand trial, on March 31, 1997, the question of his guilt or innocence seemed to have already been sidelined. The trial was to be as much about the American people's faith in their own government as it was about the man who planted the bomb.

CLOSED COURT

First however, the stage had to be set. Cowboy-boot-wearing Judge Richard P. Matsch, 67, had made it clear that he was not going to tolerate his courtroom being the scene of the sort of media circus that had surrounded the O.J. Simpson murder trial. The only live broadcast of the proceedings would be to a small auditorium in Oklahoma City, set up for relatives of the bombing's victims. A lifelong Republican who had won praise for his handling of the trial of a group of neo-Nazis accused of killing talk-show host Alan Berg, Matsch was famous for both his intellect and his short temper. It was he who granted the defense's request that the trial be moved from Oklahoma City to Denver, Colorado, to ensure McVeigh a fairer hearing.

The case for the prosecution was to be handled by Joseph Hartzler, 45, of Chicago, who had been personally selected by Attorney General Janet Reno. Suffering from the debilitating disease of multiple sclerosis, Hartzler had been confined to a wheelchair for seven years—earning the nickname "The Ironside of Illinois." He had asked to be considered for the case because, he said: "I really thought I could make a difference."

The case for the defense was to be led by the flamboyant Stephen Jones, a former legal researcher for President Nixon who had previously represented some 24 defendants facing the death penalty. His opinion of his latest client's chances? Before the trial Jones said: "Tim and I feel very good about the case."

And then there was Timothy McVeigh himself. A Gulf War veteran turned drifter who, it was alleged, had become caught up in the shadowy world of the

THE ACCUSED: Flanked by US marshals and wearing a bulletproof jacket for his own protection, Timothy McVeigh arrives at a preliminary hearing.

SCENE OF THE CRIME: The Alfred P. Murrah Federal Building in Oklahoma was completely devastated by the blast.

checked McVeigh into the Dreamland Motel, Oklahoma City. According to McGowan, two days later she saw him driving a Ryder truck—similar to the one that had been packed with fertilizer and used in the bombing. The problem for the prosecution was that this truck was rented on April 17, the day after McGowan claimed to have seen McVeigh in his truck. So were there two trucks? And, if so, why? Or did someone else rent the Ryder truck used in the bombing? Rather than have to answer these questions, the prosecution decided not to call McGowan to the stand, relying instead on the evidence of her son Eric. He too had originally told the FBI agents who were investigating the case that he had seen McVeigh driving a Ryder truck on April 16. However, he was now claiming that he was no longer sure which day it had been.

DOWNTOWN WITNESSES

Then there were witnesses Mike Moroz, Kyle Hunt, and Dave Snider, all of whom were reported as claiming to have seen McVeigh in downtown Oklahoma City within an hour of the bombing. Unfortunately for the prosecution they also claimed to have seen at least one other man with McVeigh— which would have called into question

anti-Government militia movement. A self-proclaimed "prisoner of war," he had been arrested less than two hours after the Oklahoma City bombing having been stopped for driving a car with no rear license plate. It was not until the following day that someone noticed his resemblance to the man linked by a number of witnesses to the bombing. McVeigh was charged with eight counts of murder, conspiracy to destroy the Alfred P. Murrah Federal Building, detonating the bomb, and destroying a federal building.

From the very beginning of the proceedings, the case for the prosecution looked shaky. Despite the overwhelming public assumption of McVeigh's guilt, commentators had for months been drawing attention to the large number of holes in the argument that he had acted as a "lone bomber." Much was made of the number of very good witnesses whom Joseph Hartzler and his team had decided to ignore.

There was Lea McGowan, who on April 14, 1995—five days before the bombing of the Alfred P. Murrah Federal Building—had reportedly

FAMILY TIES: Timothy McVeigh's parents, Mildred Frazer and Bill McVeigh, arrive at the Federal courthouse in Denver.

STAR WITNESS: Michael Fortier described to the jury how he and McVeigh cased the Oklahoma building before the bombing. His testimony was to prove crucial.

the contention that McVeigh was a "lone bomber." It was the same with Gary Lewis, who claimed to have seen McVeigh driving away from the Alfred P. Murrah Federal Building in a Mercury just moments after the explosion. He also maintained that McVeigh was accompanied by another man. He too was ignored by the prosecution.

In fact, Hartzler and his team were unwilling to call to the stand a single witness who could place McVeigh in Oklahoma City on the morning of the bombing. This would have jeopardized the contention that McVeigh had acted alone. But surely, commentators suggested, not calling them jeopardized the prosecution's chances of linking McVeigh to the crime. Why had a case been build around the "lone bomber" theory—albeit allowing for the fact that McVeigh's army buddy Terry Nichols might have aided in the bomb's construction—in the first place?

The "John Doe II" affair suggested one possible reason to the press. John Doe II had originally been the target of a huge FBI manhunt which had begun within days of the Oklahoma City bombing. According to Tom Kessinger, a clerk at the agency from which McVeigh had allegedly rented the Ryder truck that was used in the bombing, McVeigh had been accompanied by another man

when he picked up the truck. The FBI spent months searching for this character—identified only as John Doe II—before suddenly announcing that Kessinger had been confused when first interviewed, and was now "unsure" whether McVeigh had been accompanied at all. The hunt for John Doe II was officially called off.

JOHN DOE II

By this time however, John Doe II had already become the target of another investigation. Accountant Glen Wilburn lost two grandchildren in the Oklahoma City bombing. Determined to find out the truth about who was to blame, he had for the previous two years been following up a number of leads abandoned by the FBI. In Wilburn's investigations one name had come up time and time again—that of Michael Brescia. Brescia, a right-winger with reported links to a neo-Nazi organization called the Aryan Republican Army, had apparently been placed with McVeigh on the morning of the bombing by a number of witnesses. He was also a one-time roommate of Andreas Strassmeir—a right-wing extremist and former German Army officer whose name had already been linked to McVeigh's by another investigation.

In early 1997, Glen Wilburn, his daughter Edye Smith, and some 30

others who had lost relatives in the blast had launched a federal damages suit against the US government. They blamed the FBI and a number of other government agencies for failing to prevent the bombing, and they named Michael Brescia as McVeigh's co-conspirator. McVeigh, they claimed, had carried out the bombing under the auspices of the Aryan Republican Army. This hinted at a much wider conspiracy that the FBI was willing to accept. "This lawsuit is our way to find out the truth," said Smith, who had lost both her children in the blast. "I am sick of the government lying. I am more angry with the government than I am with Tim McVeigh."

In reply the FBI announced in February, 1997, that, despite early indications to the contrary, there had in fact never been a John Doe II, and reiterated their opinion that McVeigh had acted as a "lone bomber." Nevertheless, the following day Michael Brescia was arrested by the FBI for his alleged involvement in a series of bank robberies committed by the Aryan Republican Army. In 1995 McVeigh's sister Jennifer told the FBI that her brother had been involved in the same series of robberies.

The suspicion voiced in the newspapers and on the many Internet pages that had been set up to monitor the case was that both McVeigh and Brescia had been mixed up in an FBI undercover operation which the bureau was now trying desperately to cover up. It was a suspicion further fueled by the indictment of Carol Howe in March 1997, just days before McVeigh's trial was due to begin.

Rumors that the Bureau of Alcohol, Tobacco, and Firearms (ATF) had been warned in advance of the April 1995 attack on the Alfred P. Murrah Federal Building had first emerged in the weeks after the bombing. Witnesses had claimed to have seen a group of men wearing outfits marked "bomb squad" on the street outside the building in the hours before the explosion took place. It has also been revealed that not one of the ATF's agents had actually been in the building at the time of the blast—despite the fact that it was the center of their operations. Then, in February 1997, an Oklahoma City newspaper revealed that an ATF informant named Carol Howe had warned the bureau of the April 1995 attack for months before it took place.

Howe was a former Tulsa beauty queen who, in 1993, had begun a relationship with Dennis Mahon, an

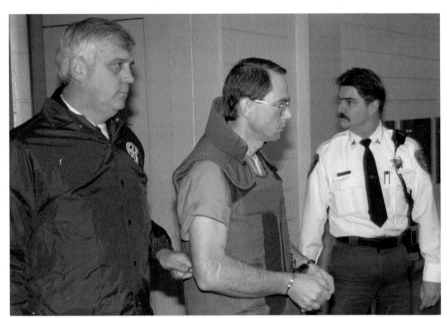

PARTNER IN CRIME?: McVeigh's alleged co-conspirator Terry Nichols is led from the Oklahoma County Jail in January 1996. He was to be tried separately.

Tulsa. She claimed that the ATF had thus known exactly when the attack was going to come.

The McVeigh defense team leaped on this information, and demanded that the ATF—which for two years had denied any prior warning of the attack—confirm or deny that Howe had been an informant, and turn over all its documents relating to her case. The bureau was forced to admit that it had employed Howe, but maintained that she had not passed on any information pertaining to the Oklahoma City bomb. However, a number of critical documents for December 1994 had apparently vanished from Howe's file.

CRUCIAL FACTS

The documents that were retrieved by the McVeigh defense nevertheless revealed a number of important facts.

First, that despite Justice Department

ex-Ku Klux Klan member who was now leader of the extremist White Aryan Resistance movement. It was while involved with Mahon that Carol Howe first began making regular visits to Elohim City, a semi-religious enclave in the Ozark mountains and a regular haunt of the radical right.

It was to Elohim City that the body of white supremacist Richard Snell had been taken after his 1995 execution for a racially motivated murder. Snell had been executed on April 19, the same day as the Oklahoma City bombing, and his last words had reportedly been: "Look over your shoulder—justice is coming." Elohim City was also the home of two alleged Aryan Republican Army members: Andreas Strassmeir and Michael Brescia.

CASING THE JOINT

According to the story in the McCurtain Daily Gazette, between June 1994 and March 1995 Carol Howe was paid $120 a week by the ATF to act as an undercover informant and report on the activities in Elohim City. It was in these reports that the plan to blow up the Oklahoma City Federal Building was first revealed. According to Howe, a terrorist group led by Mahon and Strassmeir cased the building as a possible target for an attack three times in late 1994 and early 1995. The date of the attack had by this time apparently already been set for April 19, 1995. Howe claimed that she had passed this information on to Angela Finley, her ATF case officer in

"THE IRONSIDE OF ILLINOIS": Joseph Hartzler, head of the prosecution team. Suffering from multiple sclerosis, he has been confined to a wheelchair since 1990.

GUILTY

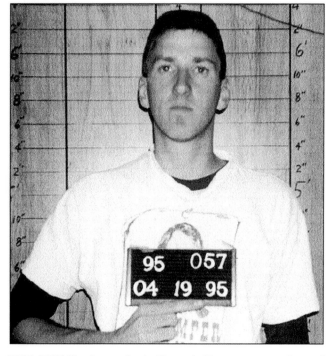

95 057
04 19 95

Jury convicts Tim McVeigh in Okla. City bombing

By Lynn Bartels
Rocky Mountain News Staff Writer

A Colorado jury today convicted Timothy McVeigh of waging the deadliest act of domestic terrorism in American history.

The 29-year-old former soldier was convicted in the Oklahoma City bombing that killed 168 people, including 19 children.

U.S. District Judge Richard Matsch read the verdict at 1:34 pm in Denver's Federal Courthouse. The jury deliberated approximately 23 hours over four days before convicting McVeigh on all 11 counts. ⊠

See McVEIGH on 48A

FOUR FULL PAGES OF COVERAGE

Timothy McVeigh as he appeared April 19, 1995 when he was arrested in Oklahoma only hours after parking a truck full of explosives at the federal building.

HARD COPY: The *Denver Rocky Mountain News* announces the verdict. Timothy McVeigh was found guilty on all counts on June 2, 1997.

claims that Carol Howe had been an unreliable informant, she had in fact passed 17 polygraph tests which confirmed that she was telling the truth.

Second, that Howe had identified Timothy McVeigh to the ATF as a regular visitor to Elohim City.

Third, that two days after the bombing Howe was given an extensive debriefing by the ATF at an underground command center in downtown Oklahoma City. During this session it was noted that Howe had reminded her interrogators of her previous warnings about the attack.

Fourth, that during the same session Howe identified a police artist's sketch of John Doe II as bearing a strong resemblance to Michael Brescia.

All of this seemed to weigh pretty heavily against both the ATF's claims not to have been warned about the attack in advance and the FBI's "lone bomber" theory. It also lent weight to the defense's suggestion that there had been a cover-up. It was beginning to look like Carol Howe might turn out to be a star witness for the defense. However, just two weeks before the trial was due to start, the US government brought criminal charges against Howe herself.

In a case that had apparently risen from an anti-government message her boyfriend had left on an answering machine, Howe was indited for allegedly possessing "a destructive device" and "conspiring to make a bomb threat." Obviously, this now all but discredited her as a witness in the McVeigh case. But to many observers, it also looked like a clear case of the government trying desperately to cover its tracks.

Either way, it seemed bizarre that somebody like Dennis Mahon had never been visited by the FBI during their interviews with over 25,000 witnesses, despite being an associate of McVeigh. It was certainly not an association that the defense was willing to ignore. Stephen Jones and his team alleged that Mahon had sent a tape to McVeigh in prison suggesting that he "sacrifice" himself. There was, maintained Jones, a "high probability" that Mahon and the Aryan Republican Army were behind the Oklahoma City bombing; that their conspiracy had been discovered but for some reason had been allowed to proceed; and that the conspirators were now being protected by a number of government organizations.

STAR WITNESS

However, the prosecution still had the testimony of its own star witness: Michael Fortier. A former army buddy of McVeigh who shared many of his extremist views, Michael Fortier took the stand wearing a suit and tie, spectacles, and a neat haircut—a far cry from the "rebellious militant" he had appeared to be when first interviewed by the FBI days after the bombing. At that time he denied having had any involvement in the bombing or any knowledge of McVeigh's part in it. However, when subsequently found guilty of trafficking stolen firearms and sentenced to 23 years in prison, he had changed his story and agreed to testify against McVeigh in exchange for immunity from prosecution. Instead, along with his wife Lori, he would face charges for failing to prevent the bombing—about which he now claimed to know a great deal.

According to Fortier, McVeigh and Terry Nichols—his alleged co-conspirator in the construction of the bombing—had planned the bombing of the Alfred P. Murrah Federal Building in retribution for the ATF's 1993 siege of the Branch Davidian cult headquarters in Waco, Texas. McVeigh, Fortier testified, had hoped to spark a "general uprising" against the US government, which would, he said, "knock some people off the fence." Fortier claimed that the Federal Building was chosen "because that was where the order for the attack on Waco had come from." McVeigh, he claimed, considered the slaughter of those in the building fully justified by the fact that, as government workers, they

SHARED GRIEF: Two women who lost family members in the bombing comfort each other outside the Denver courthouse during McVeigh's sentencing.

were part of an "evil empire." He described them as being "like the stormtroopers in the Star Wars movies."

Fortier claimed that McVeigh had originally driven him past the Federal Building in December 1994, and had told him of his plan to drive an explosives-laden truck straight through the main doors. McVeigh had apparently later modified the plan in order to enable himself to escape the blast. Fortier claimed that McVeigh and Nichols had then committed a series of robberies in order to finance the crime.

LIFESTYLES

However, responding to the suggestion that he could have prevented the bombing by informing the police about this, Fortier maintained that he had not actually believed that McVeigh would go through with it. He told jurors: "If you don't consider what happened in Oklahoma, Tim is a good person. He would stop and help someone on the side of the road. I didn't think Tim had it in him." Other than that, he said: "There's no excuse I can offer. One would have to look at my lifestyle."

However, Fortier's lifestyle at the time of his friendship with McVeigh was exactly what made him a weak witness, suggested McVeigh's defense team. A

self-confessed drug-abuser and drug-dealer, Fortier had admitted to having been under the influence of both marijuana and amphetamines during the times of his alleged conversations with McVeigh and Nichols. He had also been recorded boasting to friends about his

skills as a liar during telephone calls which were monitored by the FBI. He told one friend: "I've found my career because I can tell a fable," and talked of his plans to "wait until after the trial and do movie and book rights." After reminding Fortier that he had referred to himself as "the key man" and the "head honcho," Stephen Jones suggested that his only motivation was to make money for himself out of the trial.

So was Fortier telling the truth? And if he was, did that then mean that McVeigh (and Terry Nichols) had worked alone or alongside the Aryan Republican Army? How much did the Bureau of Alcohol, Tobacco, and Firearms know in advance about the bombing? And where did John Doe II fit into the picture? Reporters covering the trial noted that neither the prosecution nor the defense had managed to present a case that could account for all the evidence, whatever the verdict the jury returned.

On June 2, 1997, Timothy McVeigh was found guilty on all counts of the bombing of the Alfred P. Murrah Federal Building. On June 13, the jury voted unanimously that he should be sentenced to death for his crimes.

At the end of the month, an Oklahoma grand jury was selected to begin a new investigation into claims that federal agents had known about the bombing in advance. The case, it seemed, was still far from over.

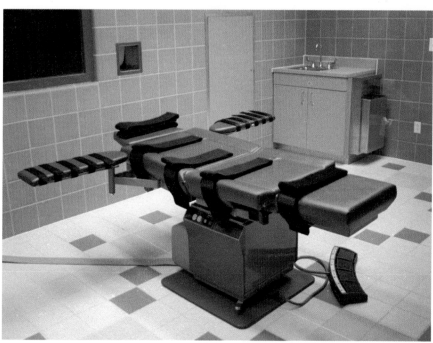

DEATH SENTENCE: The execution chamber at the US penitentiary in Terra Haute, where Timothy McVeigh could be put to death by lethal injection.

Peruvian Hostage Crisis

It looked as though the reign of terrorism that had blighted life in Peru for years was finally over, thanks to President Alberto Fujimori. In 1992 the leaders of the country's two main left-wing terrorist groups had been sentenced to life imprisonment, along with most of their comrades. Suddenly foreign investment was pouring into the country and Peru looked to be on the edge of an economic boom. Then, on December 17, 1996, the Peruvian capital of Lima was thrown into chaos—and Peru was plunged into an international crisis that would last for five months.

The garden party in honor of the Japanese Emperor's birthday had been in full swing for a couple of hours. Japanese executives and members of the Peruvian establishment mingled with diplomats from all over the world at the magnificent Lima mansion of Morihisa Aoki, the Japanese ambassador. The toast was to the recent business links between Peru and Japan that had revitalized Peru's economy. It was a week before Christmas and many of the diplomats were looking forward to going home to their families for the holidays.

Then the explosion rang out. Within seconds the air was thick with tear gas and the sound of gunfire. Startled guests flung themselves to the ground as bullets flew over their heads. Then they watched in terror as masked figures dressed in black streamed into the building.

SURPRISE ATTACK

On the streets outside the Japanese ambassador's residence, the Lima police force had been caught by surprise. Although the mansion and the walled compound that surrounded it were under permanent guard, no one had ever expected an attack to come from inside. It took the 15 terrorist guerrillas who had blown a hole in the compound wall and entered through the building next door just minutes to capture the mansion. It was, as the locals said: "El sequestro del siglo"—the snatch of the century.

As the smoke cleared, the masked bandits surveyed their prize. They had captured over 500 hostages—among them the Peruvian foreign minister, the President of the Supreme Court, the Chief of Peru's anti-terrorist police, judges, congressmen, a dozen foreign ambassadors, and high-ranking executives from some of Japan's top companies. Then the guerrillas—members of the left-wing Tupac Amaru group—removed their masks. To the astonishment of the captured party guests, most of them were teenagers. They announced: "We are here to free our comrades from prison. We are prepared

MAJOR HEIST: Smoke above the Japanese Embassy in Lima. Inside, left-wing Tupac Amaru rebels had taken over 500 hostages.

MASK OF TERROR: Flanked by armed guerrillas, Tupac Amaru leader Nestor Cerpa announces his group's demands to the world's press.

to die and to kill all of you with us."

Their demands were simple: the release of 400 of their fellow Tupac Amaru members who had been imprisoned as part of President Fujimori's crackdown on terrorism. In return they would free the hostages.

The Tupac Amaru, or MRTA, had been responsible for a string of murders, bank robberies, and kidnappings through the 1980s and 90s. Made up mostly of poor Peruvian Indians, their aim had been the establishment of a Cuban-style Marxist state in Peru. It had been thought that the arrest and imprisonment of their leader, Victor Polay, had finally crushed the movement. Instead former trade union activist Nestor Cerpa, Polay's second-in-command, had taken control of the movement. He had planned and led this one last operation with the group's few remaining members, gambling everything on President Fujimori giving in to his demands.

Cerpa's first move was to order the immediate release of all the women hostages from the residence, and then another 250 "non-essential" hostages.

But he maintained that if his demands were not met, the remaining hostages would be killed. Explosive booby traps were placed around the compound by the guerrillas, as crack Peruvian troops took up positions outside. Inside, the MRTA were settling in for a long wait.

President Alberto Fujimori was not going to give in easily. The son of Japanese immigrants, he had built his

CRY FOR HELP: Desperate hostages hold up a sign at the embassy window. Among those captured were some of Peru's highest ranking government officials and businessmen.

ACTION MAN: Wearing a bulletproof vest and using a walkie-talkie, President Alberto Fujimori enters the embassy compound.

reputation on being tough on terrorism. With an election looming, he couldn't be seen to be giving in now. His first announcement on the incident was: "I am not going to have dialogue with terrorists." However, Fujimori's position was made more difficult by the involvement of Japan, which was already demanding a peaceful end to the siege and the release of its own nationals. With so much Japanese investment tied up in Peru's economic success, Fujimori could not afford to alienate the Japanese government. As one witness put it: "If all the hostages had been Peruvian, Fujimori would have sent tanks in straight away."

Instead, the President had to stall for time. And so, as Christmas came and went, the siege of the Japanese Ambassador's residence dragged on. Inside, the hostages were getting used to their difficult situation. Red Cross negotiators had secured regular deliveries of food and water into the building. Imprisoned on the second floor and surrounded by booby traps, the hostages were doing their best to keep their spirits up. As Jorge Gumucio, the Bolivian ambassador, later described, a strong comradeship developed among them. He told the press: "We did gym together, we read the same books, we played the same games." The Japanese ambassador himself had made sure that the other hostages were as comfortable as possible, sharing his clothes, toiletries, and possessions with them. He also regularly entertained them by leading sing-along sessions—much to the bemusement of the troops and reporters gathered outside who could hear him.

Meanwhile, negotiations between their captors and the Peruvian government continued—but with little success. Although the New Year had seen a fresh wave of hostage releases, by the end of January neither side was any closer to a compromise. The 72 remaining hostages had then been held for over six weeks, but the Peruvian government still refused to countenance releasing a single imprisoned Tupac Amaru member. By now the world had learned that both President Fujimori and Nestor Cerpa had a personal stake in the crisis. Cerpa's wife, Nancy Gilvonio, was being held in the notorious Yanomayo prison, while Fujimori's brother Pedro was among the MRTA's hostages. The situation had turned into a war of nerves between the two men.

Then, at the beginning of March 1997, more than three months after the siege had begun, President Fujimori made a surprise announcement. He revealed that he had been in talks with Cuba's President Fidel Castro, who had agreed to offer the MRTA rebels asylum. Fujimori said he would personally guarantee the rebels safe passage to Cuba in return for the release of the hostages. This looked like a major breakthrough, until Nestor Cerpa announced: "We have no intention of looking for exile or political asylum. We want freedom for our jailed comrades. If there is no liberation, there is no solution."

RESCUE FORCE

Days later the talks between the MRTA and Peruvian negotiators broke down. To the eyes of the world, as well as to the MRTA guerrillas, it looked like both sides had reached a stalemate. The Peruvian government, however, had been planning for this for months.

Within two weeks of the rebels taking control of the ambassador's residence, an elite commando unit had been assembled by the Peruvian authorities in preparation for a rescue mission. Specialists had been called in from the United States' Delta Force and the British SAS to train and advise members of Peru's Leopard Police. A full-size mock-up of the inside of the residence was constructed at a military base in order to rehearse a number of possible attacks. On the streets outside the ambassador's residence the troops had begun daily maneuvers, preparing for a head-on assault which would be led by tanks and helicopters.

Only two weeks into 1997, however, the government had been rudely forced into rethinking its entire approach. On

MISSION ACCOMPLISHED: As the hostages are led to safety victorious government troops gather on the roof of the Japanese embassy to cheer to the crowds below.

January 13, the guerrillas inside the ambassador's residence had opened fire on police outside the compound. Although no one was injured, it was a sure sign that the military build-up was making the rebels nervous. The Japanese Prime Minister, Ryutaro Hashimoto, summoned President Fujimori to an emergency summit in Canada, where he demanded that the troop movements cease. He made it clear that Japan was not willing to risk the safety of the hostages in return for a quick solution to the crisis.

So instead, work began on a plan. Unknown to the outside world, a team of mining experts from the Andes were brought in to secretly excavate a network of tunnels under the compound. After installing high-powered recording equipment, intelligence agents were then able to use the tunnels to monitor the conversations and movements of the rebels above. And it was from the tunnels that an attempt to free the hostages would eventually come.

The plan was to use the tunnels to pump paralyzing gas into the ambassador's residence before launching an assault from underground. However, to carry this out successfully, the military experts would need to take advantage of as much information as they could gather about the daily routine of the guerrillas. They knew that every day the rebels played a game of soccer in the large downstairs reception room of the residence, leaving the hostages under light guard. And, in one of those hostages— retired Navy Admiral Luis Rojas—they had their trump card. Ever since the beginning of the siege, Rojas had been in secret contact with intelligence agents on the outside of the compound through a hidden radio transmitter. For weeks now, at considerable personal risk, he had been reporting on the regular comings and goings of his captors in preparation for the rescue operation. Without his information the attack could never have been planned.

It would be Rojas' job to let the troops know the exact moment for the attack to begin, and, when the moment came, to alert his fellow hostages.

On the night of Monday, April 21, the commandos began to take up positions in the tunnels under the compound. Explosives had been placed at a number of strategic points throughout the network. President Fujimori—despite his promise to the Japanese Prime Minister—had given the go-ahead. Now all the military could do was wait for the

FACE OF FREEDOM: Holding a picture of the Japanese Prime Minister above his head, a jubilant Ambassador Morihisa Aoki celebrates his rescue. President Alberto Fujimori, who is pushing the wheelchair, was praised for "seizing the chance" to free the hostages.

word from Admiral Rojas. It came shortly after 3:00 p.m. the next day.

Along with the other hostages, Jesuit Priest Juan Julio Wicht spent his time confined to the bedrooms on the second floor of the ambassador's residence. It was there that he received a whispered message from one of his fellow captives: "Get ready. We're about to be freed." At the time, as he later told reporters, he thought this was a joke. But moments later, he said: "There was an explosion from deep below the residence and all the house vibrated . . . and we all threw ourselves on the floor." Within seconds the building was filled with smoke and the sound of gunfire. No one—not even Rojas—knew what was going to happen next. Ambassador Aoki later described how: "the first thing that came into my head was . . . now my life will end."

EXPLOSIVE END

The whole operation was over within minutes. The explosives, timed to go off at exactly 3:23 p.m., had been placed in the tunnels directly below the reception room where the MRTA guerrillas' soccer match would be taking place. Ten of the rebels were killed instantly by the blast. Seconds later explosions in other tunnels allowed commandos to stream up into the compound and onto the roof of

the residence. As one squad located the hostages and guided them out over the roof to safety, the rest of the government force engaged the surviving rebels in a pitched gun battle. All the rebels— two of them teenage girls—were killed. Nestor Cerpa, their leader, died with them. Of the 72 hostages, 71 survived the rescue. Judge Carlos Giusti had suffered a heart attack after being shot in the leg during the rescue, and died in the hospital some hours later.

As the hostages were still being led from the compound, President Fujimori appeared at the scene wearing a bulletproof vest to congratulate his troops. Outside, the crowds cheered. Speaking to the world's press, Japanese Prime Minister Hashimoto thanked Fujimori for "seizing the chance" to free the hostages. He admitted that he had not been informed of the operation in advance, but added: "How can anyone criticize President Fujimori? The important thing is that the hostages were freed." From the US State Department, spokesman Nicholas Burns announced: "This incident once again demonstrates the terrible costs of terrorism."

It remains to be seen whether the bloody end to the Peruvian hostage crisis will serve as an example to other terrorist organizations across the world.

Infanticide in Delaware

Teenage sweethearts Amy Grossberg and Brian Peterson appeared to have everything going for them. Born to wealthy parents, they both had brains and good looks. They were both in their first year at college, but something happened that threatened to wreck everything. Amy Grossberg became pregnant.

No one at Delaware University realized that 18-year-old freshman Amy Grossberg was pregnant. She was petite and had taken great care to conceal her condition from both friends and family, so when she went into labor in her dormitory room on the night of November 12, 1996, she had no one to turn to. Terrified and in pain, she called the only other person who knew her secret, her boyfriend and father of the unborn child, Brian Peterson, Jr.

Peterson, also 18 and a freshman at Gettysburg College, Pennsylvania, tried to reassure her, then jumped into his car, and sped off to Delaware. He arrived three hours later at 3:30 a.m. and picked up Grossberg, who was by that time on the verge of giving birth. Together they drove to a local motel, the Comfort Inn, and booked a room under assumed names. About an hour later, Grossberg gave birth to a baby boy.

THE MISSING HOURS

What happened next is open to conjecture. It is possible that the young couple, totally inexperienced in obstetric matters, were so clumsy during the delivery that they crushed the infant's skull. More awful and, according to the police, more likely is that they deliberately killed him with some blunt instrument. Either way, minutes after his birth the baby was dead. The young couple checked out of the motel just after 5:00 a.m., one of them carrying a gray plastic bag containing the infant's corpse. They threw the bag into a dumpster at the back of the motel and then drove back to Grossberg's room at Delaware University. They slept for a couple of hours and then Peterson drove back to Gettysburg.

They might well have escaped detection completely. Certainly no one at Grossberg's college suspected anything. Shortly after 5:00 p.m., however, she started to suffer severe abdominal pains. She eventually collapsed and, from the bloodstains on her clothes, it was obvious that she was hemorrhaging.

DOCTORS' DISCOVERY

Grossberg was rushed to the Christina Hospital in Wilmington, where doctors realized that she had recently given birth. The placenta had failed to pass through the uterus during the delivery and she was in danger of infection. At first Grossberg denied having given birth but then she realized that no one was going to believe her. She told the doctors that she had a baby the previous night but that it was stillborn, and went on to explain how she and her boyfriend disposed of the body. The hospital authorities contacted the Delaware police.

In Gettysburg, Brian Peterson's nerve went too. Hours after parting company with Grossberg, he confided tearfully to a student counsellor that he had "helped his girlfriend deliver a baby," and that they had "gotten rid of it." The counsellor immediately contacted the police. Two officers arrived at the college campus within a matter of minutes. One of

TEENAGE KICKS: All-American young sweethearts Amy Grossberg and Brian Peterson had a brilliant future ahead of them—until Amy discovered she was pregnant.

SQUALID END: The dumpster behind the Comfort Inn served as a grim impromptu casket for Grossberg and Peterson's new-born child.

them questioned Peterson while the other searched his room. The second officer found a bag of bloodstained sheets under Peterson's bed and in his car a receipt from the White Glove Car Wash, stamped with 11:28 a.m., some seven hours after the baby's birth.

DESPERATE MOVE

Peterson repeated the story he had told to the counsellor, saying that his girlfriend had given birth to a stillborn baby at the Comfort Inn motel. They had panicked and disposed of the body in a dumpster behind the motel.

Peterson was arrested and charged with the misdemeanor offense of concealing the death of a baby, but within hours the police were forced to release him, because the offense had taken place in another state and they had no evidence to suggest that he had been involved in infanticide. Peterson went on the run.

While Peterson was being released from jail in Gettysburg, police in

Delaware were recovering the baby's body from the dumpster. It was obvious even to an untrained eye that the infant had been subjected to some form of assault and an autopsy the following day confirmed that he had died as the result of "multiple skull fractures, with injury to the brain, blunt force head trauma, and shaking."

Grossberg was released from hospital four days later and was promptly arrested and charged with first-degree murder. A warrant was also issued for the arrest of Peterson who was also charged with

ALMA MATER: Hanson Hall dormitory at Gettysburg College where Brian Peterson roomed in his freshman year.

IN PURSUIT: Detectives from the Nassau Police Department cannot get a reply at the home of Brian Peterson Sr.

murder. In an uncompromising mood, the Delaware Attorney General, Jane Brady, announced that she would be seeking the death penalty—in Delaware by lethal injection—against both Grossberg and Peterson.

Both teenagers came from prominent Delaware families, and that, together with the nature of the crime, made this national news—news which must have reached Peterson who went deeper into hiding, severing contact with his family and friends.

FBI GET INVOLVED

The FBI launched a nationwide manhunt for Peterson and the boy realized that he would inevitably be caught. He finally got in contact with his mother, Barbara Zuchowski, and they arranged to meet at a hotel in Wilmington. According to Mrs. Zuchowski, her son spent the night on his knees praying. At 9:30 a.m. the following day, Peterson and his mother, together with their lawyer Joseph Hurley, walked into the FBI office in Wilmington.

While Peterson was giving a statement to the FBI, a crowd of reporters and angry citizens had assembled outside and when Peterson emerged, he was greeted with taunts of "baby killer" and "fry the bastard." The sense of public outrage was so extreme that the FBI had gone so far as to fit Peterson with a bulletproof vest as they made their way to the family court. The hearing lasted only a few minutes during which

Peterson uttered "yes," when confirming his name. Joseph Hurley told the court that he intended to enter a plea of not guilty to the charge of murder and then applied for bail. The judge granted this request, saying that he did not consider

Peterson to represent a threat to society.

The defense strategy of both the accused is something of a mystery. Rather than pulling together and pooling their resources, they are considering opting for separate trials. There are even indications that Joseph Hurley is trying to shift the bulk of the blame onto Amy Grossberg. In a statement to the press he said, "I think her concerns are the major thing that led them to where they ended up. She was totally concerned with not letting Mom find out."

Hurley's assertions do carry some weight. The trouble is that precisely the same accusation could be leveled against Peterson. He too comes from a wealthy and respectable background and had as much to lose by the potential scandal. It seems unlikely that the confrontational attitude of the two lawyers will serve either of their clients well.

Meanwhile the prosecution lawyers are sticking to their guns and are demanding the death penalty. This has led to accusations of political opportunism against District Attorney Brady. The American Civil Liberties Union (ACLU) pointed out that both the accused came from wealthy families her father owned a large furniture business and his ran a large chain of video rental

COURT APPEARANCE: Brian Peterson, handcuffed, is escorted into the superior court in Wilmington, Delaware.

stores. The ACLU suggested that if the crime had been committed by a working class couple, it would not have received the same coast-to-coast publicity and that the District Attorney might not have "got caught up in the public relations of all this."

There are signs, however, that the good folk of Delaware are siding with the District Attorney. To middle-class Americans, there are few crimes as repulsive as infanticide. Not that it's that uncommon. FBI statistics show that in 1995—the most recent statistics available—249 infants of less than a week old were murdered by one or both of their parents, a ten-fold increase from two decades earlier, and the FBI admitted that this was probably only the tip of the iceberg. It appears that the number of male children killed in each of the preceding years far exceeded females. In 1995, 139 of the children murdered were male; 100 were female.

In the previous year, the disparity was even more dramatic with a ratio of 150 males to 107 females. The most significant fact that emerges from their statistics, however, is that almost all child-killers are young, poor, uneducated urban residents.

PRIVILEGED UPBRINGING

Apart from being young, Grossberg and Peterson certainly don't fit into that profile. Both their parents are millionaires. They were educated together at Rampo High School in Franklin Lakes, an affluent suburb in New Jersey. It was there that they became lovers and Amy became pregnant. She was a gifted artist and he was a bright student and an outstanding sportsman. In short, they were a couple of kids who had everything, and it is perhaps this that enraged the American public. One resident of Delaware summed it up: "They were two rich kids who had so many options— seeking out an abortion, or putting up the baby for adoption. Perhaps they were just scared, scared their parents would find out."

Others, however, were more sympathetic. "There's enormous support for the couple," says Joyce Harper, owner of a store in Wyckoff, New Jersey, where Brian Peterson is a regular customer. In an apparent attempt to foster this support, Grossberg agreed to be interviewed by Barbara Walters on ABC's 20/20 program with her parents Sonye and Alan. "I would never do anything to hurt anything or anybody, especially

OUT ON BAIL: Amy Grossberg with her mother Sonye at their family home.

something that came from me," said Amy. Sonye Grossberg went on to describe her daughter's relationship with Brian Peterson as 'very special', and described her own relationship with Amy as very close. "She's always so giving and caring," Sonye said, "I can't believe that people don't see that about her."

The move to go public appears to have backfired on Grossberg, however. The general reaction to the Walters interview appears to be one of shock at Amy's apparent detachment from a horrific crime.

While her defense team suggest that they will present mitigating circumstances in the case, Jerry Capone, another attorney from Delaware who specializes in defending disadvantaged clients, feels little sympathy for Peterson and Grossberg. "These kids from strong family backgrounds should have the proper moral background," he says. "That really frightens me. It means that this lack of respect for human life cuts across all economic classes."

The case against Amy Grossberg and Brian Peterson drags on with the inevitable plethora of petitions and adjournments which are part and parcel of the American judicial system. But they will have their day in court and then the young couple will be faced with a prospect infinitely more daunting than parental disapproval. They face the very real possibility of death row.

Obsessive Soul Mates

They met and fell in love when they were just 14 years old and looked to be the perfect couple. Outstanding athletes, and high achievers in the classroom, David Christopher Graham and Diane Zamora were inseparable all through high school. Before they went off to college, they made definite plans to marry on August 13, in the year 2000, which would be the day of their graduation. On September 6, 1996, however, the couple were arrested and charged with the brutal killing of a 16-year-old girl from Graham's hometown of Mansfield, Texas.

Adrianne Jones's body was discovered early in the morning of December 4, 1995, along a road leading to Joe Pool Lake, a popular recreation spot outside Grand Prairie, Texas. She had been clubbed over the head and shot twice in the face. The killing of Adrianne shocked the quiet town of Mansfield where she lived. High-spirited and well-liked, Adrianne, nicknamed A.J., was an outstanding student and an accomplished cross-country runner at Mansfield High.

"She always uplifted everyone around her," says Tina Dollar, the manager of the restaurant where Adrianne had worked part-time.

The brutal murder baffled the police. They arrested a friend of Adrianne's two weeks after the murder when he allegedly divulged a detail of the crime that had not been made public. But he was let go after he passed a lie-detector test, having spent Christmas and New Year's in jail. It was not until August 1996, eight months after the murder, that the first break came in the case.

On August 25, 1996 in her dormitory at the U.S. Naval Academy in Annapolis, Diane Zamora was talking with her roommates about their lives and loves. Zamora said of her boyfriend: "He'll always be faithful because I'll always have something on him." "Oh? What did you do? Kill somebody?" a roommate asked. After more questions Zamora

PERFECT MATCH: David Graham and Diane Zamora faced separation for the first time, when they gained entry to different Academies.

ABOVE AND BEYOND DUTY: A parade at the prestigious Naval Academy which Zamora attended and where she first confessed murdering Adrianne Jones to roommates.

to Colorado Springs, where Graham was training at the Air Force Academy, to warn him of the investigation. "They had the opportunity to discuss who would take the blame," says Graham's attorney, Dan Cogdell, "and agree on what to tell the police." When the police arrived to interview Graham, he too insisted that Zamora had made up the story. But on September 6, after failing a polygraph test, he confessed. That day, the police arrested Zamora who also confessed.

CASUAL ENCOUNTER

Graham was an honor student and the head of the Mansfield High School Reserve Office Training Corps program. Adrianne Jones was a fellow honor student and track team member. They often chatted during the long bus rides to track meets held across the north Texan prairies. After Jones's murder Graham was interviewed, as a matter of routine, along with the other members of the track team. It was believed he only knew Jones casually so he did not attract any suspicion. According to Graham's statement he and Jones left the school bus in Mansfield on November 4 and got into his car. He claims that she directed him to drive to the back of a grade school, where they had sex. Graham, in his stilted confessional style, describes it as a "short-lived and hardly appreciated" encounter.

Graham said he endured nearly a month of guilt, "I was letting down the one person I had sworn to be faithful to." He eventually confessed his infidelity to Zamora. "For at least an hour she screamed sobs that I wouldn't have thought possible." When she regained her composure, she demanded revenge. "The

confessed to her friends that she and Graham had indeed killed someone. The alarmed roommates informed the naval chaplain; word soon got to the police. Zamora confessed to the murder to Jay Guild, a fellow cadet, during plebe summer, the training session for first-year midshipmen. "She just came out and said he [Graham] had cheated on her with this girl and she told him to kill her," Guild told the local newspaper, Fort Worth Star-Telegram.

The Naval Academy, which Guild and Zamora attended, has what it calls an honor concept, a broad principle that a midshipman should "stand for that which is right." At the same time, there is an unwritten code that midshipmen protect one another. Guild said he stayed silent initially because he did not believe

her story. He later felt that exposing her story would have been like "turning in a family member." Guild later resigned from the Academy rather than face dismissal for violating the honor code.

The Annapolis police assumed that Zamora had told the truth and checked with the Texas police if there were any unsolved murders in the Mansfield area. Detectives immediately thought of Adrianne Jones and sent detectives to interview Zamora. At first she insisted the story was made up. "She said at the time she was just lying for sympathy and to bring attention to herself," said Sergeant Chuck Sager of the Grand Prairie police. On August 30, Zamora was placed on official leave from the Annapolis Naval Academy pending further investigation. Immediately she flew

FATAL ENCOUNTER: Adrianne Jones was brutally killed in a fit of jealousy after Zamora discovered she had dated Graham.

ORDER OF SILENCE: Jay Guild left the US Naval Academy, rather than face dismissal for violating the honor code after Zamora had confessed her crime to him.

friend of Zamora. "She even got him to quit a couple of jobs because she said it took time away from her." Others said it was Graham who ruled the relationship. "He never took his arm from around her," said Martha Kibler, Zamora's aunt. At her graduation, "Several members of the family wanted to give her a hug, but David wouldn't let go of her." Another aunt, Sylvia Gonzalez, said Zamora hadn't felt smothered: "She was totally wrapped up in him. She thought he hung the moon."

BRUTAL PLAN

It seems there was nothing they would not do for one another, including murder. Adrianne Jones had come between them; she had to be removed. Graham told police the plan was to kill Adrianne. He would "break her young neck," weight the corpse with barbells, and sink it in Joe Pool Lake.

On December 3, Graham contacted Adrianne Jones on the pretext of arranging a date. At 10:30 p.m. he picked her up and drove to Joe Pool Lake. Zamora was hidden in the back of the car with the rear seat tilted just enough to see Graham behind the wheel. Once they had parked near the lake, Graham motioned to Zamora, who clambered into the passenger seat and confronted Adrianne about having seduced her boyfriend. Then a fight broke out. Zamora told police that she feared

only thing that could satisfy her womanly vengeance was the life of the one that had, for an instant, taken her place," Graham said. According to the police, in her own statement, Zamora reportedly told Graham that the "purity" of their love could only be restored by killing Adrianne. Graham insisted to police that he was helpless to resist: "Diane's beautiful eyes have always played the strings of my heart effortlessly. I couldn't imagine life without her . . . I didn't have any harsh feelings for Adrianne, but no one could stand between me and Diane."

Graham and Zamora had been inseparable since they first met aged 14. Those who knew them believed that their relationship was disturbingly obsessive. "These two kids . . . are totally obsessed with each other, mentally," said Sergeant Sager. To many who had known them, it was Zamora who had the controlling influence, turning an icy shoulder to Graham's friends and anyone else who came between them. "She controlled most of his life," said Sarah Layton, a

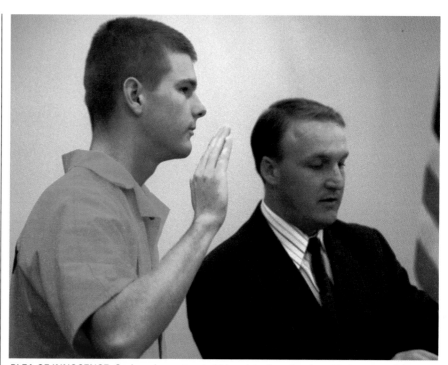

PLEA OF INNOCENCE: Graham has retracted his original confession. His lawyers claim that he invented it to protect Zamora.

Adrianne might hurt Graham so she used a barbell to strike the girl on the head. Graham then lunged to try to break Adrianne's neck. "She [Jones] was fighting from instinct," to survive, Graham told the police.

Despite having her head smashed with the barbell, Adrianne managed to crawl through the car window. The blows had fractured her skull and lacerated her brain but she staggered a little way before collapsing. "I knew," Graham told police, "I couldn't leave the key witness to our crime alive." Armed with a Russian-made 9mm Makarov handgun, he chased after Adrianne but found her lying on the ground, apparently dead. He returned to the car and reported to Zamora that Adrianne was dead. But she urged him to check again. In his confession, Graham admitted that he returned to where Adrianne lay, stood over her, and shot her twice in the face, "I just pointed and shot . . . I fired again and ran to the car."

Back in the car, "The first words out of our mouths were 'I love you,'" Graham told police. They drove back to Zamora's house and cleaned out the car. According to one police source, "Graham wasn't able to help [Zamora] because he was quite sick and vomiting."

When the police searched Graham's home in Mansfield, they found the barbell weights and the 9mm Makarov handgun hidden in the attic. But the most powerful piece of evidence in the case was the self-typed confessions of both Graham and Zamora.

DIFFERENT STORIES

Graham and Zamora are being held at the Tarrant County jail, having been charged with first-degree murder. If they are found guilty, they could face the death penalty. Their two families have hired separate lawyers, who intend to pursue separate defenses, that may mean that they will try to blame each other. The lovers have been forbidden to speak to each other. The killing of Adrianne Jones and the consequences do not appear to concern the two lovers unlike their forced separation. Mary Mendoza, who visited her niece in jail, said Zamora seemed deeply depressed. "She is not doing so good. She is terribly lonesome. She cried the whole time I was there." Her lawyer John Linebarger said that, despite her confession, Zamora pleads not guilty.

Graham's lawyer, Dan Dogdell said that his client also pleads not guilty.

PLAYING A PART: The 1997 showing of NBC's *Love's Deadly Triangle: The Texas Cadet Murders* may have jeopardized the trial of Graham and Zamora.

Dogdell has challenged the admissibility of Graham's statement, arguing that the young cadet was illegally confined for 30 hours, denied his initial request for a lawyer, and grilled nonstop before he confessed. Dogdell claimed that Graham invented his confession as a cover-up to protect Zamora. "He never intended to kill the girl. Nor did he intend to have anyone else kill her." He told the Dallas Morning News, that David's parents are concerned that Zamora holds an "unholy influence" on their son.

Despite the separate legal actions taken by their lawyers, Graham and Zamora still feel as strongly about each other. Linebarger says Zamora "wants to know when she can see [David] or talk to him." As Graham was led away to his cell, a reporter asked if there was anything he would like to tell Diane, he replied, "I love you."

NBC broadcast a dramatized version of the Graham and Zamora murder case on February 10, 1997. It was the first time that a dramatized version of a case had been broadcast before it has gone to trial. There was nothing the victims' relatives or lawyers could do after they lost a legal battle to prevent it from being aired. It seems that America's enthusiasm for broadcasting true-life murder mysteries has created an atmosphere that could potentially damage the possibility of a fair trial for David Graham and Diane Zamora.

Vacation Homicide

The youth hostel was set in the quiet rural town of Pleine-Fougères, Brittany, northwest France. The pupils of Launceston College were spending an "activity week" sampling the sights and sounds of France. But the trip was cut tragically short when 13-year-old Caroline Dickinson was found savagely raped and murdered in the room where she and her friends had slept.

On Sunday, July 14, 1996, 39 pupils from Launceston College in Cornwall, England, five teachers, a driver, and a school nurse left by bus for one of the college's many "activity weeks" in France. Caroline Dickinson was in the party that had planned visiting St. Malo, Bayeux, and Mont St. Michel, sampling French food, and practicing the language. Similar trips had been organized many times before to Pleine-Fougères. The youth hostel was chosen for its quiet, rural setting and yet it was relatively centrally located. During most of the Cornish party's five-day stay the youth hostel was full, sleeping 70 in all. Many visitors came and went leaving only a name in the register.

The evening of Wednesday, July 17, began with the pupils (34 girls and five boys aged 13 to 14), teachers, and helpers all gathered around the long wooden tables in the dining room for a dinner of tabouleh salad, chicken, and green beans. After the meal they could spend the evening as they wished, watching television, playing cards, or chatting. The hostel director, Gregoire Choleau, left the hostel at 9:00 p.m. so it was left to the teachers and the hostel's assistant director, Manuela Bernard, to herd all the children to their rooms by 11:00 p.m. Caroline had asked to sleep in the same room as her four friends, so a mattress was put on the floor between the two bunks in the tiny 12-sq-foot (1.11-sqm) space. The five girls chatted and giggled before falling asleep.

HORRIFIC DISCOVERY

At 8:00 a.m. the next morning the girls were getting up and ready for breakfast. One of them touched Caroline who appeared to be still asleep. The girl found that she was stone cold. She also noticed Caroline was discolored. Worried that she might be sick, the girls immediately went to get a teacher from a neighboring room. The teacher told the four friends to leave their room and raised the alarm. A doctor and ambulance crew soon arrived, but they were unable to resuscitate Caroline. She had been savagely raped, then suffocated with a pillow at about 4:00 a.m., as she

HOSTEL OF HORROR: Chosen for its peace and quiet, the youth hostel where Caroline Dickinson was found murdered had been used successfully many times before by her college for school trips.

lay on her mattress in the room while her four friends slept.

Within hours of Caroline's body being found, 80 gendarmes (distinct from the regular French police as they are attached to the army) had been called in from Rennes, nearly 40 miles (64km) away. An investigating magistrate in St. Malo, Gerard Zaug, was charged with coordinating the inquiry, assisted by 15 translators and a child psychiatrist. The Pleine-Fougères town hall was turned into the inquiry headquarters and surrounding streets were closed off. This was to be a high-level investigation.

Just two days after the murder, the investigating team had drawn up a composite portrait of a suspect. It was shown to villagers, but the police did not release it to the press, arguing that it could scare away the suspect. The sketch was based on information from two girls in the group who said they passed a man in the corridor on their way to the lavatory in the middle of the night—a 35 to 40-year-old man, unshaven, with dark, mid-length hair and bushy eyebrows.

INITIAL SILENCE

For reasons known only to the gendarmes, they insisted the party should remain in the same hostel. Initially, the pupils were not told of the murder. Teachers believed the news would cause mass panic among the pupils if they knew. However, Caroline's four friends and a teacher were allowed to move to the Hôtel de Voyageurs. On Friday the pupils were told the devastating news about what had happened to Caroline. The children had little time to handle this before they faced a day of questioning, in which the details of the murder came out, deeply affecting all of them.

Back in Cornwall, Alan Wroath, the head teacher of Launceston College, had to inform Caroline's parents, John and Sue Dickinson, and arrange for them to go to France to identify their daughter's body. Wroath also brought in counselors and psychiatrists in preparation for the return of the pupils. The counseling program was likely to take six months.

DNA samples were taken of the two male teachers and the bus driver but not the five boys, French regulations prevented these samples being taken. On Sunday, July 21, the grieving school party was allowed to return to England after two long days of questioning, leaving a rural community horrified and baffled at how an intruder could have crept

RANDOM CHOICE: Caroline's murder was one of several attacks on children in the area.

into the hostel and murdered Caroline.

Room 4, where Caroline and her friends slept, is centrally located on the second floor at the front of the hostel. The rooms on either side, as well as those on the opposite side of the narrow corridor, have paper-thin walls. They are connected to the second and third floors by two staircases, one of which is narrow, wooden, and creaks. Caroline lay on a mattress which filled the floor space between the two metal-framed bunk beds. Her mattress would have made it difficult for an intruder to open the door into the small room. Yet from the start, investigators insisted that Caroline was raped and suffocated while her friends slept nearby.

One of the girls in the room told the gendarmes that she had been woken by the sound of feet drumming against the floor and had assumed Caroline was having a nightmare.

According to Manuela Bernard, the assistant director of the hostel, several of the other people staying at the hostel reported being woken in the night by someone opening and closing the door to their rooms. A French motorbiker on the floor above Caroline even got up to lock his door after the disturbance at about 4:00 a.m. One teacher reported hearing footsteps and the sound of a motor scooter around the same time.

Just hours after the departure of the college party, Patrice Pade, a vagrant with a history of sex offenses, was arrested on a country road near Sourdeval, almost 50 miles (80km) northeast of Pleine-Fougères. He was detained by French police, using a portrait based on descriptions given by villagers, who reported seeing a vagrant hanging around the hostel on the Wednesday evening before the murder. Pade had been hitchhiking, allegedly on his way to his apartment at Domront,

45 miles (72km) away. During a 48-hour-long interrogation he confessed to the rape and murder of Caroline Dickinson.

FIRST ARREST

On July 23, Zaug, the magistrate, appeared at a press conference and announced the arrest of Caroline's killer. "For this kind of individual, in this kind of situation, right from the moment he had sighted his prey . . . once he had started, nothing could stop him." Zaug was asked how one man could have raped and murdered Caroline in a room with four other girls. "After a busy day, young girls of 13 to 15 sleep very deeply," he replied. For those at Launceston in Cornwall the arrest provided a measure of relief. Alan Wroath wrote to the mayor of Pleine-Fougères: "On behalf of Launceston College, I would like to express our sincere thanks for your support."

But, just two days later, Zaug was informed that a DNA test on Pade showed he was not the rapist. Apparently, he confessed just to annoy the investigating team. It took 13 days, however, before Pade's lawyer could

secure the release of his client. It was felt that crucial time was lost while Pade remained in custody. Then Zaug, using le secret d'instruction (the confidentiality of the inquiry), imposed a total news blackout. This is a legal "get-out" term which means anything that the examining magistrate considers harmful to the inquiry is not revealed. The British media reacted strongly to this silence, complaining bitterly about the manner in which the investigation was being conducted.

All kinds of rumors started circulating about suspects in Pleine-Fougères. A young blond man, wearing a parka, was reported to have threatened a German tourist two days before Caroline's murder. Just three hours before Caroline was raped and murdered, a man tried to suffocate a 14-year-old schoolgirl, before another girl's screams scared him away. French gendarmes initially dismissed this revelation, on the basis that the incident had not been reported to them. Yet it had happened only 25 miles (40km) away from the Pleine-Fougères hostel. Questions were also being asked about a possible connection with the rape and

DORM OF DEATH: The crowded dormitory where Caroline Dickinson was killed while her friends slept.

NO COMMENT: French detectives arriving at Launceston Police Station refused to comment on their findings.

murder of an 11-year-old French girl found four days after Caroline's death in the Brittany town of Redon, about 100 miles (160km) away. Michel Bazarewski, a father of three with a history of sex offenses, allegedly admitted he killed Caroline. Nothing was officially confirmed or denied.

Inspector Paul Munns of the Devon and Cornwall police had only "brief" contacts with the French police during the investigation. He had been initially informed only by hearsay through Launceston College and consular officials that the French investigators intended to interview pupils and teachers again and take DNA samples from the five boys. "They have no jurisdiction over here and any questioning would have to be done by British officers," said Munns. It took several days before the British police received a formal request from Zaug, who apparently had trouble finding a translator. In January 1997, after months of silence, French police called John Dickinson for the first time to say they had nothing to report. Despite locating everyone who had stayed at the hostel on July 17, one false arrest, and hundreds of interviews, there appeared to be no new leads as to who killed his 13-year-old daughter.

Then on March 7, French police arrested Jean-Paul Barbault at Carcassonne in southwest France.

Barbault, a self-confessed child molester, was caught trying to abduct a 10-year-old girl. He allegedly admitted abducting eight children and raping three of them. He was also suspected of raping a 10-year-old girl at St. Méen-le-Grand, Britanny, in November 1996, just 30 miles (48km) from Pleine-Fougères. Again, no statement from the French investigators was released.

COLD TRAIL

Whoever carried out the crime acted with speed and stealth, raping and killing Caroline without disturbing the girls sleeping beside her. At first it appeared to be an open and shut case with the capture of Pade. Faced with the outrage of the British press over the murder, the French investigators seemed a little too keen for it to appear that the culprit had been found. After Pade's arrest, other leads, such as the other sex attacks in the area, were not followed up, and by the time the investigators realized their error, the trail was cold. There is still anger and disappointment over the French investigators' blunders—made all the worse by the order of silence over the proceedings. But it is Caroline's parents who have suffered the most throughout this traumatic ordeal. Until the killer is caught, they have little chance to rebuild their shattered lives after the tragic and almost inexplicable murder of their daughter.

DEVASTATED: Caroline's sister, Jenny, and her father and mother attend the funeral.

Stand-Off at Justus Township

It was the longest siege in modern United States history, lasting a total of 81 days. Twenty members of the Freemen, an anti-government militia, were barricaded in a 960-acre (388-ha) ranch in Montana against 100 FBI agents. The Freemen were determined to defend their farmstead against the federal government, which, they believed, was out to get them.

On the windswept plains of Garfield County, Montana, there is a farmstead of family houses, cabins, trailers, and various outbuildings surrounded by 960 acres (388ha) of open land. Once this land belonged to the struggling Clark family: Emmett, his brother Ralph, Ralph's son Edwin, and Edwin's son Casey. Ralph Clark also owned some 4,000 acres (1,619ha) nearby. But times were tough for Montana farmers and the Clarks were no exception, finding it harder and harder to make a profit and meet mortgage payments. Eventually it all became impossible and the mortgagors foreclosed on the land.

Emmett's grandson, Dean, tried to save the farm by buying back 3,000 acres (1,214ha). He planned to plant a new crop of spring wheat and begin meeting the mortgage payments. But the farm came under siege and Dean was prevented from getting the previous year's wheat crop to the market and the current year's wheat crop in the ground. On March 25, 1996, an 81-day stand-off began between those at the ranch, now calling themselves the Freemen, and 100 FBI agents with warrants for their arrest.

CONSTANT STRUGGLE

Back in the hungry thirties, William ("Todd") Clark saw many farms foreclose, but he was determined to beat poverty and slowly bought up his neighbor's land, amassing thousands of acres, which he eventually passed on to his four sons. Like his hard-working father, Ralph was constantly struggling to meet the high mortgage payments, and foreclosure was never far away. Then in 1992 he thought his luck had changed when he attended a seminar by LeRoy Schweitzer. Schweitzer was the founder of a group called "We the People." The group claimed that the federal government had lost a huge class-action lawsuit on behalf of America's landowners, and that a trillion dollars were sitting in a settlement account. Schweitzer was selling a kit, at $300, with instructions for claiming part of the settlement.

ARMED AND READY: Justus Township, headquarters of the Freemen and the site of the stand-off, which began on March 29, 1996.

RINGLEADER: LeRoy Schweitzer, acknowledged leader of the Freemen, was named in lengthy federal indictments.

This was an elaborate scam devised by Schweitzer, which eventually earned him almost $900,000. Ralph thought Schweitzer was the answer to his financial problems. Ralph even managed to obtain some federal subsidies and loans on Schweitzer's advice. However, even with Schweitzer's help, Ralph faced foreclosure. Emmett Clark's son, Richard, also believed Schweitzer was a financial genius and would save the family from ruin. He was taken in by Schweitzer's claims that somehow the federal government owed them money and persuaded his father that he didn't have to make the mortgage or tax payments.

By 1993, led by Schweitzer, the conned Clarks had set up as the Freemen, based on "We the People." They had named their farmstead "Justus Township;" created their own "supreme court," and started issuing subpoenas to and posting bounties on elected officials, lawyers, and bankers connected to the foreclosure, and passing fraudulent checks.

Justus attracted the attention of many right-wing groups, as well as fugitives, law-breakers, and extremists, some of whom moved to the farmstead, all under the collective of Freemen, arming and defending the ranch against outsiders. Ralph was often seen patrolling around the ranch wearing a sheriff's star to signify he was the law.

Through 1996, the Freemen issued more than $1.8 million in fraudulent money orders and other financial instruments, according to federal indictments. They used those to defraud banks, credit card, and mail-order companies. They used liens filed against the property of government officials, then issued worthless money orders or checks using that property as collateral. Many companies and banks, even the Internal Revenue Service, were taken in.

HARASSMENT

For months residents of Jordan had been requesting that the Freemen be removed. The Freemen had carried out a campaign of harassment, posting bounties of up to $1 million on the heads of local officials and threatening to kidnap and hang local judges. Reporters who tried to approach Justus Township were abused; an ABC television crew had equipment worth $66,000 snatched from them. The FBI only decided to take action after exasperated Jordan villager, Tom Stanton, recruited a 25-strong vigilante group armed with hunting rifles and disclosed plans to attack Justus Township.

The Justice Department claimed they were waiting for a grand jury in Billings to hand up federal indictments on the Freemen, giving them legal authority to move against the group, who otherwise faced only state-level charges. Action was finally taken on March 25 when federal agents arrested the two Freemen leaders, LeRoy Schweitzer and Daniel Petersen. According to Newsweek, an undercover agent, known only as "Mike Manson," infiltrated the group and befriended Schweitzer and Petersen. Manson then duped Schweitzer and Petersen into inspecting a radio transmitter he was helping install on the farm. It was then other federal agents posing as technicians arrested them. This was the first move the FBI made during an 11-month undercover operation against the Freemen. The other Freemen refused to surrender and the FBI had no choice but to cordon off Justus Township.

Schweitzer and Petersen's arrest proved extremely timely. The day before, they held a meeting at the ranch where they planned the kidnap of a local judge. The meeting was caught on video and broadcast by ABC's Prime Time Live. "We are going to have a standing order," said Schweitzer. "Anyone obstructing justice, the order is shoot to kill."

At the hearings in Billings federal courthouse, Schweitzer and Petersen were determined to obstruct the course of justice first by shouting demands for a "change of venue" to their own court in Justus Township, then refusing to cooperate. Petersen threatened the court

SHOW OF FORCE: The FBI sent in a helicopter and three armored vehicles, which it called emergency rescue vehicles, to demonstrate its strength to the militant Freemen.

with talk of a bloodbath; he said of the siege at Justus Township: "This will be worse than Waco." They were both later found guilty, Schweitzer receiving 16 years for the $900,000 scam which first enticed Ralph Clark.

FUGITIVE PHONES

There were 20 men, women, and children barricaded in the ranch. The FBI, still suffering from the shock waves of the Waco siege, was determined this was going to be a bloodless settlement. Trained negotiators stayed in touch with the fugitives via a phone line. In the background there was the FBI's Hostage Rescue Team, the same taskforce involved in the Ruby Ridge siege, Idaho, in 1992. Robert ("Bear") Bryant, chief of the FBI's national security division, was sent to oversee the proceedings. He sent regular reports back to the Attorney General Janet Reno, who in turn provided the White House with updates on the situation.

By the beginning of April, 100 FBI agents had surrounded the ranch. The

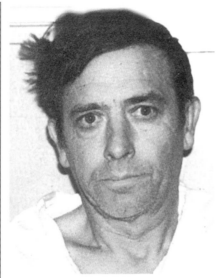

RIGHT-HAND MAN: Daniel Petersen, second in command of the Freemen, was arrested on March 25, 1996 in Jordan.

press were kept a mile away and watched the proceedings through binoculars and telescopic lenses. The first indication of any break in stalemate

came on April 3 when four Freemen met for about an hour and a half with four negotiators at the edge of the fugitives' compound. A Freemen back-up team was parked in a pickup truck about 300 feet (91m) away watching the negotiations and the FBI had a similar back-up team and a surveillance plane circling overhead. When the meeting ended, the Freemen disappeared into the ranch and the FBI went back to their vantage point. Nothing was mentioned to the press.

On May 31, the FBI moved three black armored cars and a helicopter into the area. A source familiar with FBI strategy said the arrival of the armored vehicles and helicopter was a clear message to the Freemen: "They're sending a message that 'we are prepared'." The source said the FBI decided it had to demonstrate it was serious. Since the beginning of the siege no real progress had been made toward ending it. "Despite the best efforts of the FBI and third-party intermediaries," said an FBI statement, "the Freemen have terminated all efforts at negotiations." In 68 days

NEGOTIATOR: Montana legislator Karl Ohs is allowed to pass on horseback on his way to talks with the Freemen.

GRAND FINALE: The last of the Freemen, Edwin Clark, walks out from Justus Township and surrenders to the FBI on June 13, 1996.

this was the first statement the media received. The FBI did not want the press to turn the Freemen into right-wing martyrs. The less the press knew, as far as they were concerned, the better.

On the June 3, the FBI decided to cut off the electricity at the ranch in an attempt to flush out the fugitives. This seemed to have some effect on the Freemen who began the negotiations again in earnest on June 10, when the FBI escorted three negotiators, two from the CAUSE Foundation, to the entrance of the ranch. The CAUSE Foundation represented a former member of the Klu Klux Klan and survivors of the Waco siege. The Foundation believes, "The more radical they are, the more they need to be supported for their rights." The negotiations lasted for two and a half hours before the negotiators emerged. They spoke with FBI agents at a nearby country church for an hour before returning inside the Freemen house for another hour.

While the negotiations were going on, Gloria Ward, her husband Elwyn, and her two daughters, Courtnie aged ten and Jaylynn aged eight, left the ranch. "We didn't barely have any food at our cabin," said Jaylynn. "All we had was half a loaf of bread, one jar of jam . . . and about two cookies and milk." The girls also claimed that there was very little drinking water left, with the remaining 16 people having to share three pitchers. The Wards were the first people to leave the ranch since the siege had begun in March. It seemed the FBI's patience was finally paying off.

FINAL SURRENDER

Three days after the negotiations on June 13 the Freemen surrendered. The group's 16 remaining members emerged from the longest siege in modern United States history. The siege lasted 81 days. The Freemen came out of the ranch in their vehicles and surrendered to the waiting FBI. Some hugged before being escorted away; some formed a circle and prayed. Two elderly women were free to go with no charges pending, while the remaining 14 were taken to Billings and Yellowstone County jail to await trial.

The final stages of the surrender were held up as Karl Ohs, a Republican state legislator, helped broker the Freemen's surrender. The Freemen would not surrender until Ohs had agreed to collect and guard evidence which they had compiled that they hoped would defend them in court—evidence of the government's misdeeds.

The Freemen seemed as determined as ever to carry on their battle in court. Edwin Clark said: "I stand on my objection that you have no juristiction. So I will make no plea." The thinking behind the Freemen's actions seems somewhat confused. If they believed their actions were completely lawful yet at odds with the Constitution, Common Law, or the Uniform Commercial Code, they must have known they would end up in the statutory courts where their evidence and assertions would be ignored. Did they truly believe they could beat the US Federal Government? If not, why take their evidence to court, an institution that they don't recognize? Perhaps they wanted to bring their case to court, so why resist arrest?

The Clarks were hard-luck farmers facing financial ruin; Schweitzer was a fast-talking swindler who boasted a cure-all for their financial troubles. Without Schweitzer, the Freemen seem unsure and confused about what they should really be fighting for.

Justice Saudi Style

Yvonne Gilford was found in her room at the King Fahd Military Medical Complex in Dhahran, Saudi Arabia on December 11, 1996. She had been beaten over the head with a teapot, stabbed four times, and then suffocated. Just over a week later, two friends of Gilford, Lucille McLauchlan and Deborah Parry, were arrested while withdrawing money from Gilford's bank account.

DEDICATED PROFESSIONAL: Nurse Yvonne Gilford was highly respected by her colleagues for the caring she showed patients in her charge.

Lucille McLauchlan and Deborah Parry saw the New Year of 1997 dawn in the women's section of Damman Prison. With only the most brief of meetings with a lawyer and British diplomats, and a short and desperate call to their families back home, they had plenty of time alone to contemplate their fate. If found guilty, they could face public beheading by ceremonial sword.

Their lives were very different before December 11, 1996. Earlier in the year when the two nurses signed their year-long contracts with Arabian Careers Ltd., they were offered a tax-free annual salary of $26,000, 40-days' annual leave, free accommodation, free recreational facilities, an end-of-contract lump sum, and a lifestyle that included endless parties. However, adjusting to life in Saudi Arabia can be both difficult and lonely, especially for women. Most nurses who sign up are looking for two things: the chance to make quick, tax-free money or the chance to run away. Yvonne Gilford, Deborah Parry, and Lucille McLauchlan were looking for both.

ESCAPE ROUTES

Yvonne Gilford was born in Adelaide, Australia in 1941. She began her nursing career in Melbourne and then spent five years in England before she moved to South Africa, where she was to spend the next 20 years. Former colleagues described her as a "dedicated nurse," a "modern-day Florence Nightingale." Then in June 1996, at the age of 45, she uprooted and headed off for Saudi Arabia at a time in her life when most senior theater nurses are thinking of retirement. After only six months in Saudi, Yvonne was dead.

Born and raised in Dundee, Scotland, McLauchlan began her career as an auxiliary working with the terminally ill, before becoming a state enrolled nurse. She then transferred to an infectious diseases ward. Friends described her as a bubbly and dedicated nurse, who would do anything for her patients.

Despite this praise, McLauchlan was forced to leave her job after being accused of stealing a credit card from a terminally ill patient and swindling $3,000. She fled to Saudi Arabia to

HIDING THE PAIN: Deborah Parry fled to Saudi to rebuild her life after a series of tragic family deaths.

escape possible criminal proceedings.

Parry went to Saudi Arabia to escape her bleak life back in England. When she was 21, her brother was killed in a motorcycle accident. Within weeks her mother drowned on a boating trip. Eight years later, in 1987, Parry's father died from a heart attack and her brother-in-law died from a brain hemorrhage. After four years of psychiatric treatment Parry left England for the Middle East.

In Saudi Arabia the three nurses quickly became good friends. Reports of what had led to the bloody murder varied, since there was very little official information available and the British Foreign Office refused to comment. However, according to *Al Hayat*, one of the most respected papers in the Arab world, and a source which most reflects the official line, Yvonne Gilford was involved in a late-night quarrel with Parry. As the quarrel continued, it was alleged that McLauchlan joined the two in Yvonne Gilford's apartment. *Al Hayat* quoted police sources as saying that she was being taunted with being an "old lady" who was no longer any good at her job. After being hit over the head with a teapot, Gilford fell to the ground before stumbling into the kitchen to reach for a knife. She was then stabbed four times and a pillow was used to smother her.

CAUGHT ON FILM

McLauchlan and Parry were arrested on December 20, after allegedly being caught on a security camera using Yvonne Gilford's credit card a week after her death. They had withdrawn almost $4,000 from her account.

Al Hayat quoted police officers as saying the nurses confessed to the killing immediately after their arrest. Police took the nurses back to the scene of the crime and reenacted what led up to the murder. After they killed Yvonne Gilford, the two nurses said they straightened furniture and wiped away fingerprints. This could explain why investigators were able to find only one fingerprint from one of the nurses, despite their admission that both were frequent visitors to Yvonne Gilford's apartment.

Parry and McLauchlan's lawyer, Salah al-Hejailan, was quoted as saying: "We are looking at this death as accidental and not premeditated." Hejailan's firm also said that the women later withdrew their confessions, one of them retracting a statement that she had made about having a lesbian relationship with the victim. The women said the confessions had been extracted under duress, after five days of persistent questioning.

In March 1997, Hejailan sent Yvonne Gilford's family a mercy appeal. Under Islamic sharia law, people convicted of premeditated murder are normally subject to the death penalty unless the victim's family grants clemency. But Frank Gilford, Yvonne's brother, said that the two should face the maximum punishment: "We're not going to be pushed around by the defense lawyers or the press regarding what to do here." In September 1997, however, Mr. Gilford did a smart about-face when he accepted $1.2 million in blood money. In exchange for this payment, he agreed that Deborah Parry should be spared from the ultimate sanction.

Several key questions still remained unanswered. Why was Yvonne Gilford's bedroom window left needlessly wide open when the air-conditioning was on? Why didn't security guards on duty nearby hear any cries for help or the sounds of a fight? These unanswered questions revived memories of the death of British nurse Helen Smith, killed in a fall after an illegal drinks party in Saudi Arabia in 1979. Her death remains a mystery after an inquest recorded an open verdict. The murder of a Filipino nurse at the same hospital in 1994 is still unsolved.

The case of Parry and McLauchlan fast turned into a major diplomatic problem between London and Riyadh. On the one hand, resentment grew among Saudi officials, who believed their judicial system was being falsely portrayed as unjust. On the other hand, speculation grew among British officials that the Saudi authorities were trying to discredit the nurses in advance of the trial. Behind the scenes, both governments are attempting to come to a compromise: it seems that neither side wants to see the death penalty carried out, yet are anxious to see that justice is done.

ON THE RUN: Lucille McLauchlan sought work in Saudi Arabia to avoid prosecution for theft in Britain.

Lords of Chaos

They were the most unlikely gang in history. Honors students from middle-class homes, they had everything to live for. Now four of them face the death penalty after an orgy of robbery, arson, and murder. What turned these mild-mannered, high-school students into vicious thugs who even planned to sabotage their graduation trip?

GUNNED DOWN: Mark Schwebes, a music teacher at Riverdale High School, Fort Myers.

Shortly after 11:30 p.m. on April 30, 1996, police were called to a one-storied house in Pine Manor, a working-class suburb of Fort Myers, Florida. Neighbors had heard gunshots. When they arrived on the scene, officers found a man in his thirties lying in a fetal position just inside the front door. He had been shot twice with a shotgun, once in the face and once in the buttocks. Death must have been instantaneous. Investigators had no problem in identifying the victim as Mark Schwebes, a 32-year-old music teacher, employed by Riverdale High School in Fort Myers.

There was no sign of a robbery or of forced entry. It appeared that Schwebes had opened the door to his attackers voluntarily, and that the killer or killers were probably known to him. Investigators started to check into Schwebes' private life in search of a motive and found that the ex-marine was a dedicated teacher, well liked and respected by colleagues and students alike. The only glimmer of hope came from the fact that Schwebes had a new girlfriend, a teacher at Riverdale, and had apparently had some sort of confrontation with her former lover. They brought the ex-lover in for questioning, but almost immediately eliminated him from their inquiries.

RUBBER GLOVES

Anxious to piece together Schwebes' movements on the night of the murder, the police put out an appeal for anyone who saw him that evening to come forward. They were contacted by David Atkins, the father of one of Schwebes' students, who helped the teacher organize band activities. The two men had met for a meal at about 9:30 p.m. at the Cracker Barrel restaurant in Fort Myers. Atkins told the police that Schwebes had come to the restaurant directly from work and had been a few minutes late because of an incident outside the school auditorium.

According to Atkins, Schwebes had spotted three boys hanging around outside the building, acting suspiciously. When he had stopped, one of the youths had run off. The other two he had recognized as Riverdale students but Schwebes had not identified them to Atkins. Both had been wearing rubber gloves and carrying cans of peaches. Schwebes had assumed that they were planning some act of vandalism, confiscated the cans, and warned them that he planned to report them to the "recourse

WEAPONS HAUL: A crime scene technician carries out one of three guns found at the home of Peter Magnotti.

officer," a deputy in the local Sheriff's Department assigned to Riverdale High School to try and avert trouble before it started. Atkins then told officers that he and Schwebes had left the restaurant together at about 10:30 p.m. and that Schwebes had said that he was driving home to Pine Manor.

MONUMENTAL TASK

Atkins' statement did not give the investigating officers much to go on. Riverdale High School had a student body of more than 1,200 and, even if there was a connection between the "peach can" incident and the murder, which was far from certain, it would present them with a monumental investigative task. The only thing they knew for sure was that the students concerned were male, but they had no idea of their identities or even their ages, so they were faced with the unenviable task of interviewing more than 600 boys, researching their backgrounds, and checking their alibis.

As it transpired, their first break in the case came not from laborious police work but from the indiscretion of one

Craig Lesh, an 18-year-old from Fort Myers. Lesh, a Riverdale High School dropout, was a feckless young drug addict who bounced from one menial job to another. He did have two abiding passions, however: his pick-up truck and 18-year-old Julie Schuchard.

Julie, who already had a child from another relationship, was playing hard to get and Lesh was desperate to impress her. Two days after Mark Schwebes' murder, Lesh took Julie for a walk along the banks of the Caloosahatchee River, and, in a fit of braggadocio, he told her that he was a member of a gang called The Lords of Chaos and that they had been responsible for the shooting. He added for good measure that he had been present at the scene. He named the other members of the gang as Kevin Foster, Peter Magnotti, Derek Shields, Christopher Black, Christopher Burnett, and Thomas Torrone, all of whom were known to Julie as pupils or ex-pupils of Riverdale High.

Lesh, now totally carried away, went on to tell her that, the following evening, the gang were planning to rob Hardee's,

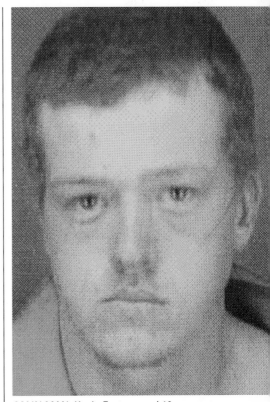

MAIN MAN: Kevin Foster, aged 19, was the leader of the Lords of Chaos.

a local restaurant, where Shields worked as a part-time waiter, and that he, Lesh, was to act as lookout. Far from being impressed, Julie Schuchard was horrified. She begged Lesh to abandon the robbery and to get as far away as possible from The Lords of Chaos. Lesh said it was too late for that. If he let them down, they would kill him, and besides he needed the money. The couple went their separate ways and Julie returned home, only half-believing her boyfriend's boasts. After agonizing for several hours, she decided to confide in her mother who persuaded her to inform the police. At 9:00 a.m. the following morning, Julie contacted the Lee County Sheriff's Department and told them the whole story.

CHANGE OF STORY

Within a few hours of Julie Schuchard making her statement, Craig Lesh was arrested. He put up minimal resistance when subjected to police interrogation. He repeated the story he had told to Julie the previous day, but with one important modification. He had not been involved in the shooting of Mark Schwebes. In fact he had not even been in Fort Myers on the night of the

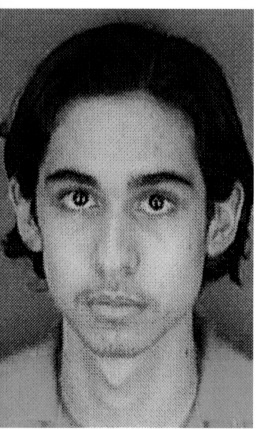

GANG MEMBER: Peter Magnotti stands accused of murder.

killing, a fact which the police quickly corroborated. He had been told about the murder by Kevin Foster, leader of The Lords of Chaos.

The Sheriff's Department issued an APB—All Points Bulletin—on all the gang members as named by Lesh. Peter Magnotti was the first to be picked up. He was walking to a friend's house where he had arranged to meet up with other gang members in preparation for the robbery at Hardee's. Sheriff's deputies spread-eagled him against a wall and, tucked in the waistband of his trousers, they found a 9mm Beretta semi-automatic, and, in his jacket pocket, a switchblade.

Minutes later, police pulled over a car driven by Kevin Foster with Christopher Burnett in the passenger seat. They were heading for the rendezvous with Magnotti to go over the final details of the Hardee's robbery. Foster was carrying an automatic pistol, and Burnett a 12-gauge shotgun.

Derek Shields was picked up an hour later at Hardee's, where he was working the night shift. Thomas Torrone turned himself into the Sheriff's Department the following morning.

Police spent the next few days interviewing the suspects who, one after another, with the exception of Kevin Foster, capitulated. What emerged was a bizarre scenario which bore a striking resemblance to A Clockwork Orange. The Lords of Chaos was not some run-of-the-mill street gang. It was a self-styled brotherhood, mainly composed of gifted middle-class students, who for some inexplicable reason had embarked upon a campaign of vandalism, robbery, and murder. There appeared to be nothing idealistic about their aims and they espoused no coherent philosophy, save their professed contempt for blacks, homosexuals, and welfare scroungers. They were, for the most part, highly intelligent and totally cold-blooded.

The robbery at Hardee's was intended to finance a gruesome mass murder. On the Saturday after the gang members were arrested, thousands of Florida students were due to celebrate their high-school graduation with a trip to Disney World in Orlando, Florida. It is a long-standing tradition, an all-night party at the theme parks where students bid farewell to school and look forward to a new phase in their lives.

If they had not been arrested, The Lords of Chaos had planned to travel on the Riverdale High School bus, armed to the teeth. Once inside the park, they had planned to mug some of the park employees who were dressed as Disney characters, don their costumes, and, in the guise of Mickey Mouse, Donald Duck, and Pluto, shoot as many black students as they could. The plan sounded bizarre to the point of being surreal, but the police were left in no doubt that the gang members had every intention of carrying it out.

As police interviewed gang members in greater depth, a clearer picture of The Lords of Chaos began to emerge. It comprised a hard core of four members and a number of hangers-on. The leader was Kevin Foster, aged 19, a dropout from Riverdale High School where he had once been an honor student. His lieutenants were Peter Magnotti, aged 17, who that spring had been voted by teachers and pupils at Riverdale the most talented artist in the school. A teacher who tested Magnotti's IQ estimated it to be 158, just two points below the genius level. "He was just a great kid," the teacher said, "one of the smartest kids I've ever dealt with."

Christopher Black was also an honor student, a brilliant mathematician, and computer expert who represented Riverdale in inter-school competitions. And then there was Derek Shields, who was probably the brightest of the lot. Having achieved top grades in math and physics, he had recently been awarded a $25,000 scholarship to the Florida Institute of Technology.

Now, all four young men face charges of premeditated homicide in the first degree, for their part in the murder. If found guilty, they could face the death penalty. Burnett and Torrone face long jail sentences for a series of lesser offenses.

NO REMORSE

So what happened? What made six intelligent young men with everything to live for embark on a vicious campaign of crime and violence? It's not even as if they were the macho types. At school they were considered "nerds". Magnotti weighed just over 100lb (45kg); Black, nicknamed "the Doughboy," stood 5ft 5ins (1.65m) tall and was grossly overweight. Foster was also diminutive and Shields was described as painfully shy. They were hardly the obvious candidates to launch a reign of terror on Florida society. Could it have been a momentary aberration? The police think not. To a man they displayed extraordi-

TWISTED FANTASY: The gang planned to don the costumes of various characters at Florida's Disney World, then unleash a hail of bullets.

nary arrogance even when facing capital charges. "They showed no remorse," said an investigating officer. "They were very matter of fact."

There is a need in Fort Myers to apportion blame, but it is difficult to know where that blame could lie. Hardly lack of parental control. All the gang members were products of relatively affluent, middle-class families and, with the exception of Shields whose parents were divorced, appeared to have been raised in stable home atmospheres. It would be hard to blame the school. These were model students. They were all academically well above average, had excellent attendance records, and none of them had ever displayed any disciplinary problems. If teachers had been asked to make a list of students likely to stray into a life of crime, The Lords of Chaos would probably have come bottom of that list.

While psychologists advance their disparate theories, The Lords of Chaos have left behind them shattered and bewildered families. Christopher Black's mother spoke for them all: "Sometimes I lie on his empty bed at home to smell him. It's all I have left."

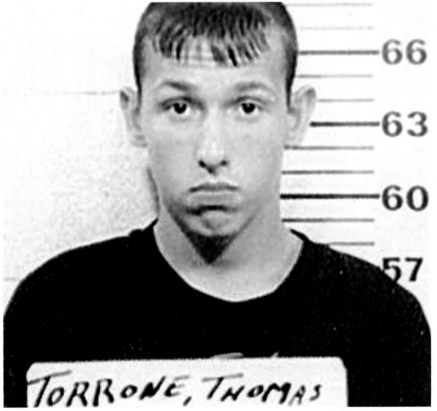

SWEET SIXTEEN: Thomas Torrone was the youngest boy in the Lords of Chaos. Like the other gang members, he was a model student.

A Family Affair

Eve Howells made her family's life hell. She allowed her husband just $50 a week pocket money and conducted a 12-year affair with his best friend. She pinned her children against the wall, and swore and spat at them; she locked them in their rooms for hours on end, and padlocked the refrigerator to stop them from having snacks. It was only a question of time before something snapped. And on August 31, 1995, it did.

SECRET LIFE: To the outside world, Eve Howells appeared a well respected school teacher with a happy family life. The reality was different.

It looked like a straightforward burglary that had gone horribly wrong. Police, responding to an emergency call, arrived at a bungalow in the village of Dalton in Yorkshire, England, to find the body of 48-year-old Eve Howells lying on the living room floor with her head smashed in. The back door of the house was open and the living room had been ransacked.

Mrs. Howells' body was discovered by her two teenage sons, Glenn, aged 15, and his 14-year-old brother John, who had returned home after taking the family dog for a walk. They raised the alarm with neighbors, who in turn contacted the police and Mrs. Howells' husband David, who was playing darts at a nearby bar.

Detective Superintendent Gary Haigh, leading the murder inquiry, gave his scenario of events at a press conference that night: "We believe that Mrs. Howells was sitting on the settee when burglars sneaked in through the unlocked back door, crept up behind her, and attacked her with a hammer or some other blunt instrument. They then ransacked the house and stole $150 in cash. This was a vicious attack on a loving mother . . . The person or persons responsible could simply have taken the money without resorting to violence."

TEARFUL PLEA

Mr. Howells, an engineer who had been married to Eve for 23 years, made a tearful appeal for help from the public. "This animal has destroyed our lives," he said. "I won't be able to come to terms with her death until he is caught. I think he's a local man who someone may be shielding. I know I must be brave for the sake of our children. Eve played such an important part in our lives that I'm not sure we'll ever get over her death."

There was a public outpouring of grief and sympathy by neighbors, friends, and Eve's colleagues at Newsome High School, where she had taught history and religious education. The head teacher paid tribute to her: "I will remember Eve as one of the very best sort of teachers. The children knew how they were expected to behave in her class, and in return she brought her subjects alive and was a source of inspiration. She set the highest standards."

As police interviewed neighbors and friends, one word kept cropping up in their description of Eve Howells—strict. Gradually, it started to emerge that, far from being a kind and loving parent, she had in fact been something of a tyrant

MAJOR ASSET: The Howells' family home, along with all the other family assets, was in Eve's name.

and life in the Howells' household had been turbulent, if not outright violent. Detective Superintendent Haigh, who had gone to school with David Howells, decided it was time to take a closer look at the surviving members of the family.

Clearly David Howells could not have killed his wife; he was in a local bar all evening, and he had scores of witnesses to attest to the fact that he had never left the building. Haigh was faced with the unsavory possibility that one or both of the boys had battered their own mother to death.

At 7:00 a.m. on September 20, Glenn and John Howells were arrested at their home. Their father accompanied them to Huddersfield police headquarters where they were questioned separately. They were detained overnight and questioned again the following day.

There were glaring inconsistencies in their versions of events on the day of the murder and, by the end of the second day, Haigh was convinced that one or both of them was responsible for their mother's death. Finally, they cracked. Glenn tearfully admitted that it had been he who had battered his mother after she had called him "a lazy little shit" for not walking the dog properly. He went on to say that his mother had been making his life, and the life of his family,

absolute hell. Told of Glenn's confession, John admitted to having helped his brother ransack the house to make it look like a burglary and also to having disposed of the murder weapon. Both boys were charged with murder and moved to separate secure accommodation run by the local authority.

FATHER'S INFLUENCE?

Haigh was satisfied that the boys had done the actual killing, but he was becoming more and more convinced that their father had been involved in some way. As he dug deeper into the Howells' family affairs, he soon found ample reason for David Howells to want to see his wife dead. Firstly, he had a financial incentive. Eve Howells had savings and investments of more than $200,000, plus her name was on the deeds of the family home. Then there was the fact that she had been having an affair with her husband's best friend, Russell Hirst, for over 12 years. Finally, as young John Howells had alleged in his police statement, Eve Howells had run the house with a rod of iron and for years had made all their lives a misery. Quite simply, David Howells loathed his wife and did not have the means or the courage to leave her. The logical, if horrific, conclusion reached by Haigh was

VICTIM AND VILLAIN: David Howells was dominated by his wife for years. Finally he conspired with his children to kill her.

that David Howells had persuaded his children to kill his wife while he established a cozy alibi for himself by playing darts with friends.

On October 19, 1995, David Howells was arrested and charged with conspiracy to murder his wife, along with his sons John and Glenn. Detective Superintendent Haigh knew that, without corroboration from the boys that their father had been involved in the murder, his case against him was purely circumstantial.

He contrived to let David Howells meet with his sons and, unbeknown to any of them, recorded their conversations. These covert recordings would eventually form the backbone of the case against David Howells.

The Howells' trial opened on January 16, 1997, 18 months after their arrest. All three denied murder. Gary Burrell, representing Glenn Howells, who admitted manslaughter under provocation, said that the boys had been "subjected to severe and repeated emotional and mental abuse and cruelty." He went on to describe in graphic detail how Mrs. Howells had terrorized her children for years and had even gone so far as to put a lock on the refrigerator to prevent them eating without her permission. Glenn Howells, he told the court, had just "snapped" after a particularly vicious outburst from his mother.

CAREFUL PLANNING

Franz Muller, lawyer for the prosecution, painted a rather different picture of events leading up the murder. He told the court that the killing had been carefully planned by all three defendants in a manner which would safeguard Mr. Howells' inheritance. The boys' father had intentionally established a cast-iron alibi for the time of the killing, knowing that he could not benefit from his wife's will if he were found guilty of her murder.

Muller backed up his claim with the covert police tapes on which David Howells told his sons: "We have just got to bluff it out. If you two break, I'm in as well, so we just have to stick together . . . We will have a good life, don't worry. I'll be waiting for you whatever happens."

Glenn Howells was the first to take the stand. He told how he hammered his mother to death through a haze of tears, then sobbed over her body: "I'm sorry . . . I love you." Glenn went on to say that killing his abusive mother was the only way to end years of torment which had driven him to the verge of suicide. "I just wanted the grief to stop. I wanted to be a normal kid like my friends and have a happy time. The only way was to get rid of the problem."

Weeping and speaking in a whisper, Glenn described the killing itself. He told how he took a rusty stonemason's hammer from under his bed, and crept up behind his mother who was sitting on the sofa addressing an envelope. "I was holding my breath and trying to keep quiet so she wouldn't hear me crying. I stood behind her so she wouldn't know what I was about to do. Even at that point, I still didn't think I would. But, as

ETERNAL TRIANGLE: Eve Howells with her husband David and their mutual friend Russell Hirst, with whom she had a long-running affair.

DRIVEN TO VIOLENCE: After years of his mother's bullying, Glenn Howells finally snapped and struck her repeatedly over the head with a hammer.

that he had "put the boys up" to killing their mother. He claimed that he only realized that Glenn had been responsible for the murder after he overheard a conversation between the two brothers after the event.

Howells agreed that over the years he had done little to stop his wife from screaming and shouting at the boys. "It was pointless me trying to interfere," he said. "I could never win. We would just end up arguing. She was clever with words. She seemed to take control."

Howells said that, after the killing, he had had "serious words" with his sons. "I asked them why they did it. What was going to happen to them? But then I agreed I would help them."

In his summing up at the end of a 19-day trial, Justice Alliott said that Mrs. Howells' conduct toward her sons had been clearly unacceptable but that did not justify the taking of a life. The jury of five men and seven women retired for three hours before declaring all three defendants guilty of murder.

David Howells was sentenced to life imprisonment and the two boys were ordered to be detained at Her Majesty's Pleasure—an indeterminate sentence subject to periodic review.

I stood there, I remembered all the bad things . . . I just looked at her and got the flashbacks, then my mind exploded. Something went in my head, and I can't remember owt [anything] until I heard my brother screaming 'No!' I said: 'Just get out!' I didn't want him to see it. When I realized what I had done, I said: 'Sorry mum, I love you.'"

MURDER OPTIONS

John Howells was next to take the stand. He told the court that his father had helped hatch the murder plot. He said he and his brother Glenn had been talking about killing their mother for more than two years and that they had discussed the idea with their father. "It got so bad," John said, "that we thought about throwing her off the balcony on holiday or pushing her into the road."

They also considered pushing her off the cliffs at nearby Flamborough Head. Finally, shortly after the family returned from a holiday on the Mediterranean island of Ibiza in August 1995, it was decided that Glenn should kill his mother with a hammer and that they should make the attack look like a bungled burglary.

David Howells strenuously denied

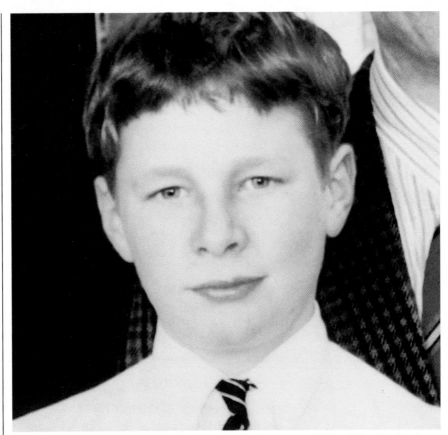

ACCOMPLICE: John Howells disposed of the murder weapon, and helped his older brother ransack the house so that police would think a burglary had been committed.

Murder by the Internet

Sharon Lopatka and Robert Glass were lovers despite the fact that they had never met in person. Their affair was conducted via the Internet. The bond between them was their shared sadomasochistic fantasies. Sharon's ultimate fantasy was to be tortured to death by her lover and he, in turn, was more than happy to comply. Finally, the day came when fantasy became reality.

Shortly after 8:00 a.m. on October 13, 1996, Sharon Lopatka left her suburban home in Hampstead, Maryland, telling her husband Victor that she was going to visit friends in Georgia. Several days passed and Victor started to become concerned. His wife was in the habit of calling every night when she was away. So far he had heard nothing. He checked with friends in Georgia but they had not heard from Sharon either. Finally, on October 20, a week after

SQUALID END: Sharon Lopatka was found dead in this shallow grave, only feet from Robert Glass's dilapidated trailer.

DEATH WISH: Housewife Sharon Lopatka sought her own destruction via the dark recesses of the Internet.

Sharon's departure, Victor filed a missing persons' report with the Maryland Police Department.

It should have been a comparatively easy matter to find Sharon Lopatka. Weighing more than 224lb (100kg) and with bleached-blond hair, she was hardly inconspicuous. The police checked with friends and neighbors but no one had seen her since the morning of October 13. They searched the family home for clues to Sharon's possible whereabouts and, tucked under a computer in her office, they found a hand-written note. "If my body is never retrieved," it read, "don't worry. Know that I am at peace." Needless to say, this changed the whole nature of the investigation. The most obvious solution was that she had committed suicide.

E-MAIL CLUES

The police hoped that her computer might hold the secret of her plans. They shipped the machine down to police headquarters where they entrusted it to Sergeant Barry Leese, head of the Maryland Computer Crimes Unit. Leese and his team found thousands of erased E-mail messages on the hard disk. Using a special retrieval program, they soon restored the files and what they read ranged from the sad and lonely to the horrific and bizarre.

Sharon Lopatka had clearly spent most of her waking hours in the "chat rooms" of the Internet, sites where strangers meet to discuss topics of common interest. These can be as innocent as stamp-collecting or bird-watching, but in her case, the area of interest was exclusively sexual. She logged into sites prefixed alt.sex, alt.bondage, alt.necrophilia, alt.masochism—"chat rooms" where like-minded sexual deviants indulge their fantasies in a murky electronic underworld.

As with other users, Sharon Lopatka used the anonymity of the computer screen to become whoever she wanted to be. She had dozens of identities. Sometimes she was Nancy, an obese giantess who liked to "crush men like bugs." In this persona she invited correspondents to force-feed her until she was 500lb (227kg). In other messages she became Miranda, a sadistic seductress, whose weight had miraculously shrunk to a shapely 120lb (54kg).

Sharon Lopatka's early E-mails were addressed to a number of different subscribers scattered around the United States but since August 1996, her correspondence had been almost exclusively with one man who styled himself as

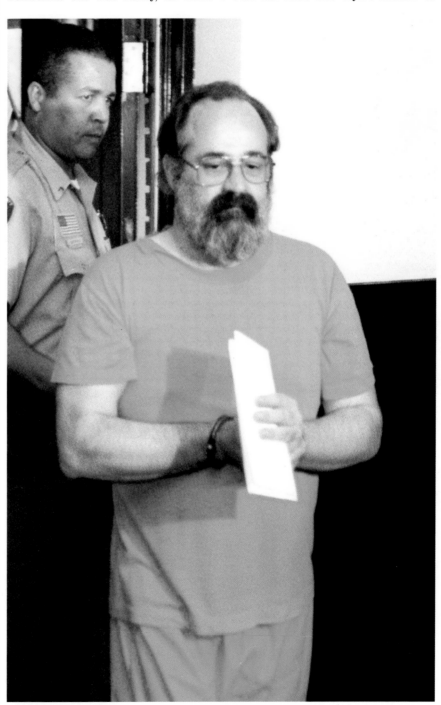

UNLIKELY KILLER: Mild-mannered and reclusive computer programer Robert Glass maintained that his lover's death was an accident.

CODE BREAKER: Sergeant Barry Leese used his computer skills to recover erased files on the victim's computer.

"Slowhand." From the E-mail number, Leese quickly identified "Slowhand" as one Robert Glass of Lenoir, North Carolina. The contents of these messages, more than 1,110 in all, were truly horrific. It was clear from the outset of her correspondence with Glass that Sharon Lopatka enjoyed extreme masochistic fantasies, the ultimate of which was to be tortured to death by Glass to whom she professed her undying love. Glass, initially tentative in his responses, soon got into the swing of things. "I will force you to perform the most humiliating sex acts," he wrote, "while I cut you with a machete and a Bowie knife." In a later E-mail he promised to "kill you very slowly in a drawn-out orgy of sex and pain that will give you the ultimate orgasm as you slip over the precipice of life into death."

Sergeant Leese, who had seen more than his share of vile correspondence in his time with the Computer Crimes Unit, still found it inconceivable that Sharon Lopatka and Glass had really gone so far as to act out their fantasy, but all the evidence pointed to the fact that they had done just that. "If it was true," Leese said, "it was an investigator's dream. It was like reading an itinerary. It was all there—the suspect, the location, the motive, right down to the train she took for her rendezvous with Glass."

On October 24, Leese traveled down to North Carolina and met with Captain Danny Barlow, chief of police in the small town of Lenoir. Barlow knew Robert Glass slightly but had never had dealing with him in a professional capacity. According to Barlow, Glass was a 45-year-old computer programer, who had been born into one of the richest and most respected families in the district. In recent years, however, he had fallen on hard times and was living in a trailer in woods which had once been part of the family estate.

FRESH GRAVE

Leese and Barlow drove out to Glass's trailer, hoping against hope that they would find Sharon Lopatka alive and well. They didn't. What they did find, however, was a freshly dug grave, less than 150 feet (45m) from the front door of the trailer. They called out a team of officers and, within a few hours, they had exhumed the naked, mutilated body of Sharon Lopatka. Beside the corpse was a length of rope. From the trailer itself, police removed a variety of weapons and tools which they later established had been used for sexual torture. An autopsy concluded that Sharon Lopatka had died by asphyxiation, but was unable to establish whether her body had been mutilated before or after death.

Robert Glass was arrested at his place of work, the County Offices, where, ironically, he was reprograming the local Sheriff's computer system. Confronted with the E-mail printouts from Sharon Lopatka's computer, Glass admitted killing her but claimed that it had been an accident. According to Glass, she had traveled down from Baltimore on the train, arriving at Lenoir late on the evening of October 13.

For three days, he and she allegedly acted out the roles that they had described so graphically in their correspondence. In the mornings, Glass claimed, he continued to go to work as usual, then at night he returned to the trailer and Sharon Lopatka. On the third night, the couple repeated the ritual of sex and torture. Glass wound a rope around his partner's neck and tightened it to the point where she was rendered unconscious. It was several minutes before he realized that she was in fact dead. He panicked and dragged her body to the nearby trash pit, where he buried her. The police were buying none of it and Robert Glass was summarily arrested, charged with first-degree murder, and refused bail.

From the investigation angle, the Glass/Lopatka case could not have been simpler, but it did leave a lot of unanswered questions. What drove Lopatka and Glass to act out their grotesque fantasies? Were the couple indulging in a deviant alliance that accidentally went wrong; or was Lopatka's death always the intended outcome of the liaison? When it comes to the trial, Glass's defense team will inevitably insist that it was the former, but given the nature of the E-mails, they will be hard pressed to convince a jury of that. And why should Sharon Lopatka have been so determined to die a violent death? For a small minority of people, pain is inexorably linked with sex and there have been numerous occasions where this has got out of hand and resulted in a fatality, but to set out deliberately to get oneself killed is virtually unheard of. To suggest that this was purely a progressive fantasy does not hold water.

An E-mail correspondence Lopatka had with another Internet user in New Jersey some months earlier reached the same conclusion. She arranged a rendezvous with her E-pal, but he lost his nerve at the last minute and pulled out. Sharon Lopatka's few friends told police that she was extremely lonely and depressed about her galloping obesity, but surely this isn't answer enough. And why should Glass, a mild-mannered, intelligent, law-abiding citizen, have agreed to go along with such a monstrous plan? He must have realized that he would be caught. True, he had told Lopatka to erase all their electronic correspondence before she traveled south to meet him, but, as a computer expert, he must have known that the police would be able to retrieve the data and that that would lead them straight to his front door.

LABYRINTH OF SLEAZE

Perhaps the answer lies in the nature of the Internet itself. There is no question that it has become an invaluable communication tool, but the Net has also become a labyrinth of pornography and sleaze where correspondents can hide their true identity. So far there is no way that it can be policed or censored. Psychologists have described the Internet as producing the "Mardi Gras" phenomenon, in which users feel that they are equipped with a mask that provides them with total anonymity and allows them to speak and behave in ways that would otherwise be unthinkable.

Since the Maryland Computer Crimes Unit was established in 1991, Barry Leese has witnessed every manner of criminal activity and human perversity, from credit card fraud to organized rings of pedophiles. "Every kind of crime is out there," Leese says. "If you can imagine it, then you'll find it there somewhere. But what you have to remember is that the same crimes were always taking place. It's just a different modus operandi. The Lopatka case may be the first murder in which the Internet has been directly involved, but it has spawned numerous other crimes of violence. For instance, there was the case of Harold Clarkson, a 55-year-old mechanic from Virginia, who posed on the Net as a 20-year-old woman in an attempt to trick another Net user into raping and mutilating his wife; and then there was that university student from New York who battered and raped a woman he met on-line."

Steve Jones, author of The Other Side of the Internet, is appalled by the potential dangers of an unpoliced Internet. "What's going on now," he says, "is people seeking people. It's like a movie, where you suspend disbelief. Only this is life, not a movie, so what you end up suspending is judgment."

When Robert Glass finally comes to trial, the Internet will be on trial along with him. The case will revolve around that hazy no-man's-land between fantasy and reality. The anonymity it affords to its users lets them explore desires that they could never otherwise reveal and, when you put two deeply disturbed people like Sharon Lopatka and Robert Glass together, there is no guarantee that they will not stray from one zone into the other.

FACING THE MUSIC: Robert Glass enters Caldwell County Superior Court to enter a plea of not guilty to murdering Sharon Lopatka.

Family Feud

Maurizio Gucci was the last member of his family to be directly involved in the company which bears his name, a name which has long been a symbol of all that is chic in Italian fashion. Behind the suave exterior lay a history of infighting, violence, and betrayal between family members. When Maurizio was shot dead on March 27, 1995, police finally decided they need look no farther than the immediate family for the perpetrator of the crime.

GUNNED DOWN: Maurizio Gucci's body is removed from the lobby of his office building where he was shot by an assassin.

Shortly after 9:00 a.m. on the morning of Monday, March 27, 1995, Maurizio Gucci kissed his lover, Paola Franchi Colombo, and strode out of his 18th-century palazzo. His office was less than a quarter mile from his home and, as was his custom, Gucci walked to work rather than face the chaos of Milan's rush-hour traffic. A suave, athletic man of 46, he turned the corner into Via Palestro and was only a matter of feet from the front entrance of his office building when he noticed that he was being followed by a well-dressed man in his late thirties.

Gucci stepped into the lobby of the building and exchanged greetings with the doorman, Giuseppe Onorato. Seconds later, two shots rang out and Gucci plunged forward onto the marble staircase. He lay there helpless as the gunman calmly walked over and shot him twice in the face at point-blank range. The gunman turned to leave but found himself face to face with Onorato, an ex-army sergeant. The assassin raised his gun again but, in an instinctive gesture, the doorman put his arm in front of his face and the fifth bullet smashed into his shoulder. As Onorato fell to the floor in agony, the killer ran out of the building, collided with a young woman, dived into a small green sedan, and was driven away at high speed by a male driver.

News of the murder spread quickly and within a matter of minutes Gucci's eldest daughter, 18-year-old Allegra, was on the scene of the crime, together with her mother, Patrizia Reggiani, his ex-wife. Both women wept copiously.

AMATEUR WORK
The police had immediately mounted a massive manhunt involving cars and helicopters, but they were unable to trace the getaway car. Eyewitness accounts from Onorato and others enabled investigators to piece the logistics of the assassination precisely. They concluded that this had been the work of an amateur. The killer had waited until Gucci got into the building before shooting. Any self-respecting assassin would have shot him in the street outside, thereby both avoiding the chance of being trapped inside the building and speeding up his potential getaway. Added to this, the murder weapon was a 7.65mm pistol, a weapon that a professional hit man would not even consider using.

Onorato was able to give the police a fairly accurate description of the killer: about 5ft 10in (1.9m), stocky, with dark

HIGH FASHION: Maurizio Gucci was one of the third generation of his family to head the internationally renowned fashion empire.

Rodolfo, Maurizio Gucci's father, died leaving 50 percent of the company to his son and the remainder was split between his brother Aldo's four children and assorted cousins. There was no love lost between any of them and the situation was a recipe for disaster.

With Maurizio Gucci effectively in control of the company, the feuding relatives closed ranks and tried to unseat him. They even went as far as to report to the authorities that he had forged his father's signature to avoid death duties, forcing him to flee the country. He returned after six months and was promptly arrested, tried, and given a one-year prison sentence. However, the conviction was overturned on appeal and Gucci walked away a free man.

LEGENDARY BATTLES

Boardroom battles between various members of the Gucci clan about company strategy became legendary and were not only unseemly in their own right but also damaging to the company's reputation and profitability. By 1989, with sales dwindling, the situation was obviously untenable and Maurizio Gucci's relatives sold out their 50 percent of the company to Investcorp, a Bahrain-based investment bank.

Gucci continued as chairman and chief operating officer of the company,

hair, and a round face. He was given mug shots of known hit men to study but he failed to identify his attacker, thereby confirming to the police that this was the work of an amateur.

Initially, the police were at a loss to provide a motive for the crime. Who would want to kill this well-liked grandson of Guccio Gucci, founder of the family's leather and fashion empire? They did not have to look for long before coming up with a myriad of possibilities. Family feuds had been a part of the Gucci clan's way of life for three generations. Guccio, the patriarch, had actively set his five sons against one another to "see what they were made of." A few years earlier Paolo Gucci, Maurizio Gucci's cousin, had turned his own father, Aldo, in to the US Internal Revenue Service, with the result that Aldo spent a year in jail for tax evasion. Paolo himself was beaten up at a Gucci board meeting and sued various family members for assault. One acquaintance quipped: "Living with the Gucci's is like having dinner with the Borgias."

But these were mere skirmishes compared to what was to come. In 1983,

GRIEF STRICKEN: Allegra Gucci, daughter of the murdered Maurizio, wipes away a tear. Next to her is her mother Patrizia Reggiani Gucci.

but his Arab partners soon became disenchanted with his business methods. Sales were falling and by 1991 the company recorded a trading loss of more than $14 million. This did not stop the flamboyant Gucci from squandering huge sums of money.

By 1993, the company had a serious cash-flow crisis and Investcorp offered to buy Gucci out for $150 million. This would have been a perfect solution, except for the fact that he had already put his shares up as collateral against personal loans totalling $11 million with Citibank and Credit Suisse. He needed to get his hands on cash to repay these debts before he could regain control of his shares. And he succeeded at the eleventh hour. Asked where he got the money, Gucci claimed that he had a dream that there was money hidden under the floorboards of his house in St. Moritz and when he looked, there it was.

His then wife, Patrizia, tells a quite different story. She claims that it was she who bailed Gucci out of trouble by per-

suading some of her wealthy friends to lend him the money. If this is true, and it is certainly more plausible than the floorboard story, was the money ever repaid? If not, public prosecutor Carlo Nocerino conjectured, Maurizio Gucci might have made himself some powerful and dangerous enemies. Nocerino spent months sifting through Gucci's affairs, but, despite their best efforts, the public prosecutor and his team were no nearer to finding a motive for the crime.

MONEY LAUNDERER

Nocerino advanced a number of theories. Was Gucci paying bribes to tax inspectors? Could he have been laundering money for drug trafficking? Fashion is a favorite route for this activity because so much of the product is exported. Gucci had recently announced his intention to open a casino in Switzerland. Could he have fallen foul of the Mafia, who consider gambling their birthright? It is possible that Gucci was involved in one or all of these activities, but after more than a year of investigation, Nocerino could not find a shred of evidence.

By the autumn of 1996, Nocerino decided he was looking in the wrong

place for Gucci's killer and that his murder was not connected with his financial affairs at all. A seemingly trivial incident made him take a closer look at Gucci's immediate family. Paola Franchi Colombo, Gucci's former mistress, was being interviewed about her lover's assassination on television. She claimed that less than a half hour after the murder, his ex-wife, 49-year-old Patrizia Reggiani, had marched into her home "as if she owned the place." Ms. Reggiani, she said, had demanded a cashmere sweater belonging to Maurizio, which her 21-year-old daughter, Alessandra, wanted as a memento of her father. She went on to say that Ms. Reggiani had behaved rudely and aggressively.

Patrizia Reggiani responded quickly, saying that when she went to collect the sweater, she had not even seen Ms. Colombo. "She was too busy packing up the family silver and paintings which were being carted away in seven or eight articulated lorries." She went on to explain that under Italian law—Gucci died intestate—all his property rightly belonged to her two daughters. Ms. Reggiani conceded that the bulk of the property taken on that day had been returned, but added:

FAMILY FRICTION: Paulo, Rodolpho, and Dr Aldo Gucci, show a united front for the cameras. The truth was very different.

MYSTIC JAILED: Giuseppina Auriemma, a Neapolitan psychic, was one of five people charged with conspiracy to commit murder.

"Not the curtains which formed the backdrop for her television interview." She went on: "Now let me tell you exactly who this woman Franchi Colombo is. The woman has said that Maurizio was always used. That's absolutely correct. He was used, firstly and mainly by her." It was vintage Gucci stuff.

Nocerino remembered a statement Ms. Reggiani had made to the press on the day of her ex-husband's murder. "On a human plane, I'm sorry, but I can't say the same on a personal one." With those words ringing in his ears, and the realization that Patrizia Reggiani, through her daughters, was the only one to benefit from Gucci's death, Nocerino established her as his number one suspect.

COLLECTING EVIDENCE

The investigation into Ms. Reggiani lasted for several months and involved covert surveillance, subpoenaing bank accounts, and wire taps. By January 2, 1997, Nocerino felt he had enough evidence to convict her of her ex-husband's murder and arrested her, along with four others who are accused of conspiring with her. They were Giuseppina Auriemma, a 51-year-old clairvoyant and ex-Gucci franchisee, 40-year-old Ivano Savioni, a hotel porter, and two Sicilian gunmen, Orazio Cicila, 58, who was already in prison on unrelated drugs charges, and Benedetto Ceraulo, 35.

Reggiani was driven to San Vittore jail wearing a full-length mink coat. She told waiting reporters that she had nothing to do with her husband's death. That night, Nocerino held a controversial news conference and gave his version of the events that had led up to the murder of Maurizio Gucci. He claimed that Reggiani had approached Auriemma with a view to having her husband killed. Auriemma contacted Savioni, whom she knew to have underworld connections, and he in turn recruited Ceraulo, who pulled the trigger, and Cicila, who acted as getaway driver. Nocerino claimed to have evidence that Reggiani had agreed to pay her four accomplices $240,000 for the hit, to be split between them as they saw fit. According to the prosecutor, Reggiani had paid out $200,000 but, for some strange reason, refused to deliver the balance with the result that the killers were now planning to exact revenge by having her shot in the knees. This had proved their downfall. The hitman they approached to maim Reggiani turned out to be a police informant.

Asked about her motives, Nocerino said they were threefold. Firstly she hated her husband, a sentiment she openly expressed; secondly, she was jealous of Paola Franchi Colombo, who had replaced her in her husband's affections; thirdly, and most important was money. Reggiani, deserted by her husband 10 years earlier and finally divorced by him months before his murder, had demanded $500,000 in maintenance. Gucci had refused and was preparing to take the matter to court. Nocerino believed that Reggiani was also afraid that her two daughters, Alessandra and Allegra, might be disinherited in favor of his mistress.

Nocerino went on to say that the police had compiled an 80-page report which included testimony by Reggiani's own lawyer, her former maid, and the maid's husband. Their evidence suggested that Reggiani had been plotting her husband's murder for years. On several occasions she had asked the maid and her husband if they could find her a "hired gun," and, according to her lawyer, she had asked him some years earlier: "How much time will I get in jail if I get rid of him?" Patrizia Reggiani will find that out herself in due course.

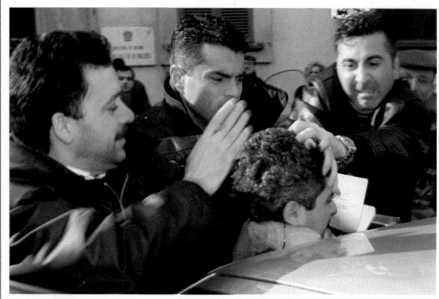

KEY SUSPECT: Benedetto Ceraulo is bundled into the back of a police car after being arrested on suspicion of the murder of Maurizio Gucci.

Born to Kill

"Killing is my business . . . and business is good. Killing for me is a mass turn-on. I was born to be a murderer." No, this is not a piece of dialogue from the latest Quentin Tarantino movie; it is a diary entry written by 12-year-old Sharon Carr. And she meant every word of it.

BLOOD LUST: Sharon Carr claimed that killing gave her a sexual thrill.

In June 1992, pretty trainee hairdresser Katie Rackliff had just celebrated her eighteenth birthday. She had also just split up with her boyfriend. On the night of June 7, she went to Ragamuffins nightclub in Camberley, a small town in the south of England, hoping to bump into her ex-lover with a view to a reconciliation. He was indeed there, but her attempt at a reconciliation was summarily rebuffed. Depressed and lonely, Katie proceeded to get quietly drunk.

According to eye-witnesses, she left the club at about 10:00 p.m., alone. Four hours later, her half-naked body was discovered dumped on a sidewalk in Farnborough, a town some five miles (8km) away. She had been stabbed and sexually assaulted. An autopsy revealed that she had been stabbed 29 times with a six-inch knife. So ferocious was the attack that some of the wounds had gone straight through her body. In addition to the wounds to her upper body and arms, her genitalia had been grotesquely mutilated with the same weapon.

The forensic pathologist had no doubt that the attack had a sexual motive, but an absence of semen and the severity of the wounding to her genitalia made it impossible for him to say whether sexual penetration had taken place. The police, however, were in no doubt that the attacker was male. Profiling suggested that he was probably in his late twenties or early thirties, of low intelligence, and possibly the same man who had murdered model Rachel Nickell on Wimbledon Common, London, some months earlier. Four years later, this was to prove a desperately inaccurate assessment.

Local police launched a massive manhunt. In cooperation with other forces, they questioned hundreds of known sex offenders, but after a year, they were no nearer to solving this appalling crime.

ANOTHER STABBING

On June 7, 1994, two years to the day after the murder of Katie Rackliff, there was another, apparently unrelated stabbing at Collingwood College, a high school in Camberley, the town where Katie had been murdered. Annie Clifford, a 13-year-old schoolgirl, was approached by a fellow pupil, 14-year-old Sharon Carr. Sharon claimed to have dropped a pound coin behind one of the lavatories and asked if Annie would help her look for it. Annie was a bit apprehensive—Sharon had a reputation for

CLUBBING: Ragamuffins nightclub in Camberley, the last place Katie Rackliff was seen alive.

being aggressive—but finally agreed.

Once inside the cubicle, according to Annie, she bent down to see if she could spot the coin. "Suddenly," she told the police later, "I felt a thump in my back on the left-hand side, just above my waist. I turned my head to look at Sharon. She was holding a knife. She was smiling and yet looked very angry as well. She told me to crouch on the floor and kept telling me: 'Don't scream, don't tell anyone, or else I will kill you.' It was as if she was in another world. She was calm and clearly happy with what she had done. Then she juggled the knife from one hand to the other, deciding what to do next." At that moment, a group of pupils walked into the washroom. Carr ran off and the girls raised the alarm. In light of what was later revealed about Sharon Carr, there is little doubt that, but for the interruption, she would have gone on to kill her victim.

Annie was rushed to hospital, where she underwent emergency surgery for a single stab wound, which had punctured her lung. Fortunately she made a complete recovery.

Carr was charged with attempted murder and, while awaiting trial at the Middlesex Lodge Assessment Center, she tried to strangle two female staff members in separate attacks. In December 1994, she was convicted of causing grievous bodily harm and ordered to be detained at Her Majesty's Pleasure—an indefinite sentence subject to periodic review.

TRAGIC WASTE: On the fateful night of June 7, 1992, Katie Rackliff lost her life, the victim of a random attack by a girl she had never met.

TERRIBLE REVELATIONS: Joe Rackcliff maintains his dignity in court, despite hearing the details of Katie's death.

Despite the location of the two attacks, and the coincidence of their both being committed on June 7, police did not make any connection between them. This is understandable. They were still convinced that Katie Rackliff had been killed by a man and besides, Sharon Carr was only 12 at the time. They did not consider that such a brutal sexual attack could be committed on a grown woman by a young girl.

TRUE CONFESSIONS

The connection between the two crimes might never have been made had it not been for the words and actions of Sharon Carr herself. While in Bullwood Hall, an institution for young offenders, Carr and other inmates were encouraged to "confront their pasts." Carr was open, even boastful about her past. During late 1995 and 1996, she told other inmates that she had killed and that she would kill again. In a letter to a friend, Simon Thompson, dated January 7, 1996, she wrote: "When I'm attacking someone, their eyes glaze . . . It is a turn-on you should try. Believe me, you might as well feel the pleasures of life before the pains, for the pains last much longer. Killing for me is a mass turn-on. It just makes me so high I never want to come down."

The consensus of opinion of fellow inmates and staff was that Carr was lying in order to impress. It was only when she developed a "crush" on prison officer, Annette Cini, and started to confide in her, that the authorities began to take her boasts seriously. Carr obviously saw Cini as an ally, someone whom she could trust. In March 1996, she wrote her a letter in which, for the first time she showed a glimmering of remorse for her appalling crime: "Dear Mrs. Cini, you are the only person who saw me cry for help and understood it. The only person I am angry with now is myself. I should never have gone so far but I did."

Prison officers searched Carr's room and unearthed diaries and letters that described how she had killed Katie Rackliff. Extracts from these diaries, which would later be used as evidence in Carr's trial, make chilling reading. They show that, almost four years after the murder, she still derived a sexual thrill from her appalling crime.

DIARIES AND LETTERS

An entry dated January 13, 1995, reads: "Remember KR. Oh God, she did get me so hot, pity really. I think about her and my head is spinning, but against the cops I am winning. Too many people trying to

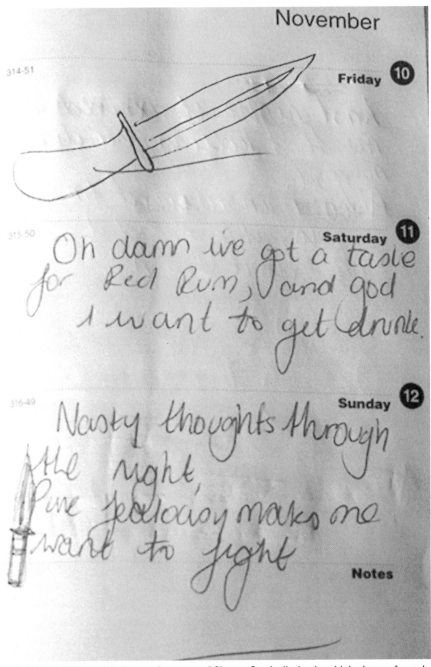

GROTESQUE FANTASIES: A page from one of Sharon Carr's diaries in which she confessed to her love of killing. The journals were used in evidence against her.

get this nigger down." Another on March 27 outlines her own sick philosophy: "I believe in pain as the mirror of the extreme perfection of man's ability, the sublimation of the ego in the physical body, the resurrection of the animal, the supreme animal, that's why she had to be killed."

On May 15, she wrote: "If only I could kill you again, I promise I would make you suffer more this time. Your terrified screams turned me on." The entry for September 25 reads: "I enjoyed putting the blade up her. It made me feel powerful. I had to overcome her serenity, her security. She needed to be raped. That showed her well."

On November 13: "I bring the knife into her chest. Her eyes are closing. She is pleading with me so I bring the knife to her again and again. I don't want to hurt her but I need to do violence to her

and that is far more powerful to me than lust . . . I know she feels her life being slowly drawn from her and I hear her last gasp." This was written by a 15-year-old girl about deeds carried out three years earlier.

Carr was questioned by police at great length and, far from denying the murder, seemed anxious to elaborate on the evidence already established against her. She described the crime in graphic detail and even went so far as to make a video reenacting the murder. Detective Sergeant Paul Clements, one of the investigating officers who interviewed Carr for more than 27 hours, later told the court: "She seemed quite unconcerned when we were discussing some quite horrific details. When the interviews were finished, she often walked away with a smile on her face. I have not interviewed anyone like her." Another

detective concurred: "In a one-to-one situation, Sharon Carr is the most dangerous woman in Britain, there can be little doubt about that."

CONFESSION WITHDRAWN

When Carr was first charged with murdering Katie Rackliff, she indicated that she intended to enter a plea of guilty, which would have made her trial a formality. At the last minute, however, she withdrew her confession and insisted on a plea of not guilty. It was too late, however. Sharon Carr might have claimed that her diary entries and spoken confessions had been fantasy. Unfortunately for her, during her interviews with police officers, she offered information that could only have been known by the killer. For instance, she admitted stealing a gold bracelet from Katie's body, a fact which had been deliberately withheld by

MOTHER'S INFLUENCE: Sharon's mother Molly McFazdean is alleged to have introduced her daughter to voodoo rituals.

CHILDHOOD SQUALOR: The wooden shack in Belize, where Sharon Carr spent the early part of her life with her mother.

the police for the specific purpose of weeding out habitual "confessors."

The trial of Sharon Carr opened at Winchester Crown Court in February 1997. Lawyer Stewart Jones, in his opening address for the prosecution, told the court: "This was no ordinary 12-year-old. We say that she was a precocious and evil girl, and we submit that this is demonstrated not only by what she did, but by what she has said and written about it afterwards."

The trial, which lasted almost a month, must have been a nightmare for Katie Rackliff's parents, Helen and Joseph, as they were forced to listen to a graphic recreation of their daughter's death through Carr's diaries and taped confessions.

There was little doubt about the eventual outcome and on March 25, 1997, Sharon Carr was duly found guilty of the murder of Katie Rackliff, making her the youngest female ever to be convicted of murder in British legal history.

Sentencing Carr to be detained at Her Majesty's Pleasure, Mr. Justice Scott-Barr described her as: "an extremely dangerous young woman. What is clear is that you had a sexual motive for this killing and it is apparent both from the brutal manner in which you mutilated her body and the chilling entries in your diary recording what you had done, that killing, as you put it, turns you on."

NATURAL BORN KILLER

Up to and during the trial, the police and the court had maintained the anonymity of the accused because of her age. Now the press had a name, Sharon Carr. The tabloid press were in a frenzy to discover more about her. Just who was Sharon Carr? Where had she come from? What had driven her to commit a brutal murder at the tender age of 12? It did not take them long to find out.

The day after the trial ended, banner headlines read: "NATURAL BORN KILLER," "A MONSTER BEHIND A SWEET SMILE," and "VOODOO PAST OF KILLER SCHOOLGIRL." Detailed biographies of her short, tragic life followed, and the story of Sharon Carr's horrific childhood makes all too familiar reading. Born in December, 1979 in Belize, Central America, Sharon Louise Carr never knew her father. Her mother was 24-year-old Molly McFazdean, a promiscuous drunk and devotee of voodoo. Their home, in a shantytown set on the outskirts of Belize City, was a tumbledown hut on stilts with no running water or electricity.

If the lifestyle was primitive, so were the local customs. One of Sharon's relatives, trying to explain her aberrant behavior, said, "In Belize we kill chickens, and goats, and other animals, and the children are right there watching. At the time they know you are killing to eat. But what's the difference? Maybe there's a thrill in it all." And visions of death for Sharon were not restricted to animals. "When she was three she watched a man burned alive in his back yard," claimed the same relative. "He was soaked with kerosene and set alight. Sharon just stood there watching. I can't believe that would not have an influence even on someone as young as her."

When Sharon was four, her mother married George Carr, a soldier in the British Army serving in Belize, after persuading him that he was the father of the child she was carrying. When Carr was posted back to England, he took Molly and Sharon with him.

It was a hellish marriage and George Carr, now 53 and the holder of a prestigious award—the MBE (Member of the British Empire)—for his charity work, remembers it with a shudder. He describes a turbulent, often violent relationship. "Molly would hand out regular beatings to the children," he said. "They lived in fear of her. On one occasion when Sharon had done something wrong, she poured pepper over her vagina. The cruelty must have had an effect on her." Carr also believes that his ex-wife's bizarre religious practices must have had an effect on her daughter. "She was a firm believer in the power of voodoo," he explained. "She believed in animal sacrifices. She used to place candles in each corner of the room. She made up her own prayers and reckoned by reciting certain prayers at certain times and in certain places, she could harm people."

By 1987, when Sharon was eight years old, George and Molly had separated. On a visit to their Camberley home to discuss divorce proceedings, George was attacked by Molly in front of the child. "The second I was in the house," Carr says, "Molly came up with this pot in her hand and poured boiling fat over me. It went over my head, my arms, and my chest . . . I think Molly has everything to do with what has happened to Sharon. If you are cruel to a child, that child grows up to be cruel."

Molly Carr was given a suspended prison sentence for the attack on her estranged husband and, for the first time, Sharon Carr came to the attention of the local social services department. They placed her, and the other Carr children, under a supervision order, but did not remove them from their mother's care. With the evidence in their possession, it was an incredible decision and one which was destined to have the most awful consequences.

By the time she was 11, Sharon could be seen hanging around street corners with a gang of older children, drinking alcohol and smoking cannabis. She frequently stayed out all night and there can be little doubt that she was sexually active.

It was at about this time that Sharon Carr apparently developed a taste for mutilating and killing stray animals. Probably fostered by the indoctrination in voodoo, which she had received from her mother, she would slaughter them with a large stone, claiming to her friends that this had ritual significance and that she drank their blood to empower her.

In the spring of 1992, several pet animals—cats and dogs—disappeared in the Camberley area. They were later found mutilated and beheaded, and there can be little doubt that Sharon Carr was responsible. It was only a matter of time before her lust for torture and death demanded a human sacrifice. That sacrifice was to come in the form of Katie Rackliff.

CHILDREN WHO KILL

The Sharon Carr case sent shockwaves through Britain. Not since three-year-old Jamie Bolger was battered to death by two 10-year-olds, was so much disgust and moral outrage expressed by the media in a case of this nature. Despite the fact that Britain has a comparatively low homicide rate—about 10 percent of that in the United States—murder by children and young teenagers is far from unknown.

In April 1996, 13-year-old Louise Allen was kicked to death by two other girls, aged 12 and 13. They were convicted of manslaughter. In June 1996, an 11-year-old boy was convicted of the manslaughter of 74-year-old Edna Condie. He had dropped a slab of concrete on his victim's head from the top of a tower block "for a laugh" when he was 10. In September 1996, when he was 15, Learco Chindamo was convicted of stabbing headmaster Philip Lawrence to death. The following month two boys, aged 15 and 17, were charged with the murder of 29-year-old Lesley Fox. In January 1997, a 14-year-old boy was charged with battering 82-year-old Lucy Marshall to death in Scotland.

February 1997 saw the trial of Sharon Carr, but she was not alone. John and Glenn Howells were found guilty of killing their mother, Eve, when they were 14 and 15 respectively. A 13-year-old boy in Scotland was found guilty of stabbing his brother to death after an argument over who should do the housework; and in the same month, 14-year-old Brian Smith was convicted of the murder, when he was 13, of nine year-old Jade Matthews. The list goes on.

The question is, what should be done with these children who kill? In Europe, attitudes differ greatly, from the ultra-liberal to the draconian. Ages of criminal responsibility vary widely too. In Scotland it is eight years of age, in England and Wales it is 10, in France 13, in Germany and Italy 14, in Norway and Sweden 15, and in Spain 16.

LUCKY ESCAPE: George Carr fled from a life of hell with his wife and step-daughter.

So what awaits Sharon Carr? She was sentenced to detention at Her Majesty's Pleasure, a sentencing system devised to handle juvenile criminals that dates back to 1908. The length of the sentence is indeterminate, giving the authorities the flexibility to release offenders once they are considered to have been rehabilitated. Juveniles convicted of murder are given sentence terms of 10 years or more—that is, they are to be detained for that period before release can even be considered. The length of the term is set, not by the courts but by the Home Secretary, acting on the advice of the Parole Board. The sentence for Sharon Carr is likely to be set at not less than 15 years.

Heaven's Gate Suicides

Members of the Heaven's Gate religious sect were waiting for a sign, a sign that it was time for them to be liberated from their earthly bodies. They found it in the brilliant form of the Hale-Bopp comet. The cultists, who were all fans of science fiction, the Internet, and surgical castration, were assured by their leader, Marshall Herff Applewhite, that they would be transported by aliens to a higher place. And so, 39 men and women, between the ages of 26 to 72 prepared themselves for the journey by taking massive doses of barbiturates washed down with vodka, and then suffocating themselves with plastic bags.

On Wednesday, March 26, 1997, Rio DiAngelo, a computer programer and ex-member of the Heaven's Gate cult, arrived at his place of work, InterAct Entertainment in Beverly Hills, to find a Federal Express package waiting for him. Inside were two video tapes, two computer disks, and a set of instructions. It was in effect a suicide press kit from Heaven's Gate, explaining how they were about to abandon their "human packages" and proceed to a "Higher Place." A horrified DiAngelo knew what this meant. He went to his boss, Nick Matzorkis, and told him that he was sure that the cult members were either about to commit suicide or had already done so.

At first Matzorkis refused to take him seriously. He knew quite a few members of Heaven's Gate personally. For some time they had been designing Internet Web sites for him and, while he readily admitted that they seemed a bit weird, he had never felt them to be a danger to themselves or anyone else. But DiAngelo was adamant. He knew for certain that ritual suicide was one of the long-term objectives of the sect. In fact that had been one of the reasons he had left Heaven's Gate, some six months earlier. Matzorkis suggested that DiAngelo contact the cult's headquarters, a rambling mansion in Rancho Santa Fe, near San Diego. DiAngelo said he had already tried calling but there had been no answer. Even Matzorkis was forced to admit that this was strange, and reluctantly agreed to drive DiAngelo to San Diego to investigate.

Two and a half hours later, Matzorkis parked outside the Heaven's Gate mansion and DiAngelo went in alone. When he emerged 20 minutes later, according to Matzorkis, he was "as white as a sheet." He got into the car and said quietly: "They did it."

Matzorkis contacted the San Diego Sheriff's Department and within an hour, officers were at the scene. As soon as they entered the house, they knew what to expect. The air was thick with the putrid smell of decaying human flesh. On beds and mattresses they found 39 bodies—18 men and 21 women—in various stages of decomposition. Each was dressed identically in black pants, a black shirt, and brand-new black Nike running shoes. In all but two cases, their

THIRTY-NINE DEAD: Members of the Los Angeles Coroner's office take away bodies after the mass suicide at Rancho Santa Fe.

LIVING IN LUXURY: The multimillion dollar ranch that was home to the Heaven's Gate cult. The ranch was paid for by profits from the sect's computer company.

faces were covered with diamond-shaped purple shrouds.

There was no sign of a disturbance or struggle. In fact, one of the officers explained later: "Save for the acrid stench, the place was calm, even serene." All the deceased had packed an overnight bag for their journey to a "Higher Place," containing a change of clothing, a spiral-bound notebook, and a stick of lip gloss. Each of them had five dollars in his or her pocket, presumably for traveling expenses. Alone in his bedroom, they found the corpse of the cult's founder and leader, 65-year-old Marshall Herff Applewhite. He too was ready for the journey.

FAREWELL

According to the San Diego medical examiner, the cultists had died in three waves. Fifteen of them had died on Saturday, March 21, some five days before their discovery. Another 15 had followed the next day; and the remainder had died on the Monday. The last two women to die were not wearing shrouds, but still had plastic bags over their heads. It had presumably been their grim task to lay out the others, a privilege they had to forego themselves. All had died by ingesting phenobarbital mixed with apple sauce and washed down with vodka. In this drugged and drunken state, they had fastened plastic bags over their heads and lain back quietly, waiting to die.

Apart from the tapes and disks sent off to DiAngelo, individual Heaven's Gate cult members left a number of videos as farewell messages. Against a backdrop of a brilliant Californian sky,

there was absolutely no sense of sadness or foreboding as each member stepped forward to say his or her piece to the camera. Said one woman: "We couldn't be happier about what we're doing." Another laughed as she said: "People in the world thought I had completely lost my marbles—they're not right. I couldn't have made a better choice." "Beam me up," squeaked one young woman.

One of the eerie things about the farewell video tapes was that it was hard to tell the cultists apart. All of them had close-cropped hair and wore androgynous clothing. It is easy to understand why the sheriff's deputies initially thought that all the victims were young men. Shedding all vestiges of sexuality

was central to the ethos of the Heaven's Gate cult, and a postmortem revealed that six members, including Applewhite himself, had gone so far as to have themselves surgically castrated. "In order to be a member of that kingdom," explained one former cult member, "one had to overcome one's humanness, which included one's sexuality."

Even relatives of the victims had difficulty recognizing their loved ones, some of whom had had no contact in many years. Mary Ann Craig, whose husband John abandoned her and their six children in 1975, was not surprised at the news of his death. "I've been waiting for this for 22 years," she said. Nichelle Nichols, who played Lieutenant Uhura in the original Star Trek series, was equally philosophical about the death of her brother Thomas at Rancho Santa Fe. She told CNN: "He made his choices, and we respect those choices."

DO AND TI

So what was Heaven's Gate, and what convinced its members to take their own lives, in the worst case of mass suicide in the United States? The cult in various guises and under several different names dated back to 1970, and was the brainchild of Marshall Herff Applewhite. The son of a Presbyterian minister, Applewhite was a man who appeared to have everything going for him. He was blessed with good looks and a fine singing voice. Married with two children, he was appointed music professor at the University of Alabama in 1963.

EX-MUSIC PROFESSOR: Marshall Herff Applewhite expands on his philosophy in a video he made for his followers. Sex, drugs, and alcohol were banned.

Then, five years later, the marriage collapsed and Applewhite left his job suddenly among rumors that he had been having a homosexual affair with one of his students.

He wandered around the South and the West for a while before obtaining a post as a music teacher at the University of St. Thomas in Houston, Texas. He didn't last long. In 1970, he resigned from the post, giving his reason as "health problems of an emotional nature." He checked into a private clinic, hoping to be "cured" of his homosexual desires. It obviously didn't work because shortly after he was discharged, he underwent his surgical castration.

It was about this time that he met his true soul mate, Bonnie Lu Trusdale Nettles, a nurse who was an aficionado of astrology and new-age religions. Bonnie abandoned her husband and two children, and took to the road with Applewhite. The relationship was platonic; the couple extolled the virtue of shedding all base desires, saying that they had both been "infused with higher, heavenly spirits."

Nettles and Applewhite gave each other nicknames—Tiddly and Wink, Guinea and Piggy, Nincom and Poop. Finally, they settled on Do and Ti, names they would use in the Heaven's Gate cult. Between them, they devised a philosophy which was a mixture of Christianity, new-age spirituality, and science fiction. They believed that they, like Jesus, would be assassinated, rise again from the dead after three days, and be carried off in a space ship.

They had their religion, and now they needed some disciples. Do and Ti went on a recruiting campaign around the southern states and gradually built up a modest following. Do must have had considerable charisma to have succeeded in persuading grown men and women to leave their families, homes, and jobs to follow him on his quest for immortality, telling them that they must be prepared to: "Walk out the door of their lives."

TOUGH TRAINING

At this stage, the sect was known by the acronym HIM—Human Individual Metamorphosis—and its membership numbered around 50. Recruits were obliged to take reeducation classes from Do and Ti and were subjected to a tough regimen. Sex, alcohol, and drugs were banned, and all ties with families were to be severed. HIM supported itself with money from the trust funds of richer members and, when that ran out, by doing odd jobs and begging.

In 1985, Ti died or, as Do described it, "left her human vehicle," and the HIM went into sharp decline. But Do wasn't finished yet and, in 1993, he relaunched the cult under the new name of Heaven's Gate. He took out an advertisement in USA Today, declaring that: "UFO Cult Resurfaces with Final Offer." "This was," the advertisement warned, "the last chance to advance beyond human." It went on to explain that, while Do did not agree with some of their philosophies, nor did he condone all their actions, Heaven's Gate was aligned with other millennial groups such as the Branch Davidians—who would later be responsible for the massacre at Waco, Texas— and the Solar Temple—who have since conducted three mass suicides in Canada and Europe that have resulted in the death of 70 members. Do considered they were all set against a common enemy, a corrupt world.

It is ironic, therefore, that Heaven's Gate should then go on to make itself a comfortable living on the proceeds of the very modern technology it claimed to eschew. For years, cult members had been using computers to track stars and search for UFOs and other signs of life in outer space. In the process they had acquired a high level of computer skills and, in 1996, Do announced that Heaven's Gate was launching a computer business called Higher Source to design Web pages for the Internet.

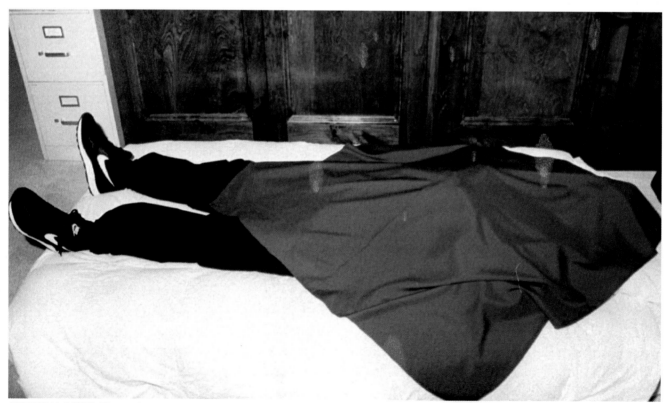

IDENTICAL DRESS: The 39 dead cult members were all found wearing the same clothes and covered with purple shrouds.

HIGH TECH: The Higher Source website, an advertisement for the Heaven's Gate cult's computer services division. Most cult members were middle class and well educated.

Their rates were extremely competitive and they quickly established an impressive client list, ranging from the San Diego Polo Club to the InterAct Entertainment Group in Beverly Hills.

"They were faster, cheaper, and more efficient than most designers," said Greg Hohertz, a former employee of InterAct. "They all went by their forenames, but then there are a lot of people who go by one name in Hollywood. We live in a world of Chers and Madonnas. They were very polite and that should have tipped me off because no one in Hollywood is polite."

PARANOID THOUGHTS

Heaven's Gate was soon earning enough to enable members to move into a $7,000-a-month mansion in the exclusive community of Rancho Santa Fe. Neighbors described the cultists as quiet and polite, without being too friendly. If they had looked closer, they would have seen that Applewhite and his followers, like so many cultists, were also becoming paranoid. They insisted that the phone remain in the landlord's name and paid their rent and all other bills in cash.

They had no bank accounts, no Social Security numbers, nothing that could link them with the government.

Despite the swimming pool and Jacuzzi—neither of which was ever used—life at the luxury mansion was spartan. Members generally rose at 4:00 a.m. and studied the night sky for signs to guide them to their true home in the heavens. The rest of their time was spent designing Web pages and watching endless reruns of Star Trek, The X Files and Star Wars.

Applewhite meanwhile embarked on a recruiting campaign via the Internet and, within a matter of months, he had doubled his membership.

JOURNEY PREPARATIONS

But all was not well at Rancho Santa Fe. Applewhite was convinced that they were being investigated by the FBI and the CIA. It was Jim Jones and Jonestown—where more than 900 died in a mass suicide—all over again. Paradoxically Applewhite was also depressed by the lack of recognition Heaven's Gate was receiving. He described this in an Internet bulletin as "a signal to us to begin our preparations to return home." He went on to write that "the weeds of humanity had taken over the garden," and that it was "time to go to the level above, or what humans call dead."

Applewhite also became convinced that there was a UFO, four times the size of earth, trailing the Hale-Bopp comet, and that his beloved Ti was aboard and would come down to collect him and the other members of Heaven's Gate. As the comet became visible in mid-March, and Easter approached, the cultists knew the time was right and got ready to shed their "earthly containers." They had their own version of the Last Supper—chicken pot pie and cheesecake—and prepared to go to a "Higher Place."

BEAM ME UP: Cult members believed the Hale-Bopp comet concealed a massive UFO that would come and take them away after their deaths.

INDEX

Note: page numbers in *italics* refer to illustrations.